Media Mash Up

Big Stories, Bold Opinions and Blazing Hot Takes from Today's Top News Media Voices

By Rick Schultz

Thank You

First and foremost, I'd like to thank Jason Barrett and BarrettNewsMedia.com, the premier outlet covering the news and sports media industries. Watching what J.B., Stephanie and their team have built in the sports media space, and now also in news media, has been astounding. It has been an honor to contribute to Barrett News Media, as the company continues to increase its reach and influence across the media industry.

The following essays are recaps, summaries and encapsulations of what was delivered at the time by the media personality involved. The messages, expertise and knowledge are, thankfully, their own. My goal was to capture the opinions and viewpoints of these news media leaders, and bring it to the reader in a concise, entertaining and easy-to-consume format. My agreement or disagreement with their point of view is irrelevant. While I do, in fact, agree with many of their viewpoints, I certainly don't see eye-to-eye with every one of them. And hopefully, neither will you. Their opinions may excite you, enthrall you or anger you....so be prepared! They are the experts, bringing their unique worldviews, education and experience in the way they deliver these news stories to us every day. I thank them for delivering this material to us in the unique way that only they can.

I'd like to thank the news media professionals and opinion leaders appearing in this book, including Will Cain, Glenn Beck, Richard Baris, Robert Barnes, Joseph Cotto, Paul Gottfried, Marty Glickman, Kevin McCullough, Grant Stinchfield, Eric Metaxas, Brain Buffini, Laura Ingraham, Raymond Arroyo, Sean Hannity, Rush Limbaugh, Mark Levin, Jesse Watters, Dan Bongino, Daniel Hannan, Charles Payne, Scott Adams, Tucker Carlson, Brandon Straka, Greg Kelly, Sean Spicer, Michelle Malkin, Dick Morris, Bob Sellers, Howie Carr, Chris Salcedo, John Bachman, Dave Ramsey, Chris Hogan, Nicole Arbour, Michael Savage, Robert Kiyosaki, Grover Norquist, Tom Wheelwright, Bill O'Reilly, Lou Dobbs, Dr. Robert Jeffress, Dr. Ben Carson, Peter Lavelle, Tara Palmeri, George Szamuely, Joe Concha, Linette Lopez, Julie Hyman, Dan Robert, Jim Cramer, Stuart Varney, Chris Barron, Eva Ados, Cheryl Casone, James O'Keefe, Matt Walsh, Mark Robinson, John McLaughlin, Erick Erickson, Harry Dent, Kim Kiyosaki, Dr. John Delony, Nic Newman, Derek Hunter, Joseph Wulfsohn, Dan Miller, Andrew Wilkow, Greg Gutfeld, Ken Coleman, Rachel Cruze, Christy Wright, Anthony O'Neal, George from Cryptos R Us, Rachel Maddow, Lachlan Cartwright, Brian Stelter, Janice Dean, Shannon Bream, Pat McAfee, Pete Hegseth, Lawrence Jones, Dagen McDowell, Jessica Tarlov, Eric Bolling, Joy Reid, Don Lemon, Joe Scarborough, Chris Hayes, Jay Caspian Kang, Larry King, Michael Saylor, Pastor Rick Warren, Liz Claman, Carl Runefelt, Jack Murphy, George Stephanapolous, Lester Holt, Brett Baier, Ted Siedle, John MacGregor, Jedediah Bila, Harold Ford Jr., Michael Malice, Dave Rubin, Sean Duffy,

Judge Jeanine Pirro, Arthur Milikh, Ina Fried, Jeff Rosen, Joe Rogan, Robert Breedlove, Michelle Makori, Doug McKelway, Megyn Kelly, Michael Clemente, Mike Huckabee, Kirk Cameron, Mike Rowe, Matt Crouch, Tony Perkins, Jon Stewart, Chris Stirewalt, Soledad O'Brien, Sean McLaughlin, Robert Iger, Jeff Sottolano, Nicky and Moose, Don Martin, Ari Melber, Steven Greenhouse, Peter McCormack, Natalie Brunell, Diane Sawyer, Barbara Walters, Oprah Winfrey, Stephen Moore, Katrina Szish, Neil Cavuto, Dinesh D'Souza, Ben Shapiro, David Asman, Dana Perino, Bill Hemmer, George Kamel, Greta Van Susteren, Aubrey Strobel, Clarissa Ward, Mike Lindell, Brian Glenn, Christina Bobb, Laurie Roberts, David Catanese, Karen Kerrigan, Andy Stanley, Alison Kosik, Anastasia Amoroso, Ryan Ermey, Isabel Brown, Mike McGlone, Rob Schmitt and Kristina Ellis.

Dedication

For Tessa and Emma, the two best gifts - among an unending list - that God has given me. May your beauty continue to shine bright like the beautiful stars you are. And may you continue to read, learn, grow, experience, take chances, and formulate your own opinions…rather than settling to be sheep in the herd.

Also, for the courageous media voices across America who bring us the truth with their unique style and flare.

About the Author

Rick Schultz began his media career in 1993 and is an experienced writer, anchor, host and play-by-play broadcaster. He has been a weekly columnist for Barrett News Media since 2020.

Rick is the former Sports Director at Fordham University's highly-acclaimed WFUV Radio, where he lead and mentored a team of 50 student sports broadcasters.
He has been an adjunct professor for sports broadcasting at The Connecticut School of Broadcasting, Marist College and Fordham University.
Today, in addition to his business career, he provides sports broadcasting content and coaching at SportscastersClub.com

Rick has held various news and sports media roles throughout his 30-year career, with outlets such as The Hudson Valley Renegades, The Norwich Navigators, Army Sports at West Point, WATR Radio, 1340/1390 ESPN Radio, Pamal Broadcasting, Cumulus Media, Scorephone, ABC Sports Television, NBC Sports Television, Metro Networks and WFAN Radio.

Follow Rick Schultz on Twitter - @RickSchultzNY

Other Books By Rick Schultz - available on Kindle, Paperback and Audible

Secrets of Sports Broadcasting: Practical Advice for Sportscasting Success

Minor League Baseball Revealed: A Secret Tour Inside Our National Pastime

Untold Tales From the Bush Leagues; A Behind The Scenes Look Into Minor League Baseball, From the Broadcasters Who Called the Action

A Renegade Championship Summer: A Broadcaster's View of a Magical Minor League Baseball Season

101 Things I Wish I Knew Before I Bought My First Home

101 Things I Wish I Knew Before I Sold My First Home

How to Buy or Sell Your Home: 202 Real Estate Tips for Success

Sales Surge: 50 Secrets to Propel Your Sales Career With Less Stress

Sales Surge Sequel: Another 50 Secrets to Boost Your Sales

Table of Contents

Table of Contents   7

Introduction   12

Will Cain, Still in the Game   14

The Coming Civil War   17

The Peril of Polls   20

Debate Moderators Should Follow Marty Glickman's Example   22

A Trump Landslide Victory is Coming   24

Marionettes Keep on Dancing   27

America Exposes the Media   30

Conservative Voices' Call to Action   33

The Unstoppable Optimism of Charles Payne   36

Finding Truth Through the Fog   38

Fox News Tells its Audience to Pound Sand   41

The Dawn of a New Era in Cable News   44

The Career Opportunity of a Lifetime   46

The Pandemic Did Not Cause Economic Hardship   49

Pulling Back the Curtain With a Laugh   52

Talk Radio Voices Roar in 2021   55

The Economic Tune is Changing   57

The Shifting Media Spotlight   59

Americans Become Their Own Media   61

Is the Media Starting to Catch On?   63

Media Already Rolling Over for Biden   65

Elon Musk Leaves Media Scratching Head   68

Rush Limbaugh's Lesson for Aspiring Broadcasters   71

Stuart Varney Connects in the Morning   74

Joe Biden, Already a Failure   76

Media Unimpressed by Bleak Presidential Address   78

A Call to Protect America   80

Beware of the Climbing Stock Market   82

Today's News is So Cliche   84

Project Veritas Fights Back   87

Woke Bullies Unmasked   89

Leaders Say Time To Secure Voting Rights   92

Liberal Backlash Begins in Liberal Bastions   94

Could This Be Our Next President?   97

Cable networks highlight split on "global warming"   100

Prepare For the Bubble to Burst   103

Why is Cleaning Up Our Financial Act a Bad Thing?   105

Remembering America's Greatness   107

Bypassing the Media, Right to the People   109

Biden Already Polling Poorly   112

Faking the News Without Worry   115

Reveling in CNN's Ratings Demise   117

You Don't Have to Be a Jerk   119

More Please, Sugar Daddy   121

Media Forced to Cover the News   123

Planning for the Next Generation of Financial Talk Radio   125

The Impeachment Boomerang?   127

Media Cheap Shot Over Bitcoin   129

Maddow Wins Big   132

America Aghast Over Biden's Early Results   134

Janice Dean, America's Storm Chaser   136

Democrats Fret Over Their Divide-and-Conquer Strategy   138

Another Mark Levin Masterpiece   140

Glenn Beck's American Optimism   142

Many in Media Support Aaron Rodgers   144

Media Fanning the Flames of Hate   146

Punishing Americans By Design   148

America's E-Bike Future   150

The Art of the Interview   152

Grocery Store Cashier Headed to the Moon   155

Silver Lining in Media's Self-Serving Behavior   158

Who is Really to Blame for Inflation?   160

Your Pension May Not Save Your Golden Years   162

An Insider's View of the Media Game   164

Dave Ramsey and Those Evil Millionaires   166

Entrepreneur Literally Saves the Children   168

The Golden Era of Media Just Beginning   170

Bitcoin's Call Option on Morality   173

BSM Summit Unmasks the Secret for a Successful Media Career   176

Doug McKelway's Change of Pace   179

The Problem with Television News in America   182

Ramsey Solutions' Lesson on Legacy   186

Surprising Delivery for New York Employees   190

A New Media Face for Bitcoin   193

Some in Media See Impending Recession   197

Media Responds to the Speech Censors   199

Michael Malice Takes on the Media, Again   202

Katrina Szish: Charting the Uncharted Path   204

Dinesh D'Souza Fires Back Over 2000 Mules   206

The Biggest Story in America   209

Freedom From Media Anxiety   211

The Media's Oversized Influence on Financial Markets   213

DeSantis Basking in the Media's Ire   215

Brats to Get a November Beating   218

Financial Media Finds an Example on the Hardcourt   220

Media Fed Up With Biden and His Party   223

Van Susteren Captures Both Horrors and Kindness Amid Ukrainian War
226

Rising Star Offers Perspective on the State of Journalism   229

Mike Lindell Still Pursuing 2020 Election Truth   233

Political Polling: Cream Rising to the Top?   236

Calling Out the Inflation Shell Game   240

Democrats Raise Taxes on Americans Again   243

Secrets to Finding News Media Mentors   245

The Days That Create Fortunes   248

Gen Z Needs a Break From the News   250

From the Gas Pump to the Grocery Store and Back Home Again   253

Massive Market Crash Still Looming   255

A Promise to Save America From "Living Hell"   258

30 Years of Ramsey   260

Thanks for Reading!   263

Introduction

Anais Nin once said, "We see the world not as it is, but as we are."

More accurately today, we see the world as our media is.

Can we all agree that it has been a crazy couple of years?

From the shutdown to the cultural frenzy over issues of the day, our media has had an awful lot to report on. It has truly been a period of change, raw emotion and breathtaking new developments.

And while sharing these eye-opening developments over recent years, the very journalists who *report* the stories have often *become* the story.

Their opinions, biases and worldviews often shape the story we hear. For better or worse, we absorb the news based on the journalistic bent of those bringing it through our phones and into our homes.

Over the past two years, I have penned weekly essays for Barrett News Media, which details the news media's coverage of the hottest topics of the day. From politics to Bitcoin, economic collapses to emerging business trends, our trusted media sources of choice have delivered the news, in a style and tone that only they can. And BNM has become one of the world's premier outlets for news, analysis, opinion and storytelling on the daily happenings in the news media world.

These essays share the news, as dissected, delivered and opined-upon by the media personalities we hold in such high esteem. As much as they could be in 1000 words or less, these are recaps of the stories they delivered in their own unique way.

The opinions are mostly theirs, from the topics chosen to the style in which they package and share the stories with us, the media consumer.

My goal was simply to be the messenger.

What follows in this book are 100 such essays, spanning every week for almost two years. You'll read about some of the hottest topics in the news media, as covered by some of the most well-known personalities of our day.

You'll also hear about some lesser-known journalists, podcasters, YouTubers and emerging professionals making a name for themselves through alternate avenues of media and opinion.

You'll hear from names you know, such as Bill O'Reilly, Glenn Beck, Rachel Maddow, Sean Hannity and Dave Ramsey, as well as others you may not be familiar with, such as Ben Armstrong, Richard Baris, Nicole Arbour and Natalie Brunell.

You may not like all of the personalities; most definitely you will even loathe some. Most of these media voices, although certainly not all, presumably find their niche on the right side of the political spectrum. But be warned, conservatives may find agreement with most, albeit not all, of their opinions shared in the following essays.

The point of this book, and of the weekly articles for Barrett News Media, is to bring you stories you may have missed, through the lens and voice of media personalities you may, or may not, be familiar with.

Their unique voices and points of view shape our understanding of the news, and I hope they open your mind to new points of view. Perhaps they will reinforce your current thinking, and even expand your frame of reference.

If you enjoy the news media and appreciate the diverse personalities who bring the stories to our attention, I hope you savor these opinions and viewpoints from the past two years.

September 13, 2020

Will Cain, Still in the Game

Goodbye to curveballs and slam dunks. Hello to mob riots and campaign trails. For Will Cain, this is the perfect time to change uniforms.

Cain has completed his transition from sports back to news, and if his first few weeks co-hosting Fox and Friends Weekend is any indication, he seems quite comfortable. Like a free agent ballplayer changing teams in the prime of his career, Cain has grabbed the opportunity to build the next successful chapter of his on-air life.

Although he did appear on Fox and Friends a decade ago, this is the broadcast veteran's first stint as a regular with the network, after previously starting successful media companies and working on-air in television news for other networks.

His background in the news world, however, was all before he landed at ESPN and truly made his national name. After joining the "Worldwide Leader in Sports" in 2015 and hosting his well-regarded ESPN Radio afternoon-drive program since 2018, Cain anticipated a successful leap back into a world far from pitching changes and 3rd down conversions.

"I am excited to join the team at 'FOX & Friends Weekend' and look forward to building upon my experience in sports, news and politics on the number one morning show in the country," Cain told FoxNews.com before his first show last month. And what a time it is to be back in news for someone with the broadcasting chops and opinionated delivery such as Will Cain.

If you watched or listened to Cain work at ESPN over the past five years, you could tell he was unique. After all, this was a conservative-leaning guy working - actually *excelling* - at ESPN! That alone made you take notice. Whether delivering a radio monologue or taking part in a television debate with Stephen A. Smith, Cain came prepared to deliver compelling programming each day. At the same time, he quietly developed a behind-the-scenes reputation as a class act, always willing to help others in the field.

Take, for example, the day he helped entertain a group of students from Fordham University's sports media powerhouse, WFUV Radio. After spending time behind the scenes discussing the sports media business, Cain allowed the students to watch his radio/television simulcast program from the control room. As if that weren't enough, he invited one of the college broadcasting students onto the air for a 20-minute debate about one of the hot topics of the day. That just doesn't happen in national sports radio! Cain helped give those aspiring sportscasters a day they'll never forget, while creating a compelling segment of radio.

Will Cain worked on the television news side in the past, including hosting a show on Glenn Beck's *The Blaze* network, as well as working as a CNN political contributor. By most standards, it looks like he hasn't missed a beat in jumping into some of the day's more sensitive and divisive topics with his co-hosts Jedediah Bila and Pete Hegseth. The task has been made easier because he has a history with the duo, co-hosting a news talk program on The Blaze.

"Some years ago we spent every night around a table, debating the issues that were important in that day's news cycle," Cain said during an introductory segment on Fox and Friends in mid-August. "Chemistry is one of those things that every television executive would like to think he can create, but it's often magical. It takes trust, confidence and mutual respect. I can say walking in that the three of us genuinely have those three characteristics. I genuinely like these two people. I trust them and I respect their points of view. That does not mean I'm going to always agree with them, but I truly trust and respect them."

Together, the three create a young, hip vibe for the Fox News morning program, and Cain has been willing to jump right into the mix and tackle some of today's most contentious stories.

For example, with rioting and looting running rampant in many major U.S. cities this summer, Cain recently spent some time talking with New York City police officers, residents and business owners. One current officer, who asked to be disguised so his identity wouldn't become public, told Cain, "I never thought I would have to put this uniform on and be looked at as the enemy, and to be hated." He followed up by telling Cain, "you would be crazy to take this job now in this day and age." Quite a jarring difference for Cain - and one he has handled adroitly - after only weeks ago he was spending his afternoons discussing, for example, the challenges for baseball and football beginning their respective 2020 seasons.

Cain also waded into the political waters, commenting on last month's Democratic National Convention by saying nominee Joe Biden's speech "crossed the bar of being a smooth speech," but also added "I found criticism of this president, criticism of this country, criticism of our history, but not much substance on how they would fix it."

Will Cain has never been shy to offer his opinion, whether it be on *The Will Cain Show* or during his appearances on ESPN"s *First Take*. He has promised to continue bringing his unique style and wit to the more weighty and significant topics of the day with Fox.

"I can't wait, I'm so excited to be back with these two and on Fox News," Cain said. "We're gonna have fun. We're gonna pursue the truth.

As far as we can tell, Cain is fitting in just fine so far. He certainly hasn't lost his fastball.

The Coming Civil War

"There is a clear choice - good versus evil," the talk-show host implored his audience recently. "We are headed towards a revolution and a civil war." And quite possibly, he thought, by the time we reach Christmas.

For many, the words of radio talk show host Glenn Beck seem a bit far-fetched. Just shock-jock talk aimed at drawing a reaction. This is what Beck is known best for, no? And isn't generating a response - good or bad - the *goal* of the talk-show host?

Beck does have a flair for the dramatic. He has often gone out on the proverbial limb, predicting impending doom and crisis. The sky was falling under our last president, and initially he didn't expect much better from this one. Is this latest prognostication nothing more than strategic hyperbole cooked up by one of the country's leading experts in riling up an audience?

How could any talk-show host compare 2020 to the 1860's? Could the riots of today actually be the precursors to a second War Between the States? Perhaps it would be easier to put the mind at ease, dismissing his claims without a second look - if only Glenn Beck hadn't been correct about many other similar issues over his on-air broadcast career.

Beck has predicted, over the years, that we would see increased division and bloodshed in the streets, with Americans pitted against one another. On this account, one cannot question his prescience. For more than a decade he has foreshadowed the type of events we are currently watching in our neighborhoods or on our television screens. He has been sounding the bell since his days hosting his nightly Fox News television show. And today we see cities, streets, homes, businesses and police under attack.

Yes, he's been vindicated for promoting the Overton Window theory over the past many years - where a society advances the most radical, extreme positions, only to come across as sensible by eventually settling for much more "centrist," acceptable positions in the end. Even though such a position would have been seen as too radical at the outset, it now seems tolerable relative to the extreme alternative. In other words, you tell your parents you expect to get an F on the test, so then actually coming home with a C seems acceptable. Partial government-controlled healthcare seems reasonable when juxtaposed against total Medicare for all. Removal of some statues and flags seems acceptable to many who otherwise would never go along with tearing down our National Monuments. Extreme environmental regulations are tolerable compared to a complete ban on fossil fuels. Beck foreshadowed many of these changes through the Overton Window effect he espoused.

But his record is not blemish-free. To this point, the markets have not completely melted down, bringing with it the entire world economy. The Cloward-Piven strategy of "overwhelming the system," if it was indeed attempted over the past decade, was unable to bring forth the extreme, rapid transformation of American Society. And to his credit when Beck, in his opinion, has been incorrect with his predictions - as he recently, and quite publicly, announced he was during his negative barrage against then-candidate Donald Trump - he has admitted so publicly and forthrightly.

America is undoubtedly politically divided. From 2008 to 2016, half of the country looked on in horror as the American heritage was in the crosshairs from within, and many things they hold dear were attacked and demonized. For the last 4 years, the other half of the country has felt similarly.

America is divided on masks, divided on the weather and divided on the roll of God in our society. Just to name a few. And this was all before a vacant Supreme Court seat stole the headlines.

According to Gallup, in 2012 69% of Americans felt we were divided. In 2012, that number had risen to a record-high 77%. Today Gallup says 55% of Americans believe race relations in the country are poor. According to Rasmussen Reports last Friday, 53% of Americans approve of the job President Trump is doing. 48% disapprove. Is it not the job of the talk-show host to point out these divisions and ruminate on where that may be leading us as a country?

With these national trends as a backdrop, should we give Glenn Beck's prognostication more credence? Simply because he has been correct on some accounts, could we really be staring down the barrel of another Civil War in America?

"The plans have been laid by revolutionaries who have very high connections and lots of money," Beck said on his nationally-syndicated radio talk show last month, as he pointed out the rapid rise in rioting and looting this summer. "Why won't the Democrats come out against these protests, calling them peaceful protests?" he asked. "They are riots! They are burning our streets down!"

Beck theorizes that mayors and governors of these ravaged cities are sitting by on their hands, hoping President Trump will overstep his Constitutional authority and take action - a move that would act as the catalyst and spark the true revolution. He also shared a first-hand discussion with a business owner who joined an organized militia group as a means of protecting his business and his family.

"This is the clear fault of the Democratic Party," Beck said. "This party is a threat to the Constitution. They know exactly what they're doing. The press is in bed with them."
He then pointed to House Speaker Nancy Pelosi inflaming tensions by calling out her supporters to "mobilize and organize," while referring to her Republican political opponents as "domestic enemies."

Glenn Beck often touts his ability to predict future events, albeit without precise timing. On this account, he has both won and lost. Regardless, Americans continue to listen.

Let's hope 2020 is the biggest miss of his career.

The Peril of Polls

Political polls are everywhere, and we can expect to be barraged by them for roughly the next five weeks. The real question may not be what they say, however, but rather how much importance the news media should give them in the lead-up to the 2020 Presidential election.

We all remember how the majority of polls turned out in 2016, in terms of their predictive value. Many were wrong in the end, as they consistently predicted an outcome that did not, in fact, materialize. The same can be said, and arguably more so, for the 2018 elections. Our question here, however, is not the validity of the polls, or even their methodology. The question here is about reporting these polls as news, when such a weak case can be made, through recent history, as it relates to their predictive value.

When news organizations report on and publicize polls, even when conducted by their own network, should we view their results as *news*? Or should these polls be reported as the subjective *opinions* of those doing the polling or reporting?

Tune in to a cable television network this week, and you are likely to hear reporting about a poll predicting Joe Biden will win the 2020 election by 10 points. The same day, chances are you can tune in to a national radio show and hear about another poll predicting the re-election of President Donald Trump by a comfortable electoral margin. How can they both be true? And as a result, how can these results be classified as *news*? Shouldn't news be objectively factual?

Networks pump up their political polls and treat them as though their proprietary methods and data sets are head-and-shoulders above the rest. Chris Stirewalt and Bret Baier will go to all lengths defending recent Fox News polls, and the results are then parroted day and night as unassailable facts. The same can be said for hosts promoting and reporting on their own polls on the more overtly liberal networks CNN, CBS, ABC, NBC and others. Sometimes the large groupings of reported polls coincide with each other. On other days, networks report as news poll results that vary widely.

Meanwhile, there has been a growing number of alternative news outlets recently, going deeping into polling and pointing out where some of the network names have gotten it wrong. Richard Baris, through People's Pundit Daily, broadcasts nearly every day on YouTube and social media, with his polling news show, *Inside the Numbers,* that goes deeper into data collection and statewide trends. Baris, director of Big Data Poll, spends hours on end, dissecting and sharing his methodology and geographical breakdowns. This transparency is both refreshing and enlightening.

Baris sees substantial changes in the coalition that elected President Donald J. Trump in 2016, and questions whether pollsters and poll-aggregators are fully on top of these shifts and capturing the full extent of these shifts. "This is a very complicated election cycle," Baris said on his program recently. "Very complicated. And there is no way, no chance, no how that these pollsters are going to get it with the distribution and the participation rates that they are getting. If they do, it will be dumb luck." Baris specifically points out many erroneous polling results stem from incorrect weighting breakdowns for education and geographic distribution. He also gets quite worked up while pointing out the lack of standards and transparency from many outlets in the polling industry.

Baris also broadcasts weekly with co-host Robert Barnes, an accomplished and nationally-renowned attorney, on their program, *What Are The Odds*? The duo's extensive broadcasts amount to master classes on election polling, devoted to statewide voter registration trends, party affiliation and the nuts and bolts of weighting and "nesting" data when conducting surveys. Viewers learn more about Minnesota's "Iron Range" and Pennsylvania's Bucks County than they ever imagined wanting to know.

On a similar note, YouTube broadcasters Joseph Cotto and Paul Gottfried go deep into cultural trends and polling, often coming to the same conclusions as Baris and Barnes. Cotto's program frequently includes the only pollster who correctly predicted Brexit and the 2016 presidential election, the Democracy Institute's Patrick Basham. On a whole, these digital news outlets offer an extremely detailed and exhaustive dive into polling leading up to the election. They also happen to largely disagree with the 2020 election results provided, to this point, by national media outlets and universities.

So on one hand, you have the national media and university polls, leading us to believe a specific result is extremely likely on November 3rd. The same result they told us was a stone-cold lock four years ago. On the other hand, you have new, online media voices and public polling veterans predicting wildly different results. They won't both be correct. If so, should what they are "reporting" on today be considered news?

Or is it more opinion, wishful thinking, or shaping of a narrative?

Many of these questions will be answered on November 3rd and in the days that follow. In many respects, the credibility of news outlets hangs in the balance.

October 4, 2020

Debate Moderators Should Follow Marty Glickman's Example

"The only person who tunes into the game to hear the broadcaster is his mother," proclaimed immortal sports broadcaster, Marty Glickman.

Think about it. Have you ever tuned in to a sporting event to hear the *broadcaster*? Of course not. You flip on the television, radio or device for one reason - to watch the *game*.

If only Glickman was moderating this year's first presidential debate.

The great Marty Glickman was a pioneering voice of sports play-by-play, beginning his career in 1940. He practically invented the art form and quite literally became the standard. The basketball term "swish," when a player makes a basket without hitting the rim, was a Marty Glickman creation. He also invented much of the basketball court geography we still use today - such as "elbow", "key", etc. And aside from his broadcasting accolades, Glickman later went on to become the world's preeminent sportscasting coach. His generosity and impact on the world of sports broadcasting were equally immeasurable.

But the thing that made Marty Glickman the world's top play by play broadcaster, even more so than those technical inventions, was his philosophy. He had a simple mindset to which he believed every play by play broadcaster should adhere when calling the action of a live event.

The underlying premise behind everything Glickman taught was simply this - *people tune in for the game.* Whether in sports or news, viewers tune in for the *event*. It is never about the broadcaster.

The sports radio play by play broadcaster's job is to describe the action, or "paint the word picture," so the listener can see the action in his or her mind. On television, the broadcaster should complement the action the viewer can already see. But in either case, the game is the one and only focus. The broadcaster is simply the conduit to bring the listener into the action.

Before last week's presidential debate, the debate's moderator, Fox News host Chris Wallace, said his goal was to become invisible. He said he wanted viewers to forget he was even there. Indeed, Wallace was channeling his inner Glickman, as if he had just spent a critique session with the Dean of radio play by play. In voicing this pre-debate strategy in the lead-up to the highly-anticipated event, Wallace gave the country a tremendous amount of hope. As a professional, we expected him to deliver on the promise and give us, the viewers, what we wanted. Specifically, we expected a clear, unfiltered view of the two verbal combatants.

It only took minutes before our hopes were dashed.

From his first interruption of the president, Wallace was continually in the middle of the action. Rather than a mono-on-mono between President Trump and Joe Biden, viewers were bombarded with what often became a two-on-one. Regardless of the fact that he seemed intent to join Biden in trapping Trump, he should not have been in the scrum to begin with. Not one of the millions of viewers tuned in to hear Chris Wallace!

So how, then, could the moderator have done what he obviously felt was his duty, to maintain order and control? Perhaps early in the debate, when the two men were interrupting and speaking over one another, Wallace could have said, "Gentleman, you are obviously disregarding the debate rules and jumping in when it is your opponent's turn. But my role is not to play kindergarten cop. If you two want to continue with these tactics, I'm going to be here and our viewers can make their own judgements." In that way, Wallace could have re-stated the ground rules, to viewers and the participants, while not becoming the story. In other words, he would have trusted viewers to make up their own minds.

But far too often, that is not how elite news journalists see their role. Many of them, in fact, have very little confidence in the American public to make up its own mind, without the journalist setting the premise. Their inherent belief is that they, as the smartest folks among many, need to explain what we should think. Whether during debates or otherwise, many journalists just can't miss an opportunity to tell us what to think or how to view an argument.

Much has been written about the content of the questions, and why Wallace seemed to pick sides early in the debate. Why did he ask the president a pointed question about white supremacy, when just four years ago he asked the same question and received an unambiguous answer from then-candidate Trump. Those angles of Wallace's performance have been covered extensively elsewhere over the past week.

Our focus here is simply directed at Wallace's philosophy of handling the debate, both in his pre-event resolution and then in the actual outcome.

Why did we tune into the debate in the first place?
To hear Trump and Biden, or to hear Chris Wallace?

His plan was the right one. It was Marty Glickman.
On execution, however, he became part of the story and the resulting aftermath.

Here's hoping that viewers get the contrary approach they deserve next time.

October 11, 2020

A Trump Landslide Victory is Coming

President Donald Trump will win reelection on November 3rd, and by a larger margin than his 2016 shocker.

That's the opinion of KMC Radio talk-show host Kevin McCullough, who made the declaration recently on Twitter and during subsequent appearances with Grant Stinchfield on Newsmax TV and on the Eric Metaxas Radio Show.

"The only thing I can find right now in American culture that says Trump is going to lose are these polls that continually come out, the RealClearPolitics average puts them together," says McCullough, pointing out big media and university polls that many think are missing a wide swath of Trump voters and under-representing Republicans. "I think if you have properly-weighted polls and you don't talk to registered voters, but you talk to likely voters, you start to get a different story." Specifically, he points out the massive enthusiasm advantage for President Trump, as well as rapid job expansion as the economy roars back from the pandemic-induced shutdowns.

"Trump voters will literally crawl over glass to get to the polls for President Trump," Stinchfield agreed. "That's not the case for Joe Biden. He just happened to be the person Democrats offered up."

McCullough's bold prediction comes on the heels of a new Gallup survey, which says that 56% of American's consider themselves better off than they were four years ago at the conclusion of the previous administration, even during a worldwide pandemic. The survey also shows that most voters agree with Trump on the issues and find him to be a strong, decisive leader.

McCullough, KMC Radio host and founder of BingeThinker.com, has a history of correct presidential predictions, including calling Trump's victory in 2016. Instead of dissecting granular, district-by-district political minutia, McCullough relies heavily on overarching national trends in formulating his electoral predictions. He first broke onto the stage in 2006, when he published an article predicting a Barack Obama presidency.

McCullough's recently-released 2020 electoral map predicts a Republican tidal wave, with Trump not only winning the states he carried in 2016 - including Florida, North Carolina, Pennsylvania, Michigan, Wisconsin, Ohio and Arizona - but also picking up Nevada, New Hampshire and Minnesota.

"I think Donald Trump is going to blow Minnesota out of the water," he said on the Eric Metaxas Radio Show, pointing to the key issues of law and order and the economy. "I think it is going to turn the darkest red that it has ever thought of being in the modern era. The enthusiasm in Minnesota is so raging...they are ready to walk through fire, crawl over glass, pick the analogy of your choice. They want to get to the polls."

Overall, he has Trump winning 331 electoral votes, compared to just 207 for Biden. A candidate needs 270 electoral votes to win, and this prediction would be an increase over Trump's 2016 winning tally of 306.

"It's all red. We're not talking just swing states" said Stinchfield, as he showed McCullough's predicted map of the electoral outcome. "We're talking a massive, Reagan-style landslide."

Many others, including high-profile attorney and political gambler Robert Barnes, have also been singing the same song, noting the long list of trends favoring a comfortable Trump victory. Barnes often points to traditional objective data points, such as search engine volume, social media support, voter registration trends and models based on party primary turnout. All strongly favor Trump in 2020.

In addition, many other political voices point to a growing list of related, objective measurements that also foreshadow a Trump win. These include a dramatic rise in gun purchases, who polled Americans *think* is going to win, the stock market's current rise over the three months leading up to the election, expected record-setting 3rd quarter GDP growth, younger candidates and incumbents almost always winning and the total number of small-dollar donors. Many experts point out that these data points all favor Trump, while only one - the group of big media and university polls - favors Biden. McCullough says both campaigns understand the real state of the race.

"They both know that the media polls are not accurate," McCullough. "I know this because I've spoken to the Trump pollster and he's told me directly, 'yeah, they're not even close.' Biden people know they're not accurate either, and if they tell the real story of what it looks like, it's not gonna be good."

In the conversation with Metaxas, who refers to McCullough as "Vote-stradamus," he points specifically to the support that President Donald Trump enjoys among the Republican party, which is far superior to what either Barack Obama or George W. Bush garnered from their parties during the runup to their successful reelections. Also important is the Rasmussen Reports daily Presidential tracking poll, where Trump's job approval numbers have been consistently higher than those of president Obama during the month of September leading up to reelection. And that is *with* massively favorable, idolatry-like media coverage for Obama, compared to the opposite for Trump.

"While I don't have an exact science to why I'm coming to these conclusions, there is certainly a lot of data, not anything that is indicating to me that Biden has this huge lead, other than those media polls that keep getting published on every media channel," he said.

McCullough says he will update his 2020 map as the days tick down until the election, but that his current prognostication is about far more than just Trump's appeal. As he sees it, this race is also about what many see to be the shortfalls of Biden's long tenure in government.

"When you've been in Washington for 47 years and you've not really gotten any accomplishments to your credit, except things that you are kind of embarrassed by, like the prison reform package that he put together that jailed more African Americans than anything before it, youre talking about a very troublesome record that he's got to depend upon, " McCullough pointed out. "This is one of the reasons even president Obama was slow to endorse him."

Kevin McCullough has traditionally been spot on when he puts out an electoral map projection, and since making this prediction last week he has gained nearly 30,000 Twitter followers.

These thousands join millions more who are hoping his streak continues in just a few short weeks.

Marionettes Keep on Dancing

They might keep pulling our strings, but we don't have to dance.

The next two weeks promise to be a time of nearly unrivaled angst and division, continuing the ramp-up of emotion and anger we have experienced for at least a decade. Drooling with anticipation, the media seems to take every chance they can get to whip us into a frenzy and separate the masses into opposing camps. It's good for ratings and the bottom dollar.

With tensions rising for every reason imaginable, and even for those made up and built out of thin air, there are some voices calling on our better angels. One man behind the mic has emerged recently with words of wisdom for an embroiled nation. It is not unusual that he would offer this countenance today, because Brian Buffini has done similarly for years.

On a recent podcast episode, the Brian Buffini Show, the host made his call for the Power of Persuasion. As he sees it, it is in our power to disagree during this season, while maintaining healthy relationships and connections. His episode, like his program in general, did not focus on our political climate or current events. He stays above the fray, teaching in overarching themes, rather than getting into the mud with each week's tabloid developments. But buried in this recent broadcast were kernels of pertinent advice for an anxious nation.

Buffini's broadcasts have been a blessing to countless real estate professionals over the years, and more recently he has slid into the personal development and growth space, drawing on years of inspiration from greats such as Zig Ziglar, Earl Nightingale and Russell Conwell. Buffini delivers splendid weekly programming, devoted to the values that pushed him to emigrate to America, and then to succeed wildly once arriving and putting in the work.

Amid our current cultural angst, Buffini sees a complete breakdown in the way we talk to one another.

"Discussion is dead. Debate is dead," Buffini pointed out as he set the table for his recent episode. "Having differing opinions....you get censored online for having differing opinions."

During the program, the renowned speaker relied thematically on two classic books - *How to Win Friends and Influence People*, by Dale Carnegie, and *Influence: The Psychology of Persuasion,* by Robert Cialdini.

In a day and age when we are often at each other's throats, Buffini points out that no matter how our friends, colleagues and the media turn up the rhetorical temperature, *you really can't win an argument.*

"Winning an argument is actually losing," he said. "A man convinced against his will is of the same opinion still." Even if we win a heated political exchange, it is the "small satisfaction for a bridge possibly burnt." We make the point - CHECK MATE! - but lose a friend in the process. Very little actually changes. Dale Carnegie said if you lose an argument, you lose. And if you win an argument, you lose. Wise words we can carry with us long past November 3rd.

"An open mouth is a closed mind," says Buffini. "If you were wrong would you actually want to know it? For most people, the answer is no!"

Buffini goes even deeper behind the back and forth to ask *why are we arguing?*
"Our news media is no longer news media," Buffini pointed out. "I've watched press conferences and I've watched the questions afterward, and I go 'These are not interviews. These are not questions. These are activists.'" Buffini reasons that with 24-hours of "opinion, opinion, opinion," it's no wonder we are all amped up and ready to argue!

Buffini often points out that we are all salespeople, in some form or fashion, and *we all need to be skilled at persuasion.* This is a skill that translates from business, to politics to the Sunday night dinner table.

"You can change laws. You can clamp down with political correctness. You can weaponize speech," Buffini said, before paraphrasing a passage from Carnegie's classic book. "But if somebody's will is the same, and you haven't reached the heart, then you haven't done anything."

During this broadcast, Brian Buffini laid out many perfectly reasonable and wise points. He pointed out that the art of persuasion is about both sharing our way of thinking AND maintaining relationships, even when opinions remain far apart.

Indeed, just two weeks ago, Judge Amy Coney Barrett offered similar remarks during her Supreme Court nomination speech, saying that "arguments, even about matters of great consequence, need not destroy affection."

Throughout this episode, Buffini demonstrated his knack for combining historical wisdom and common sense. He quoted Carnegie. He quoted Cialdini. He even quoted Mark Twain! And every piece of advice they offered made perfect sense.

Many of us will hear his words and appreciate them.

Then we'll flip to our favorite media outlet to get our daily fix of the "news," as usual.

Old habits are hard to break, and the puppeteer is calling.

October 25, 2020

America Exposes the Media

America is currently experiencing unprecedented levels of unity. Agreement is everywhere, spanning across political, cultural and geographic divides. Among all issues, there is one on which Americans of all stripes can agree - the media should not be trusted.

On Friday's Ingraham Angle, Fox News hosts Laura Ingraham and Raymond Arroyo hosted a panel of swing state voters in Columbus, Ohio. This panel of Republicans, Democrats and Independents voiced a common concern - they do not trust the mainstream media or big tech.

During a discussion about the newly-uncovered evidence and corruption charges against Joe Biden, a panelist named Deb pointed out that many viewers most likely hadn't even heard about the uncovered laptop and email allegations.

"What bothers me is our news has become so personalized, that if you're a Biden supporter, you're not getting that side of the story," she said. "If you are a Trump supporter, you are, so the Trump supporters are going to continue to believe that this is a Joe Biden corruption piece, and the people who are Biden supporters are going to believe that this is a bunch of hooey."

NPR - partly funded by Americans' tax dollars - blatantly admitted they would not even cover the new revelations about the alleged pay-for-play scandal engulfing the Democratic nominee.

"We don't want to waste our time on stories that are not really stories," NPR announced as it's reason for not covering the shocking developments. "And we don't want to waste the listeners' and readers' time on stories that are just pure distractions." Interestingly, there was no such blackout during many similar stories that, while lacking evidence, targeted the president over the last few years.

The truth is, the veil has been lifted, and America no longer believes in or counts on the media. According to Gallup in 2020, only 40% of Americans have a great deal or fair amount of trust and confidence in the mass media - such as newspapers, TV and radio - when it comes to reporting the news fully, accurately and fairly. On this, there is a large degree of national unity. Some Americans believe this media deception is purposeful, because forcing us into our respective camps is good for business.

"The response of the media and the press is symbolic of what it takes to create the system that we are under," said Sadie, a self-described Independent. "The divisiveness is just advanced and supported, split, that's exactly what democracy requires under a two-party system, and they did it very effectively."

Americans knew something was wrong when, last decade, the media as a whole refused to look into a presidential candidate's web of shady ties and anti-American network of friends. They knew, of course. They just felt it was their solemn duty to keep their audiences uninformed. As Sean Hannity has repeatedly, "2008 is the year journalism died."

Then, in 2016, the same media went from celebrating and glorifying a cultural icon, only to do a 180 and go into full demonization mode once he announced a run for president. Same guy, same media. Americans watched the flip, which validated what they've always suspected of the mainstream press. As a result, that year saw only 32% of Americans admitting they had trust in the media's truthfulness - a record low. The charade is over.

Regarding the current scandal, some voters admit they don't care about the content or the media's motives.

"This is actually, for Democrats, a non-issue, a non-story. It's not being covered like it is on Fox, and quite frankly I'm kind of tired of it," said Lauren, a Democrat. "I don't believe that it's a thing, and even if it is, it doesn't matter."

"She's right, it's not being covered," responded Kevin, a Trump voter. "The question is, why? Why don't you see it on NBC, ABC or CBS? That's the question we should be asking." Proving the point, a Democrat named Mark admitted that, even though the initial email and laptop revelations had been made many days earlier, this was the first he'd heard of the allegations. How can Americans agree on anything when we don't all hear the story or get the facts?

Americans of all stripes know the truth. The media, as a whole, is not fair and balanced. News is not really news. In actuality, news is now a reflection of a point of view. If you agree, you like it and gravitate to it. If not, you are drawn to the opposite media view elsewhere. In some circles, this philosophy is referred to as "advocacy journalism," which is short for picking a side and anchoring your "reporting" accordingly.

Ingraham wrapped up the segment, asking the live panel, "How many people out there think a media outlet, again regardless of who is in the White House, should regard stories about our adversaries funneling money to family members of a sitting president, that's not a story. How many of you think that's the way a media organ should react?"

Not one member of the panel raised a hand. Democrats, Republicans, Independents. Not. One. Hand.
On this, Americans are unified.

November 1, 2020

Conservative Voices' Call to Action

The message is going out loud and clear - re-elect President Donald Trump or face the reality of an America that is unrecognizable.

Many of the country's premier conservate voices have sounded the alarm bell and called on their fellow citizens to protect their nation from the socialist nightmare they say awaits if Trump is defeated tomorrow. The "most important election of our lifetimes," they say, in the leadup to tomorrow's climactic vote.

On Friday, the "King of Talk Radio", Rush Limbaugh, began his program with a healthy dose of optimism.

"We can absolutely win this thing," Limbaugh began. "The bottom line is, we *have* to win this thing. I cannot imagine what our country looks like if we don't, folks." Limbaugh, a consistent defender of the President, had Trump join him recently and turned his entire three-hour program into a virtual rally.

For the past year, Sean Hannity has been calling on fellow Americans to reject the left wing radicalism so many legal immigrants are flooding to America to escape. He has consistently pointed out the Democratic ticket's extreme liberal positions, and urged his viewers to understand the choice before them.

"When they tell you who they are and what they plan to do, you've got to believe them," Hannity implored his television audience Friday. "For Joe and Kamala Harris and other Democrats, this election isn't only about higher taxes and government policy. This is about power. They want one-party rule in America."

Hannity has been on a year-long roll, warning of the dangers posed from cancel culture and the bullies on the left with their "doom and gloom" wish list, including the Green New Deal, open borders, defunding the police, eliminating fracking and fossil fuels, abortion on demand, packing the court with countless additional liberal judicial activists, adding more democratic senators, locking down schools, restaurants and churches, punishingly higher taxes and a government takeover of healthcare....to name a few.

"Will you bow to the angry mob that is demanding that you vote for Joe Biden, or will you vote for freedom," Hannity asked. "For prosperity, for energy independence, for judicial restraint, the Constitution, lower taxes and less bureaucracy and peace through strength. That is all on the ballot - safety, security, law and order is all on the ballot."

Talker Mark Levin, who has warmed greatly to President Trump over the past four years, made his plea during a weekend Facebook post. As he made clear, his focus is not simply about our nation's current outlook, but rather on preserving our traditions for generations to come.

"Donald Trump is a great president. He deserves reelection. We need to make sure he is reelected in order to protect our liberties and secure our republic" a measured Levin explained. "That's how important this election is. If you haven't voted, or your family hasn't voted, or friends, or colleagues, or neighbors, or co-workers, you need to make sure that you and they all vote. So we can pass to our children and our grandchildren the republic that we have lived in and enjoyed. When the Democrats say that everything is on the table, they're not kidding."

On his Saturday night episode of *Watters' World* on the Fox News Channel, host Jesse Watters highlighted the President's back-to-back-to-back winning weeks, culminated by our nation's record-setting 3rd-quarter GDP of 33.1%.

"I mean, I could be wrong. Maybe Covid is going to kill Trump's reelection. Maybe his style is going to hurt him with some groups. Maybe the big tech billionaire media alliance rigging the race for Biden is just too powerful," the rising conservative star pondered. "That could happen. But I don't believe it will. It won't happen if you vote. The people are what make Trump powerful. He's going to win re-election if the people turn out. I can feel it."

On Twitter, contributor Dan Bongino drew attention to Trump's unprecedented final push, where the President is holding up to five rallies a day and engaging with hundreds of thousands of supporters across battleground states.

"There isn't a more powerful force in politics than THE BIG MO," Bongino tweeted Saturday. "And the "mo" doesn't get any bigger than the Trump "mo" right now.

Daniel Hannan, on this weekend's edition of *The Next Revolution* on Fox News, ticked down the domestic and foreign policy victories over the past four years under Trump's leadership.

"On the substance, in any fair election, Trump would be resoundingly reelected," Hannan pointed out. "But we don't have a fair election. NBC, ABC, CBS, CNN, NPR, New York Times, Washington Post, Facebook, Twitter.....all of it, non-stop, wall-to-wall Biden propaganda. The alliance of bias, colluding to suppress information and suppress the Trump vote." Still, Hannan feels optimistic that America has seen the dishonest media for what they are. "Don't let them do it," he urged. "Don't let them win. Don't just rage against the machine....vote against it."

As Limbaugh's listeners and political allies remain anxious about the election, they often wonder what they can do to have an effect on the outcome.

"The best thing you can do is VOTE. It's the single best thing you can do," Rush said. "Make sure you vote and then convince four other people to vote for Trump with you. Or five. Or six. We have the power. We can save our country."

By early Wednesday morning, we may find out if this group of conservative stalwarts have effectively made their contribution, galvanizing enough support to aid in getting the President over the finish line.

November 8, 2020

The Unstoppable Optimism of Charles Payne

Even after the last week, Charles Payne is a well of optimism. While the official outcome of the 2020 Presidential Election will remain undecided for perhaps a month or more, one can bank on the fact that Payne will continue to rally for America's economic rebound.

Payne is an unabashed champion of American prosperity. He has been a leading voice this year, promoting both the pre and post-pandemic economic boom, which has brought opportunity for citizens across the economic spectrum. He has been talking on air for years, explaining what needs to be done to ensure an all-encompassing rising economic tide.

Over the last few years, we've seen those policies come to fruition, bringing with them astounding economic growth. From boardrooms to warehouse floors, wages have risen and take-home income has grown for the vast majority of Americans. From Payne's perspective, much of those advancements will be maintained for the foreseeable future.

Many Americans understandably fear the economic implications of a possible shift in policy. An assault on fracking and fossil fuels would have incalculable effects on the way many citizens make a living. In addition, new regulations on energy production or use would "naturally cause energy costs to skyrocket," as predicted by former president Obama.

Regardless of the current investigations into election fraud and the eventual 2020 presidential election outcome, Payne urges many Americans to take a breath. Republicans surged across the country - in state houses, as well as the U.S. House - while maintaining control of the U.S. Senate. This red wave bodes well for the preservation of many of President Trump's economic gains, and divided government, on the whole, usually sets the stage for solid stock market increases.

"Markets and economy (especially blue collar workers and farmers and so many others typically left out of economic booms) love President Trump," Payne tweeted last Friday. "Now that most of his work cannot be undone is a major plus."

On the whole, Payne feels that congressional gridlock will prevent any mass-elimination of the policies that have supercharged the economy over president Trump's first term.

"The good news is there is no Biden mandate for full frontal assault on your industry," Payne tweeted to an upset oil field worker, now scared of losing his job. "Voters in Ohio and Texas and Pennsylvania spoke loud and clear about their frustration, but there will be a lot of executive actions that won't help."

As a champion of the little guy, Payne is the epitome of the American dream, rising from poverty to success over the course of his life. His recent book, *Unstoppable Prosperity,* is a how-to for readers wanting to learn his philosophy of picking stocks. Through his on-air work, Payne has developed a bond with his audience based, first and foremost, on his unending optimism.

"My success has been built from my strong work ethic, augmented with fiscal discipline and investing," Payne says in the book. "I never let being poor hold me back from acting on my dreams so I plunged into the stock market as a teenager."

When he's not writing books and tweeting about his grandkids, Payne hosts Making Money With Charles Payne from 2pm-3pm daily on the Fox Business Network. You may also catch him filling in or appearing with Neil Cavuto or another host on Fox News or the business channel.

As the legal challenges mount in our divided nation, Charles Payne remains hopeful. He has always been bullish on America. On our economy, but more importantly, bullish on our spirit.

We don't know exactly what the future holds. What we do know is that Charles Payne will continue to have his eyes fixed on a bright, uplifting future for America.

November 15, 2020

Finding Truth Through the Fog

Who should we believe?

Amid the confusion, legal battles and post-election dust settling, Americans are left wondering, "Where can we find the truth?"

Not the Trump truth. Not the liberal truth. The *real* truth, as if there were any other kind.

Perhaps in bygone eras, citizens would flip on the nightly news to find out what was going on in the world. They saw and believed. After all, there was no reason not to.

They read in the morning papers, and they believed. There was no reason not to.

Over the past few decades, however, Americans have been conditioned to question the news, based solely on where it emanates from. Liberals believe CNN and MSNBC. Conservatives, who for years have believed Fox News, now rely on Newsmax, One America News and others. The dangerous trend has solidified - we don't trust or believe those on the other side.

Much of the credit for the democratization of our news consumption goes to Rush Limbaugh. Before his program took off in the 1980's, a largely liberal news media delivered its programming to an unsuspecting America. Essentially one source, with the same worldview, delivering the news. Not until Limbaugh emerged did listeners realize that there was actually another side to the story. What consumers had been fed for years had come through a liberal prism. Before Rush, it wasn't possible to notice, because the media variations were all bananas from the same bunch. After Rush, eyes have been opened.

The media has been proven to lie and mislead. Dan Rather. Brian Williams. 4 years of breathless proclamations that our President was a Russian asset. Perhaps the most impactful contribution from President Trump has been his ability to allow the mainstream media to bare all and present themselves as they are. Partisanship and extremism for all to see. From this evidence has come the mistrust.

The issue at hand as we conclude 2020 is that America has been split along partisan media lines, and nobody knows where to get the truth.

Was the election really stolen, using dead voters and mass election fraud, while preventing the other side from observing the count?

Were millions of votes changed through secret use of ballot-switching software, as has been alleged in some media circles this weekend?

Or was the President simply rebuked over his forceful and sometimes-unrefined personality, while a red wave washed across the rest of the country, lifting Republicans to unexpected levels virtually everywhere else?

Pollsters told us he would be beaten badly. The media said he had no chance.
Yet, we saw a huge Trump lead by early morning November 4th, only to watch hundreds of thousands of supposedly-mail-in votes dumped into the mix, overtaking the President in the hours and days since.

Were these additional ballots faithfully tabulated in accordance with the law?

Were nefarious characters manipulating the totals in the dark shadows of night? Not one American citizen hopes that is the case.

Is it possible that Republicans, with President Trump at the top of the ticket, maintained control of the Senate, picked up perhaps a dozen seats in the House, maintained all state legislatures and picked up more...but the President still lost? Even while he received nearly ten million more votes than he did in 2016 and performed markedly better with black and Hispanic voters. Yet he lost to a candidate lacking an enthusiastic base or energetic ground game who blew past the vote totals of the first black president and the would-be first woman president?

What is the truth?

The problem is we don't yet know. And, more importantly, we don't know who to believe.
Most American voters, as up to a million Trump supporters demonstrated Saturday in Washington D.C., won't take to the streets to riot, loot and cause violence if their chosen candidate is declared the loser. But that depends completely on us trusting the outcome. And right now, very few do, because very few trust those delivering the news.

Scott Adams of Dilbert fame put it best.

"The most corrupt institutions and individuals in America have declared that the election was free of fraud," Adams tweeted sarcastically this week. "That's good enough for me. What's wrong with the rest of you?"

The issue at hand is not who rightfully won on November 3rd. Americans of all stripes would, and should, accept the winner of an honorable, truthful election.

The concern is that we don't yet know. The lack of trust has created a dense fog, one that shows no signs of lifting any time soon.

November 22, 2020

Fox News Tells its Audience to Pound Sand

"It's been nice having you around for 25 years. Really, you've made us quite wealthy and successful. We gave you what you want. But it's time for you to hit the road, because we don't share those values anymore. We're done with you. You've served your purpose, and please don't let the door hit you on the way out."

In essence, these were the unspoken words delivered by Fox News to its legions of viewers on November 3rd, 2020.

One of the first signals came early in the night, as many viewers were just settling in for a night of watching the election returns, when the Fox team announced gleefully that not only would Democrats hold the U.S. House of Representatives, but they would actually surge and gain at least five seats.

In reality, Fox news was quite wrong, as Republicans rode a red wave to massive double-digit gains in the House.

The climactic moment when Fox News unofficially gave it's viewership the royal salute was shortly after 11pm, when the network's brainiacs declared Joe Biden the winner in Arizona. That was the first call of the night to cut against the grain in President Trump's most direct path to re-election. The problem, of course, is that the Grand Canyon state has yet to be officially decided...21 days later. It may indeed flip from red to blue. Or it may yet stay in Trump's column, after looming recounts and/or legal challenges.

Regardless, Fox was ready, willing and eager to kick its loyal audience to the curb. And truthfully, that is their prerogative. Changing leadership and, with it, a change in philosophy has foreshadowed this evolution for years.

Out were Glenn Beck, Bill O'Reilly and others. In are Donna Brazile, Leland Vittert, Chris Wallace and other voices skewing left.

And many other changes have been noticeable for quite some time.

Neil Cavuto, a once-staunch espouser of free markets and conservative principles, has seemingly joined his pal, Mitt Romney, in the destroy-Trump-at-all-costs mission. Just two weeks ago, Cavuto cut away from White House Press Secretary Kayleigh McEnany's press conference, as she was pointing out mounting evidence of voter fraud. Cavuto simply couldn't allow such assertions to go out over the Fox News airwaves.

Dana Perino, a mostly-fair yet non-Trumper, responded last week to current vote-altering allegations by wondering on air if, or when, the Dominion company would sue the Trump legal team. She tweeted that she wouldn't be surprised if they do. Certainly she may be correct, if one presumes the allegations of corruption are unfounded. The facts have yet to be heard and the process has yet to play out. Still, her gut reaction seemed to be to attack the Trump team. Same for many other contributors heard on the network.

Some of the shifting attitudes inside Fox News began to show prior to the election. One example came in September, when contributor Newt Gingrich brought up the influence of George Soros when discussing the violent rioting and looting in Democrat-controlled cities across the country. The startled panel of hosts chided Gingrich for making the remark and shut down the train of thought.

The change inside Fox News has even escalated and attached itself to the network's biggest name, at the moment. Tucker Carlson recently announced he'll continue to host his network program, and then last week took what many felt was a personal aim at Trump attorney, Sidney Powell. Carlson correctly noted that he has yet to see verifiable proof of Powell's claims of massive voter fraud, but then descended into personal attacks on her demeanor and credibility. Through text message exchanges, she has refused to appear with evidence on his program, and Powell says it was Carlson who was rude and unprofessional. Regardless, the last two weeks has taken Tucker down a couple pegs in the eyes of some of the more than 73 million Trump supporters. Many of these same viewers had, until recently, even put forth Carlson's name as a future presidential candidate.

The big winners so far, as Fox News has summarily dumped its loyal customer base, seem to be NewsMax and One America News. Like Trump himself, both growing networks play to a conservative, traditional American base. They have seen skyrocketing interest and ratings over the past few weeks, as viewers search for an alternative to what they could count on for more than two decades at Fox News.

As Fox dismisses claims of voting irregularity and proclaims Joe Biden as "President-Elect," One America News recently aired a feature entitled, "Dominion-izing the Vote," which went in-depth into the "glitches, errors and money trails" related to the voting systems used in many swing states.

The Fox News slide is now far more than anecdotal. RedState reported last week that MSNBC's *Morning Joe* beat Fox News' *Fox & Friends* in the ratings for the first time in 20 years.

The Daily Caller quotes a Morning Consult survey that reports while 67% of Republicans viewed Fox News favorably before the election, only 54% view them favorably now.

And depending how the 2020 election eventually ends up, these networks may have a new leader to glue them together with the Republican, conservative and populist base. At the moment, that leader still has plans for the next four years.

As he is fond of saying, "We'll see what happens."

November 29, 2020

The Dawn of a New Era in Cable News

The astronaut has planted his flag on the moon.

As we witness the evolution of the news media, with established networks lurching further left to please the woke, liberal audience, younger outfits are jumping in to fill the void.

A tweet last week from conservative activist Brandon Straka summed it up perfectly.

"Watching @Newsmax is really exciting to me bc I see the great potential," he said on Twitter. "It's like watching early MTV when it 1st launched. It's going to become something big & something unlike anything that's been done before. I love tuning in & seeing the faces of up-and-comers in our movement!"

As the mental images of 1981 MTV flood back - complete with REO Speedwagon, Pat Benatar and Rod Stewart - the responses came rolling in. Followers told Straka his analogy was a strong one and that they, too, could feel the excitement of something new. Many remember the fledgling music video network that featured an astronaut planting an MTV flag on the moon, and they appreciate Straka's metaphor.

One theme echoed by many of the responses was that viewers are sick and tired of being herded, like sheep. They don't want to be told what is true and what to believe, when their eyes - and common sense - tell them otherwise.

"Tuning in more and more! It's nice to hear honesty and respect," tweeted a fourth-grade teacher, in her compliment of NewsMax. "I'm also enjoying reporters that report the facts and let their viewers make their own minds up. Keep it coming! I'm not even watching my local news anymore; sick of hearing them vomit at the mouth!"

A retired firefighter commented, "That's a great comparison! It's obvious they don't have the state of the art sets or graphics yet, but if they stay true to the conservative base, the sponsors will follow the viewers away from @FoxNews and they will catch up and pass other networks!"

The point about the set and graphics is a solid one, and it is here that you occasionally get the feel you are watching something new emerging from the very beginning. Just last week, high-pitched feedback filled the air as anchor Greg Kelly began his program. Kelly paused, and moments later a member of the stage crew appeared from behind, reached to the side of Kelly's suit jacket and adjusted the levels on his IFB transmitter. Live, unfiltered TV. Hard to be more authentic than that. Kelly rolled with it, and proceeded smoothly into another stellar monologue.

Founded in 2014, after their website precursor launched in 1998, NewsMax TV has become a landing spot for anchors, hosts and national personalities who first gained notoriety elsewhere. The list includes Kelly, Sean Spicer, Michelle Malkin, Dick Morris, Bob Sellers, Howie Carr and others. Adding to the list are upcoming talents such as Grant Stinchfield, Chris Salcedo, John Bachman and many more.

As we enter 2021 and the top three cable TV powerhouses stake their leftward claim, NewsMax TV, along with One America News Network, has a real opportunity to fill the void and become the counterbalance. As the mainstream legacy media continues its decades-long charade of bias, Americans are jumping ship and heading for dry land.

Viewers demand credibility. They crave intellectual honesty. They appreciate creators who produce something real, while expanding into unoccupied territory to deliver that which is missing. Rush Limbaugh hit radio gold thirty years ago, when he spoke from the heart, voicing traditional opinions that, up until that point, hadn't been heard broadly on television or radio. NewsMax now attempts to tap into that recently-vacated cable television void in a similar fashion.

In 1983, viewers and music-lovers gathered to experience the spectacle of Michael Jackson's *Thriller* video. It was fresh, unique and entertaining. Exactly what fans expected from MTV.

In today's evolving media landscape, viewers are excited to challenge the status quo and again feel the growing pains of something new and authentic.

They want to plant their own flag on the moon.

December 6, 2020

The Career Opportunity of a Lifetime

As young adults pause for reflection over the upcoming Christmas break, non-traditional as it is this school year, many will ponder their future. Where they are, and where their aspirations may take them in the years ahead. The holiday slowdown is the optimal time for introspection and goal setting. High school and college students may, and should, be plotting their steps toward future employment.

"Where do I want to be in five or ten years, and what do I want to do with my life?"

Although many of them may not see the following response through the thick clouds of COVID, it could be staring them straight in the face.

This may be the perfect time to pursue a career in news journalism.

You read correctly.

On the face of it, this sounds absurd. In fact, ridiculous. After all we've seen and heard over the past decade - fake news, alternative facts, opinion-laced broadcasting, hate-filled group-think and much more - why would anyone want to join that bunch?. As we enter 2021, society as a whole holds about the same opinion of news "journalists" as they do used car salesmen, ambulance-chasing attorneys and politicians.

In fact, reporters and journalists have quite the distinction in terms of negative opinion. And they have truly earned the honor. Last year *Moneywise* reported on Gallup's latest findings and ranked occupations based on trustworthiness. Members of Congress, lobbyists and car salespeople were the three most dishonest professions. The next two least-respected jobs on the list - TV Reporters and Newspaper Reporters.

In other words, America doesn't trust politicians, attorneys or journalists. (Our apologies to the ethical politicians and attorneys across the fruited plain.)

But in this fact lies the biggest opportunity for the youth of today! Look at many of the revolutionaries and history-makers of our time - Warren Buffett, Steve Jobs, Russell Simmons, Elon Musk. When society and popular opinion go one way, they go the other. The masses say "sell," so Buffett buys. Americans flock to SUVs, so Musk dives head-first into electric.

Going against the popular and easy flow is a crucial choice. It puts you on the island, standing alone against the tide. Immediately, you are unique. You stand out. You will garner the spotlight that has been abandoned in recent years, because you differentiate yourself from the monolithic mainstream media thought patterns.

So the next time you turn on the TV and hear a network television anchor rambling on with his interpretation of the news, including, most notably to him, what you should think about it, take this as the bright, flashing green light of opportunity!

Most of these "journalists" want to tell viewers what they should think about an issue. They want to insert opinion and treat it as fact. You, on the other hand, will stand out by simply reporting genuine facts and allowing viewers to make up their own minds and formulate their own opinions. What a novel concept!

Who, what, when, where, why and how. Remember when this was the definition of a career in journalism? Lay it out there for the consumer, and let them feel about those facts how they will.

News directors, reporters and "journalists" often feel they are much more important these days to stick to that simple set of guide posts. That old way of thinking is so 1950. They are uber-smart and, therefore, feel they must pass along just a touch of sophistication and opinion to help shape the little people. As such, many profess to practice "advocacy journalism."

From their holier-than-thou viewpoint, "advocacy journalism" means reporting on the stories that matter and teaching you why you should care too. In the real world, the term "advocacy journalism" simply means slanting the news to highlight their favored point of view. Very similar to the use of the term "social justice" to highlight preferred left-leaning policy positions.

So the next time a news director or professor urges you to pursue advocacy journalism, why not stand out by simply covering the facts. Your readers or viewers can make up their own mind. In that respect, who do you think will come across as fresh, unique and trustworthy? You!

Common sense might lead one to believe that real news gathering and journalism is a dead profession. A career path from a bygone era that has melted away, much like the milkman or phone book advertising rep.

But fear not!

There will always be room for honest, ethical news reporters and writers who do the research, dig for the facts and lay them out transparently for their audience. They begin and end with the facts, with little eye toward any desired outcome.

The way news journalism was meant to be pursued.

The time might be right for you to travel this path and build a career to be proud of.

December 13, 2020

The Pandemic Did Not Cause Economic Hardship

Not one American has been affected financially by the worldwide Covid-19 pandemic.

This opinion from the 3rd-ranked talk radio host in the nation, Dave Ramsey, may catch some off guard.

Perhaps you heard the segment on *The Dave Ramsey Show* last week. You may have recoiled in disbelief, or turned up the volume to see if you heard correctly. After all, you've seen the economic destruction this year with your own eyes.

Businesses have closed. Many restaurants are teetering on the financial edge. Hard-working taxpayers are struggling to pay the bills. Hourly employees rushed to collect unemployment. Even now, many Americans wait on Congress to approve another Covid-relief payment, one that the Democrat Speaker of the House admitted this week has been purposely stalled so it would not help the President get re-elected.

With so much financial suffering among American households over the last ten months, how could Dave Ramsey ever say the pandemic wasn't the cause.

"The financial challenges are not brought on by the pandemic," Ramsey stated clearly. "They're brought on by the economic shutdown. It's brought on by your government."

Ramsey's rant began when co-host Chris Hogan handed him an article from USA Today, stating that over 68% of Americans had financial setbacks in 2020 amid the pandemic. The article highlighted a new 3000-person Fidelity survey, which cited job loss, declining household income and drawdown of emergency savings as some of what most Americans experienced this year.

"When you shut down people's ability to make an income, then they're going to have financial trouble. "Ramsey said. "That really wouldn't be an insight, USA Today. That would be a fairly obvious conclusion."

"Cause and effect," Hogan added.

"But it's not the pandemic. The pandemic didn't cause it," Ramsey continued. "People being sick with Covid did not cause the economy to collapse. These shutdowns by the government caused the economy to collapse."

This is a particularly touchy subject as we approach Christmas, with many states - including New York this week - announcing another round of restrictions, once again forcing restaurants and businesses to slow down or close. In these states, governors are repeating the financially-destructive cycle.

Many medical professionals and politicians, including President Trump, have continually warned that the nation cannot allow the cure to be worse than the sickness itself. Indeed, some studies show little correlation between strict lockdown measures and positive effects in slowing down the spread of Covid-19. In fact, many scientists say the same for mask-wearing.

"One of the biggest problems with the economic shutdown, brought on by the government, in an attempt to control the pandemic, is that it has affected attitudes more than reality," said Ramsey. "Depression is up. Suicide is up. As (Ramsey personality) Dr. Delony calls them - the diseases of despair are up."

The study reported that 23% of respondents lost a job or household income this year, and 20% had an unexpected, non-health emergency. 18% had to provide unexpected financial aid to family or friends.

Ramsey continued, saying that what Americans are hearing and seeing from the news media is causing them to perceive that things are actually worse than they are. This mindset, in turn, has caused them to lock down their finances, feeling they are actually in a worse situation than is actually the case. Seeing constant doom and gloom in the news makes one feel as though his own financial house is crumbling, whether backed up by reality or not. Hogan referred to this feeling of personal financial doom as a self-fulfilling prophecy.

"It's not a mathematics thing. It's - I'm freaked out because I've watched the news so much, that told me it's coming to an end," Ramsey asserted. "I listened to the Governor of California, and I listened to the Governor of New York, and I said we're all gonna die. It's over. We just need to stay inside and wait on death to come."

Ramsey and Hogan, as has become their mantra over the decades, urged listeners to stay focused on the long term and make decisions based on facts, rather than feelings.

"If you believe things are going bad and you start taking all your decisions based on things going bad, you're going to cause them to go bad," Ramsey said.

Ramsey and team head into 2021 continuing to focus on the personal side of finance, keeping listeners focused on kitchen-table reality, regardless of the feelings and narrative presented by the news media.

December 20, 2020

Pulling Back the Curtain With a Laugh

"I saw the man behind the curtain, and I went to Oz. I just saw who these people really are."

Comedian and social media influencer, Nicole Arbour, recently spent some time with Glenn Beck, sharing her perspective on the current state of our country and the Hollywood elite, as the condition of each has been laid bare for all to see.

Once a member of the Hollywood crowd, Arbour no longer sees in the majority of that group much to admire.

"I saw that every charity that they pretend to support, they don't support that charity. They show up to the event to walk the red carpet, to get their photo taken, to wear a dress that's $20,000, donate zero to the actual charity, and then do an interview that says, 'I support this'. All of them are fraudulent human beings."

Beck has built a career standing for the common man against the powers of the elites in government, Hollywood and media. He touted populism a decade before Donald Trump came marching into town carrying the populist flag. It was Beck who, years ago, implored his audience to read Amity Shlaes' *The Forgotten Man*, which offered a look back - and, unknowingly, a prediction of coming events - into the current populist American revival.

Arbour, meanwhile, has gained notoriety partially due to her quick comedic wit and its applications on social media, and also because she has shared her life authentically with followers. Her Go Team Academy website reveals she was disabled, suicidal and in bed for most of her 20's. Today, Arbour contributes a light, honest, uplifting approach from a younger point of view.

After time as a cheerleader and inside the Hollywood world, Arbour now pokes fun at,the fake entertainment culture being presented to normal Americans.

"They don't have any values. Their only value is the dollar, and they don't care how they get it," Arbour said. "Everything I care about in my life - they *don't* care about. It's just a hollow existence in Los Angeles, and I'm glad to be out of it."

In the shorter interview, airing during the live Glenn Beck Radio program, Arbour discussed the mainstream media narrative being pushed, claiming that Joe Biden won the 2020 presidential election. She, like half of America looking at data and evidence, doesn't buy it.

"A good portion of the country feels like they just had their teeth kicked in," Beck said. "I know you're a Trump supporter. You can't believe those guys won."

"Well they didn't, that's why I don't believe it. We know that it didn't happen," Arbour responded. "So now the country has to rally and decide who we are. I am a Canadian that has taken on this country as my own, but we have to decide who the heck we are and what we stand for."

Arbour echoes the feelings of many Americans across the country who see scores of statistical anomalies that simply don't add up.

"Even if, for some reason, Harris is the....I'm not even going to say Biden, because he doesn't know where he is. If Harris is suddenly the president, how are we going to act," Arbour asked rhetorically. "The masks and the veils are off everybody, we can see who everybody is, so now we get to move on from here."

Arbour discussed the time she was speaking to an audience on the campus of USC in 2016. She was not a supporter of either presidential candidate, and was speaking about social media and the upcoming election. She told Beck that before going on stage that day, members of the Hillary Clinton campaign were "strongly suggesting" that she endorse the Democratic nominee during her presentation. She refused, only to have them introduce her falsely to the young audience as a Clinton supporter.

"I was like, game on! Flip table, now you guys have an enemy, let's go!" she told Beck. "That was my first real inkling that this Hollywood crowd is not what they say they are. And then as more and more has come out over the past few years, I'm just standing there saying I told you so! I feel like I'm Spartacus or something."

With the curtain now pulled back, and Americans taking sides, both Beck and Arbour made the case for the goodness of America overcoming the nonstop deception and hate.

"I have so much faith, maybe I'm just a happy cheerleader by nature - which I am," Arbour said. "Yes, Avengers Endgame is coming, but we're on the right side. I see people who were the opposite of what we think going 'Wait a minute' every single day. They're waking up. From the entrepreneurs that are fighting back and opening their businesses, from people saying these lockdowns are ridiculous. From people saying, 'I know you say election fraud didn't happen, but I'm watching the video with my own eyes!'

Yahoo Finance named Arbour the top influencer to follow in 2020, and during the radio interview she shared some of her personal growth journey. She admitted that a few years ago she thought the worst of anyone supporting Donald Trump. She recalled visiting a friend who was already on the Trump train.

"You're a garbage human," she thought of her friend, at the time. "Oh my gosh, you're a homophobic, sexist racist."

Arbour now says she has naturally changed her view. And although she has seen so many great American citizens supporting the President, she says she doesn't let the media or Hollywood culture decide what she should think.

"I was like, whoa Nicole, that's a *you* thing, for you to automatically think that this person is X, Y, Z because you've been told to think like that."

Nicole Arbour pulled back the curtain for Beck's listeners, and even found time to tell him he could easily be mistaken for Colonel Sanders.

The full radio interview, as well as a longer podcast episode, can be heard on Glenn Beck's website.

January 4, 2021

Talk Radio Voices Roar in 2021

Conservative talk radio is undergoing a major shift, perhaps the medium's biggest in the last few decades.

As we ramp back up to normal life after the Christmas and New Year's break, talk radio is also getting back to business as usual. However, this year promises to deliver a changing talk radio landscape where much is still unknown.

For the last four years, conservative talk radio, aka successful and profitable talk radio, has had proven results delivered by the Republican Trump administration to admire every day. More money in working-folks' pockets, zero foreign wars and judges who admire and follow the constitution make up just a few of the items top talkers have had to praise over the past few years. Plus plenty of drama, some created by the President, along with even more drummed up by his Democratic opposition.

As such, the biggest shift in 2021 for conservative media is playing the role of the opposition, with their preferred party no longer holding control of the White House. In fact, as a business model this vantage point has traditionally held the biggest upside, in terms of ratings and revenue. It pays very well to vocally beat the drum of opposition and point out your opponent's mistakes. Fear, anxiety and anger sell, and we are certain to see it from the right, as we have for the last few years on the left.

This assumes, of course, that Joe Biden is in fact the president as of late January. For a moment, we'll go with that assumption and disregard the mountains of evidence indicating it was actually President Trump who swept most of six swing states, and with them the Electoral College.

Relating to this current political battle over the validity of the election results, some talk hosts will have to find their sweet spot. Sean Hannity, for example, spent four straight years loudly praising and lauding the accomplishments of President Trump, only to seemingly roll over and pronounce a Trump loss immediately as we woke on November 4th. While other hosts fought, as they do to this day, Hannity was much slower to come around to supporting the 75-plus million voters who believe their legal choice was subverted and corrupted. Only as the waning days of 2020 approached did Hannity seem to tap into the anger and frustration of his radio listener base. In 2021, he'll have to stake out his territory.

Other hosts, such as Mark Levin, have been 100% behind the #StopTheSteal movement, immediately pointing out the unconstitutional nature of this election process, and becoming especially critical of most of the post-election judicial rulings. Levin has never wavered, and his posture will undoubtedly remain consistent as the new year unfolds. Rush Limbaugh has hit a similar tone, urging America not to back down and allow its will to be subverted.

Abnormal this year will be the afternoon or evening airwaves devoid of Michael Savage. After 26 years opining about politics, culture and meatballs on his syndicated radio talk show, Savage now moves to a podcast-only format, where he says his program may be a bit more edgy, due to a lack of FCC constraints.

The biggest change in 2021 - in fact the elephant in the padded radio studio - may be the world of talk radio without Limbaugh leading the charge. In an emotional sendoff to 2020, Limbaugh concluded his final broadcast of the year by admitting the day will come when he cannot host his daily radio program. The eternal optimist and "Mayor of Realville," Limbaugh has been open about his battle with lung cancer, especially after missing shows due to the effects of treatment. Limbaugh literally resurrected the talk radio format in the 1980's, hit a nerve with the traditional, conservative majority of America, and helped give rise to a generation of hosts and personalities following his lead. A broadcast day without Limbaugh, whenever that should come, will surely be as abnormal to the medium as one can imagine.

We don't know exactly what the 12 months of 2021 will bring, let alone the first 12 days of this new year. Americans are hoping for health. To quote Warren Harding, who lead our nation at this time 100 years ago, they are hoping for a return to normalcy. Harding and his successor, Calvin Coolidge, led a rebirth of the nation and the rise of the roaring 20's.

American talk radio is now experiencing a rebirth of its own. We will hear their voices roar anew in 2021.

January 11, 2021

The Economic Tune is Changing

The sweet music of a strong economic era could very well be coming to an end, with Americans from coast to coast anticipating a slowing, if not complete cessation, of the nation's economic renaissance.

Media and talk personalities are sounding the alarm bells, as Joe Biden and his globally-focused team of economists are set to take the reigns of power next week.

On a recent episode of *The Rich Dad Radio Show*, host Robert Kiyosaki opened with a warning. Joe Biden has announced he will nominate Janet Yellen as his Secretary of the Treasury. From 2014-2018, she was the chair of the Federal Reserve. A student of economic history, Kiyosaki is both amused and alarmed at the news.

"We've just gone centralized, we've gone communist," Kiyosaki said, during his episode titled *Your Taxes in 2021*. "She was head of the Fed, and the centralized bank called the Fed is supposed to be separate from the Treasury. If you understand that, they should not be together."

In a November 30th article on FoxBusiness.com, Grover Norquist opined that economic hardship is quickly headed to the kitchen table of American families.

"Personal income taxes will increase, your 401k will drop in value as the Biden administration and Yellen increase the corporate tax on the corporate stocks in your 401k, and your cost of gasoline and energy will increase," Norquist, the President of Americans for Tax Reform predicted.

Norquist noted that the liberal Yellen will "gladly carry out Biden's tax-hike plans," starting with the elimination of the Trump tax cuts, which put more money in the pockets of the American middle class.

"Such a repeal would impose a $2,000 annual tax hike on a median-income family of four and a $1,300 tax hike on a median income single parent with one child," Norquist said.

Kiyosaki, for his part, has mostly sidestepped the expected siege of Americans' rights to free speech, religious liberty and the right to bear arms. His radio program's focus has always been "the good news and bad news about money." During the episode, tax advisor Tom Wheelwright summed up his expectations of the next few years.

"The Democrats have this magic money theory, I'm sorry, *modern* money theory, that's the Fed," Wheelwright said. "They think they can just print money and everything's going to be fine, and then you tax people and enact your social policies. Taxes have become social policy more than they've become even raising revenue, under that theory."

After experiencing the past few years of record-low unemployment and unprecedented levels of economic prosperity for virtually all socioeconomic groups, Americans are now preparing for a reversal, expecting a tsunami of new taxes and regulations aimed at the hard-working middle class. They remember keenly the economic malaise the last time Biden's party controlled the White House.

Bill O'Reilly thinks this will have a drastic and personal effect on American voters, as they see their economic gains of recent years wiped out by a looming leftward shift in economic policy.

"The economy is the first thing they're going to try to do," O'Reilly told Glenn Beck on his radio show last week. "The first thing that Biden and his crew want to do is raise taxes. Now that's not going to help the economy, everyone knows that."

Longer-term, O'Reilly thinks the result of the approaching economic policies will most likely be a slowing down by businesses, along with economic contraction.

"I don't hope for that," O'Reilly added. "But if that happens, in 2022 there's going to be an enormous backlash against the Democrats. "There are 32 Senate seats up in '22, and the Republicans could well take both houses if there is an economic contraction."

For his part, Kiyosaki has long-believed that as the United States economy falters, there will be opportunity and safety in precious metals, such as gold and silver, as well as in cryptocurrencies like Bitcoin. His criticism of money printing has spanned decades and administrations of both parties.

While America braces for its economic fate, all ears are on these and other voices, as they try to predict the country's financial future.

In their assessment, the music is about to end.

January 18, 2021

The Shifting Media Spotlight

2021 brings a new focus for the media, as frustration and anger linger across the country relating to journalism's role in the rancor and discord enveloping American life over the past couple decades.

Fox Business host Lou Dobbs had an insightful conversation Friday with Dr. Robert Jeffress, the pastor of the First Baptist Church of Dallas, Texas. The two recapped the lasting achievements of Donald Trump's administration, the media's deceptive coverage of his Presidency and journalism's once-revered role as our nation's watch dogs.

"The President again is being fraudulently impeached by the Dems, and there is not even a whisper of dissent or opposition to that in the national left-wing media," Dobbs said, also pointing out the recent attacks on Jeffress by some members of the Republican establishment.

"Lou, this is something we're going to see more and more over these next four years," Jeffress began. "That's an attempt to shame people like you and me who strongly support this President, and to repenting of our support of him. Well I'll guaran-dang-tee you I'm not repenting of anything, certainly not my support of this great President."

Jeffress told USA today this week that he had no regrets in supporting Donald Trump. None whatsoever.

"I told him this week that I believe he is the greatest President of my lifetime, and he will go down as the most pro-life, pro-religious liberty President in American history," Jeffress added. "Nothing anyone says is going to change that. Lou, he's leaving office next week with his legacy intact."

Dobbs, who has for four years pointed out nonstop media deception relating to President Trump's accomplishments, went further to recap the incessant attacks on the 45th President of the United States.

"It's an extraordinary legacy all the more because of the efforts of the radical Dems, the deep state, from the beginning almost of his candidacy for the office - they tried to deny him - and then their efforts to overthrow him and block his agenda throughout. He accomplished more than any President in the first three years of his term. His four years in office are remarkable in achievement, all the more so because of the naked, corrupt opposition of the radical Left and the deep state," Dobbs said.

Jeffress, an early and consistent supporter of candidate and then President Trump, added that the President knew what he was in for, as the entire establishment swamp of both parties was not simply going to sit back and allow him to disrupt the normal way of doing things in Washington.

"I remember sitting in the oval office and telling him 'Mr. President, you have an axis of evil that is going to conspire to take you down. Not only the media and the Democrats, but the establishment Republicans,'" he recalls telling Trump. "And that proved to be true. They conspired together but they couldn't stop his tremendous achievements in spite of all of those headwinds. I am grateful, eternally grateful, for what he has done for our nation, even though he's leaving office for now. His legacy will endure."

The news over the weekend was how Dobbs summed up the conversation in his synopsis of the non-stop attacks from the left and the media, designed to take down Trump politically and personally.

"It is the most vile, venomous assault ever conducted against a President in our country's history," Dobbs pointed out. "Short of the assasignation of Abraham Lincoln. This is a nation that cannot heal, that cannot come together, until we understand the truth and reality of what we have witnessed over the course of the past four years of this man's presidency."

"We're going to depend upon you over these next four years to point out what is going on - the darkness, the lies that we're going to see," Jeffress implored Dobbs. "Yes, we need to pray for our new president, president Biden. The Bible says we need to pray for all of our leaders. But we also need to be ready to push back against the unGodly policies that are sure to come. These are days for God's people to stand up and be courageous like never before."

If recent history is any indication, both Dobbs and Jeffress will remain standing strongly on the front lines, illuminating the truth, as the next chapter of our nation's history unfolds.

January 25, 2021

Americans Become Their Own Media

As the mainstream, corporate media has transformed from watchdogs and information disseminators to cheerleaders, suppressors and protectors, citizens now have to take on the aforementioned traditional roles themselves.

If the truth is to be told, shared and understood, many Americans now believe they have no choice but to act as their own media.

Grant Stinchfield devoted part of his Friday Newsmax program to laying out why he believes the rapid, deleterious changes that have overcome our nation in just the last week will only serve to weaken the country. He was joined by former Housing and Urban Development Secretary, Ben Carson, who set the stage for what the country must be aware of as we enter a period of adjustment in America. Neither man targeted the mainstream media by name, but their discussion contained an unmistakable call for citizens to be alert and vigilant. They need to do the job that, in years past, was the duty of the media.

"With only three days in the White House, Joe Biden claims he wants to 'Build Back Better,' yet every move he has made leads you to believe he wants to tear it down worse," Stinchfield began, noting the Biden quickly removed both the Winston Churchill bust and military battle flags from the Oval Office. "We went from America First to America Last in a matter of three days, and the D.C. swamp is reemerging."

Presidents have traditionally entered office experiencing a "honeymoon period," characterized by unsustainably high approval ratings. Not so this year, as Rasmussen Reports pegs Biden's approval at just 48%, lower than the starting point for both Barack Obama and Donald Trump. Many Americans, possibly most, understand that sans a flood of mail-in ballots with a lack of signature verification, the likelihood is high that Donald Trump would still be president. Many citizens also fear what will be the immediate dismantling of the Trump policies that led to unprecedented peace and prosperity across the nation.

"There will be a lot of things that will not be able to be torn apart, and we need to concentrate on those," Carson noted. "I hope people are paying very close attention, because you see two very distinct philosophies on how things should be run."

The mainstream media, once a protector of the individual, has now become a protector of the ruling class. While not calling out the liberal media specifically, Carson has for years called out the true duty of government, as laid out in the Constitution.

"When this country was created, it was created as a place where there would be individual freedoms, where you could live your life the way you wanted, believe what you wanted. You had religious freedom as long as your rights didn't impinge on the next person's rights. But then there's always been a group that has felt that the government should be in charge, that true utopia is a place where you give the government full power from cradle to grave, and they take care of you." In just the past few days, American watchdogs and a sliver of the national news media has called out this overarching theme enveloping the new administration's executive orders and policy proposals.

"I implore the American people - pay attention to what's going on," Carson said. "Remember what's happened over the last four years, how the economy just skyrocketed because of the policies - removing all of those regulations, letting people spend their own money and determine their own way. Those are the things that had a very, very rapid ameliorating effect on America."

Carson is right to put the onus on citizens to track the changing effects over the next few years, knowing much of the American media will attempt to deflect, deceive and obscure the truth from viewers.

Stinchfield played a clip of President Biden, after months of blaming his predecessor for everything related to COVID-19, saying that "there is nothing we can do to change the trajectory of the pandemic in the next several months." A far different tune than he and his party of resistance sang for the past year, and a clear example of what Stinchfield and Carson want viewers to be on the alert for.

"The way that the previous administration was able to get business, and industry and science and universities to all work together, to come up with a vaccine in record-breaking time. No one thought it could be done, and yet it was done because of the push there to try and save lives."

Carson did not mention the press as he summed up, however his all-encompassing point cannot be understated.

"China is not going to destroy us. Russia is not going to destroy us. Iran is not going to destroy us. North Korea is not going to destroy us. What will destroy us is us, if we continue to listen to the purveyors of hatred."

Americans can no longer trust the mainstream press to present truthful reality. They must now take that burden upon themselves.

February 1, 2021

Is the Media Starting to Catch On?

Americans are speaking up, standing against the elite system and looking toward a bright future for hard working citizens. And with the exception of the election of President Donald Trump, this past week may have been the biggest leap forward in the current populist American revolution.

In 2016, American citizens declared that they'd had enough by electing a business-minded outsider, who promised to shake things up. At long last, there stood a leader to represent regular citizens against the Deep State and the interests of the global elites of all parties. It was the movement that created and gave rise to his presidency, not the other way around.

In November of 2020, the establishment swamp fought back, using a flood of dubious mail-in ballots to vanquish the populist leader, one way or another.

This past week, the little guy once again took the fight to the elites, this time using Wall Street hedge fund tactics to drive up the price of GameStop stock. This created a huge loss for some large Wall Street funds. But not to worry, because Democrats were quick to come to the defense of the institutional elite.

"It's not a surprise that the media attributes the GameStop revolution , these populist traders taking on the biggest hedge fund boys and beating them at their own game, to the point where they go crying to mommy and asking mommy to intervene to stop the mean bullies on Reddit from beating up these poor billionaires, who only have two yachts apiece," attorney Robert Barnes said this week on Peter Lavelle's The Gaggle You Tube Podcast. "That probably happens more because of what Trump exposed, almost unintentionally. All of these people are just emperors with no clothes."

While the mainstream media attempts to shape public opinion by echoing the deep state narrative, regular American citizens across the fruited plain are sharing the truth and acting accordingly - flocking to alternative media, creating and disseminating fresh content, increasing independence through Bitcoin, abandoning corporate media and walking away from platforms and businesses that engage in censoring.

Still, the media persists, albeit out of sync with growing sentiment. Popular content-creator Scott Adams summed it up this way Sunday on Twitter…

"Here are a few things that Q followers do NOT believe, but CNN DOES believe: Fine People Hoax, Drinking Bleach Hoax, Russian Collusion Hoax, Capitol protest was a coup attempt, courts ruled that the election had no widespread fraud."

Unlike past attempts in bygone eras, the media disinformation of 2021 is falling flat.

Politico reporter Tara Palmeri told MSNBC this weekend that Trump's populist movement - or rather, the populist movement that created Trump - is, in fact, gaining steam.

"I think the base is getting stronger, truly," Palmeri said after traveling to Wyoming to gauge sentiment. "I hate that they're so distrustful. It feels like another world but that's what's on the ground and I don't think we can ignore it and I'm really happy that I went out there and saw it because I think that there's a huge disconnect between Washington and the rest of the country."

The *People's Pundit*, Richard Baris, followed up by tweeting, "Absolutely agree there's a populist majority in America. Without a doubt. Whether someone comes along to unite it, is the million-dollar question."

The way many now see it, the tables have been turned. It is now the Democratic left aligning with Wall Street and the powerful D.C. swamp, against the American people.

"To the extent that these ideas had existed 20, 30, 40 years ago, they were ideas on the left," The Gaggle's co-host, George Szamuely commented. "It's fascinating to watch the migration of these ideas to the right. It's the right now that talks about the Deep State, and what you'd call the left saying 'these are good guys, these are patriotic, loyal Americans,' and they have to protect the country from the likes of Trump and Putin and the rest. And even with what we've had in the past couple of days of GameStop, it's the right that's suddenly railing against Wall Street. These hedge funds, these vulture capitalists who are screwing the little guy and how all the institutional mechanism is protecting the hedge funds. This is an extraordinary transformation."

Barnes summarized by saying, "the peasants just keep finding new pitchforks."

The populist movement is clearly rising, and eventually the mainstream media will have no choice but to acknowledge the revolution en masse.

February 8, 2021

Media Already Rolling Over for Biden

Among his many initiatives and their numerous positive reverberations, one accomplishment may stand out as President Donald Trump's crown jewel. That achievement - laying bare the partisanship and duplicity of many in the mainstream American media.

Stretching back nearly a century, Americans traditionally received only a singular view of the country, and the world. The media all slanted in one direction, which made it difficult for viewers to notice. Then, in the 1980's, Rush Limbaugh entered the stage and provided the other view of America, one based on traditional values and national pride. The presupposition that our founders created a nation that has become the greatest cause for good in the world.

Most of the media still cling to the left-leaning core belief that America remains, at best, just another in a conglomerate of nations and, at worst, the cause of much of the world's trouble. Many in American news media, including much of the new tech world, buy into these liberal, Democrat-party beliefs. The daily praise hoisted upon extremists on the left, both in Congress and in the media, is unending.

The problem for the media, however, is that most Americans still believe in the country as the last, best place for individual citizens of any race, creed, belief or background to prosper to the highest levels possible. And President Donald Trump proved that conservative, populist policies indeed helped Americans advance to levels not seen in recent history. Citizens experienced peace and prosperity first hand. And even those who disagreed with the former President's style or dislike his personality instinctively felt the positive policy impacts.

Set against this backdrop, Trump's greatest achievement may be laying bare the truth felt by real Americans across the heartland, juxtaposed by the story being fed by the mainstream media. Through their approach, viewers can clearly see where the media stands.

From day one, the media went into attack mode against Trump, like a pack of vicious hyenas, ferocious and unrelenting in pursuit of their prey. Truth and facts were far less important than narrative and the feelings they intended to ignite. And viewers noticed.

A new poll last week from Rasmussen Reports found that 55% of likely voters feel the media is being easier, kinder and gentler toward President Biden as they were to Trump. Voters see the media backing up their friend.

Rather than taking the same antagonistic tone and tenor toward Biden as the media aimed at Trump, they've reverted largely to asking such hard-hitting questions as "what flavor ice cream are you eating." That piercing question was lobbed at Biden during the later stages of the presidential campaign. One can also recall fondly when former President Obama was asked what kind of tree he would be if he were a tree.

The Rasmussen poll, largely considered to be one of the most accurate based on their using likely rather than registered voter participants, found only 13% of respondents think the media is more aggressive toward Biden than Trump. 77% of Republicans feel the media is going easier on Biden than they did Trump. Only 33% of Democrats feel this way. Sure, Republicans already know the media is unfair, so most telling is that 55% of unaffiliated voters feel that the media is going far softer on Biden than Trump.

Regardless of the facts on the ground, including an unprecedented flurry of executive orders pushing largely unpopular policies, the media has their boy's back. No matter what. Just as it's always been. At the same time, Rasumussen pegs Biden's early job approval at only 49%, traditionally low for a president this early into a fresh term in office.

This week the Daily Beast reported that White House staffers prescreened reporters in advance of daily press conferences, to find out what they planned to ask. Would any such luxury have been afforded to Trump or his spokespeople Sean Spicer or Sarah Huckabee Sanders? Can anyone imagine such kid-glove treatment for Kayleigh McEnany, who was able to take difficult questions and immediately respond with fact and insight? To their credit, the White House Correspondents Association has reportedly told its members either to ignore the requests or not to comply.

Joe Concha wrote in January in the Hill, "Coverage of presidential inauguration week underperformed already-low expectations, with the usual measured accolades and sober analysis for the incoming president mostly sidelined for fawning praise and outright activism." It hasn't gotten any more objective in the two weeks since.

For years, Americans have been conditioned to receive, and accept, one side of the story. The liberal, progressive side. But among his many positive achievements, President Donald Trump was able to pull back the curtain and show how far many in the corporate media will go to lift up a Democrat and demonize a Republican.

Concha summed it up way back in November, writing in the Hill, "We saw it throughout the campaign. We see it now in the transition. And we'll see it in a Biden administration — a carefully choreographed, risk-averse and packaged president who will provide a fraction of the access that Trump has." And a strategy that only works with a complicit media.

Over the past four years, President Trump validated the disconnect many Americans were already seeing and feeling from much of the mainstream media. Among so much during his term in office, this may be one of the greatest pillars of his lasting legacy.

Elon Musk Leaves Media Scratching Head

It has been more than a week, and yet many in the mainstream media still don't know what to make of it.

The financial world was jarred awake recently by news that Elon Musk and Tesla had invested $1.5B into Bitcoin. Many talking heads remain confused. Many seem to be honestly sorting through the decision and its ramifications. Others are downright apoplectic.

The news initially spiked Bitcoin's price by more than 10% and Tesla's by about 3%, yet most news talkers were initially dismissive of the move.

Will Musk prove again to be a visionary, courageously leading the way to a future most cannot yet see. Or will he rue the day, watching the 12-year-old cryptocurrency crater into irrelevancy?

The initial invective aimed at the CEO of Tesla and SpaceX came across as somewhat unwarranted, especially while many more institutions, such as Greystone, Mastercard, PayPal, Twitter, BNY Mellon and Venmo, have made major moves toward, or investments in, Bitcoin in recent months.

Is this because Musk is disrupting the status quo and giving regular people more say in their financial futures?

Is the news media circling the wagons to protect its elitist sense of control?

Or do they simply believe Musk is making a foolishly irrational decision?

Linette Lopez of Business Insider told CNN last week, "I think Elon Musk is more, as always and ever, a fan of Elon Musk, and Elon Musk has figured out that when Elon Musk tweets or does something in the market, the market quickly follows him." Other reporters have noted that Musk only began talking up Bitcoin after Tesla made the investment.

Is Musk simply blazing the trail as Mavericks do from time to time?

"Maverick is a funny word for someone who paid 20 million dollars to the SEC for lying about whether or not they would take their company private," Lopez added. "He did that in the summer of 2018 and he seemed to get away with it pretty much scot-free, he paid a parking ticket here in the United States. Maverick is probably not the right word. He's not necessarily known for being honest."

Last week's developments come after Musk himself had been rather dismissive of Bitcoin as recently as December, tweeting that it was "almost as bs as fiat money." And in January he said, as the world's wealthiest individual, he personally owned only a quarter of one Bitcoin.

Michael Saylor, the CEO of MicroStrategy, recently created headlines by investing his company's reserve cash into Bitcoin. It was a shocking and courageous move, regardless of the long-term results. Two weeks ago, Saylor hosted nearly 7000 companies at his recent corporate conference. For two days, the host unveiled its corporate playbook on how, and why, he invested his corporate treasury into Bitcoin. The way Saylor sees it, the real risk is in keeping your cash in the dollar, which is losing value at an increasingly fast pace. It is widely believed that Musk and Saylor have connected, perhaps to discuss the topic.

Is it possible Musk has taken this corporate approach to heart? In the announcement, he also said Tesla will pursue eventually taking automobile purchase payments in BitCoin.

"I still have trouble understanding, how exactly....if I wanted to buy a Tesla with Bitcoin, like how is that gonna work," asked Yahoo Finance host Julie Hyman. "How is it a viable currency when the value fluctuates so much? How are you going to do the transfer? I have a hard time wrapping my head around, just concretely how that's going to work right now."

"If you're a company and you're going to accept payment in crypto, you better only do it because you are ready for the volatility and you are trusting that eventually the value is going to go up," said Dan Robert of Yahoo Finance. "Otherwise, right, it's very simple. Why would a company take something that tomorrow could be worth a lot less money. But clearly, if you're Elon Musk, if you're Jack Dorsey, if you're Dan Schulman, you believe in the future of this stuff."

Regardless of what the future holds, some think the move will leave investors holding on for the rocky ride.

"I think they should wonder why he's not investing it in Tesla," Lopez added, pointing to the company's upcoming factory expansion.

If other CEOs see Musk as a crypto trailblazer, countless more could follow the path he, Saylor and others have created. Apple has been mentioned, among others. And so far, the market has reacted with an increase in the overall value of Bitcoin to almost $48,000 per coin.

"I think this is really driven by Elon Musk saying, you know what, regular currency's no good anymore because everybody's printing it and this is the more valid storehold," said CNBC's Jim Cramer. "Musk is driving so much of this market it's fascinating."

Elon Musk has lived his career on the edge, pushing toward what others cannot yet see. Still, many in the media are clearly not ready to jump into the Bitcoin car he is driving.

The move took guts, and time will tell if the media is correct in its reservations.

February 22, 2021

Rush Limbaugh's Lesson for Aspiring Broadcasters

Rush Limbaugh's impact on the world may never be fully understood or appreciated. Even as we've heard many heartfelt tributes over the past week, they fail to capture the landscape-changing consequences of his 30-year rise and domination of the talk-radio airwaves. This piece, too, will fall well short.

Still, one lesson for aspiring broadcasters sticks out. From the up-and-coming student at the college radio station, to the neophyte media professional cutting his teeth for ten bucks an hour somewhere in middle America. This lesson is for one, and for all.

It isn't to learn all you can about Conservative policy and Republican party history, although Rush certainly did. He figuratively, and literally, wrote the book, while making complex philosophy simple. His ideal America? Create a strong and powerful country where people of all types, colors, backgrounds, sexes and ethnicities can flourish to the greatest of their God-given abilities. This was one of his overarching beliefs, but not the key lesson we are referring to here.

It wasn't his side-interest in tech products, specifically those designed by Apple. He was quick to silence his devices when they talked to him during a broadcast, and he loved sharing what he had learned from the liberal tech blogs. Yet he always knew when to return to the topics of the day, pleasing the "stick to the issues crowd."

Yes, he was a "household name in all four corners of the world," but that took time. To aim toward such lofty heights could paralyze a young newbie just trying to get on the air for the first time. Rush's notoriety grew over years and decades. Many of his loyal listeners of 2021 began as "Rush babies," or first heard him while catching the EIB network during high school lunch breaks back in the 1990's.

Limbaugh path required perseverance, which became a driving force for his career. While his family of lawyers would have been pleased had he followed in their footsteps toward a stable and lucrative career, he blazed a different path. He shunned formal advanced schooling and pursued radio. A brief stint in professional baseball helped him grow and continue, following his heart all the way. That tenacity helped sustain him through personal and health challenges over the years.

Once identifying his first love - radio - he mostly stuck to it. Brief stints with television, from the bright-ties on weekend talk to a short-lived sports gig never made him lose focus with radio.

Rush learned to nourish his "talent on loan from God." In this way he balanced the necessary media ego with the acknowledgement of where the talent truly came from, and to who it ultimately belonged. He was simply a steward of the gifts.

Limbaugh was never afraid to challenge someone who "got all up in his chili." He was a serious and thoughtful broadcast professional, and not one to waste time with the "phony-baloney, plastic banana, good-time rock n rollers." A solid lesson, sure. But not the big one, from a broadcast perspective.

He idolized "Ronaldus Magnus." He distrusted the "wizards of smart." He promoted Rush Revere and Liberty, while sipping Two If By Tea. He stood with Betsy Ross against the modern detractors of America, and he took major career risks each and every "Open Line Friday."

Yet, these still were not the big lesson Rush Limbaugh imparted on aspiring broadcasters.

That major lesson, the one that helped him grow a career to lengths never before seen, was simple.

The big lesson is this - *He built an unbreakable bond with his listeners.*

Rush knew his audience. He thought like them, and he spoke like them. He said what they thought, with words they themselves often could not come up with.

This was the biggest lesson for aspiring broadcast professionals. If you listened every day, you could sense its significance. Rush was honest. He was authentic. As he said many times, he had nothing to gain by misleading his listeners. One failure in this regard would have been catastrophic and career-crushing. He delivered not what his audience wanted to hear, but what his heart and mind authentically believed.

For example, at noon Eastern time the day after the 2012 presidential election, Rush got straight to the point. "It is nearly impossible to beat Santa Claus," he said that day, referring to the challenge of unseating a president intent on spreading the wealth of hard-working citizens around.

When you listened to Rush Limbaugh, you felt as though he was speaking directly to you. Not to a crowd or a group, but to you. The connection was natural - a friend talking to a friend, complete with the emotion and fact. When he was frustrated, you knew it. When he felt good, you instinctively did too.

Rush was real. He was original, as all unique humans are. For broadcast professionals, this genuine approach is the key to long-term success. Authenticity attracts the audience - your bona fide broadcast tribe.

Watch and listen to the really great ones throughout history or in today's media landscape. Whether in news, sports, finance or entertainment, the most successful broadcasters are the ones who know who they are and effectively share that vision with the audience. This built his incredibly attractive brand, lassoing the masses by their own volition.

Rush Limbaugh was authentic. He connected because he was the real deal.

This is a lesson for aspiring broadcasters across the fruited plain, who dream of success and dare to achieve it.

March 1, 2021

Stuart Varney Connects in the Morning

Oh, the pain of selling your shares of Microsoft, only to have the stock proceed to hit record highs. Especially after years of proudly standing by the holding and proclaiming great pleasure in it's slow, steady and safe growth. Such was the plight of the jovial, ever-informed and curious Fox Business anchor, Stuart Varney. (he has since re-purchased a chunk of Microsoft.)

On any given weekday morning, you're likely to hear Varney mentioning his infamous sale, or discussing gas prices near his home in New Jersey and near his vacation spot in upstate New York. In Varney, viewers get exactly what so many of them are searching for as they reach for their next cup of morning coffee. Most notably, he is able to build a bond and a connection with his viewers. Yes, he knows the market. He knows trends, PE values and economic indicators. But you also feel as though you truly know *him* as well.

The qualities that set Stuart Varney apart are priceless and sometimes rare for network business anchors to possess. You start with knowledge. Sure, he knows his niche - the market and its impact on the everyday Americans who tune in to see him every day. He can tell you what the numbers say and what it all means. He also matches that knowledge with a real-world persona that viewers can identify and connect with.

For example, he sold that Microsoft stock too soon.
"I did that too!," says Joe Six-Pack.

But he turned around and bought some shares of Boeing.
"Ok, we'll see," you think.

During the prosperity of the Trump years, Varney was downright giddy, and happy to say so, about the falling price of gas.
"Hey, I can fill MY truck up for a few bucks less too!"

He came to this country from the United Kingdom and learned the value of hard work by washing dishes in a restaurant.
"I washed dishes at my first job too!"

Through his stops at other networks, including CNN and CNBC, Varney has always been able to connect - with the market and, more importantly, with people. He asks the questions we want answers to, and follows up with a non-pretentious curiosity. If he doesn't understand how Peloton works, he asks for clarification. If he is still confused about Bitcoin, he asks for clarification from his expert guests. As a result, his morning program, "Varney & Co.," has the feel of a gang of buddies, rather than some stuffy money show.

In his role as the traffic cop, Varney spends his mornings discussing issues and stock trends with market analysts, network correspondents, CEO's, political leaders, entrepreneurs and socialites. In one minute, he'll be asking his correspondent, Susan Li, about the latest move on the big board. In the show's next segment, he's talking football with Joe Namath or economics with Art Laffer.

Varney's intellect and knowledge brings us in, but it is the connection that keeps us. That, and his unbridled pride in being an American citizen, which he became in November of 2015.

"I became an American because I believe America is fundamentally good," Varney told his audience in January of 2020. "Where else in the world can someone with a foreign accent go on national television and tell people what's going on in *their* society?"

And tell us he does. Legions of Americans wouldn't start their day any other way.

March 8, 2021

Joe Biden, Already a Failure

It may be only six weeks, but that is plenty to offer an early report card. The grade - F.

Bill O'Reilly didn't mince words when he joined the Glenn Beck Radio Show on Friday. When asked what the week's biggest news story was, O'Reilly said it was the early and clear failure of President Joe Biden.

"I said I would give Joe Biden a chance because he asked for one,and in our Judeo-Christian tradition, if somebody asks you for a chance, and they're not a convicted felon, you give them a chance" O'Reilly said. "But after six weeks, we have absolute pandemonium in the country."

The hard-hitting O'Reilly laid into Biden, criticizing the President's change in border policy, which effectively invites illegal immigrants to flood America's borders.

"How exactly is it helping the country to allow undocumented people to cross into the United States, request asylum, hand them $1100 in cash so they can go anywhere they want, and not test them for Covid," he asked.

O'Reilly noted that 106 undocumented people tested positive for Covid-19 in one day alone.

According to Beck, 6% of illegal border-crossers have tested positive for Covid-19, and he added "I'd rather have children locked in cages, as they say, that are protected, waiting for someone to claim them that can be clearly tested to be a parent or a relative, rather than this system now of colored wristbands by the mob and the cartels down across the border, that are smuggling these children into America, clearly for the sex trade."

O'Reilly has spent much of this week, both on his website BillO'Reilly.com and in interviews, such as this one with Beck, detailing the 180 degree difference between the immigration policies of former President Donald Trump and the new Biden administration. He and his guests, such as Trump immigration advisor Stephen Miller, have documented how children are being smuggled across the border into the United States, after which authorities are helping them locate and bring over their parents and families as well. He added, "it is absolutely astounding, and the reason it's happening is because the media does not report it. So people listening to us now don't live on the border, they don't know what's happening. This is going to lead, in the next two years, to hundreds of thousands of undocumented people coming into the United States."

The push to help Americans see the impending danger from the administration's radical change of course came at the same time Trump voiced his anger and concern about the effects of these extreme policies, which favor non-citizens over Americans.

"The spiraling tsunami at the border is overwhelming local communities, depleting budgets, crowding hospitals, and taking jobs from legal American workers," the former President said. "When I left office, we had achieved the most secure border in our country's history. Under Biden, it will soon be worse, more dangerous and more out of control than ever before. He has violated his oath of office to uphold our Constitution and enforce our laws."

Trump continued, saying "Our border is now totally out of control thanks to the disastrous leadership of Joe Biden. Our great Border Patrol and ICE agents have been disrespected, demeaned, and mocked by the Biden administration. A mass incursion into the country by people who should not be here is happening on an hourly basis, getting worse by the minute."

Bill O'Reilly has been one of the most vocal news personalities informing the country about the crisis in recent days, pointing out what many see as the resulting deleterious effect on America's economy and neighborhoods. His urgency stems from the media's common suppression tactic of hiding negative impacts of the policies of their protected class of Democrat politicians. He adds, "nobody will know, because the media blacks it out."

The way O'Reilly sees it, there are three developing trends that will eventually combine to crush Biden's approval ratings and turn public opinion decisively against him.

"The economy, and you're seeing a shaky stock market now. Immigration, and cancel culture," O'Reilly listed as the big three areas where Americans are beginning to feel the negative effects of radical Democratic policy shifts. "Those three things are going to undermine his administration. But here's the really frightening part about it - if you, and me, and Stu were talking to President Biden right now he could not explain, and does not know, what is happening on that border. He does not have the capacity, in my humble opinion, to absorb information and analyze anything."

In Bill O'Reilly's opinion, the honeymoon is over. National chaos and pain are only beginning to kick in. Even if the media refuses to share the facts.

Media Unimpressed by Bleak Presidential Address

As birds begin to chirp and the smell of spring is in the air, gloom and Doom is the order of the day in America. This was the overarching theme of President Joe Biden's first primetime television address, and many in the objective media were not impressed.

On Friday's episode of *The Gaggle* on YouTube, hosts George Szamuely and Peter Lavelle shared their opinions of Biden's speech to the nation.

"It was a very strange affair," Szamuely began. "Rather lachrymose and depressing, long on flights of rhetoric. You get a sense that the writers were people who enjoy writing and like to pile on the adjectives and the repetition of phrases."

Szamuely criticized Biden for falsely taking credit for the vaccination program, which was designed, developed and put forth by former President Donald Trump.

"He has a history of plagiarism," Lavelle noted about Biden.

Szamuely opined that in his speech, the president had "dishonestly suggested that Trump had somehow, even though he didn't mention his name, that Trump had somehow responded passively to the virus, he didn't do anything, he was silent about it and so on, which is untrue." They pointed out that it was Biden, democrats and their media allies who criticized Trump for being xenophobic when he acted decisively, halting travel from China in January of 2020.

The pair discussed Biden's rather grim view of the foreseeable future, where Szamuely said, "everyone's going to get vaccinated and maybe - just maybe - he will allow Americans to celebrate July the Fourth, not having big parties, but just with immediate friends and family members….but only if they behave themselves."

"This very, very dire, gloomy tone that he took. First of all, most people are going to use their own personal responsibility on how to move forward here," said Lavelle, a seasoned political analyst. "He doesn't give any sunlight to that, which is a very big mistake. As far as allowing us to do something...well who the hell are you, Joe Biden, to say what we can do? You don't have that power."

The real darkness from the speech stemmed from the authoritative tone, with the president sounding more like a dictator or king than president of a democratic republic.

Lavelle continued, "I don't know who wrote it, but whoever did is a 20-something who doesn't know anything about separation of powers." He added, "Saying what we can do and can't do, and essentially he will allow us to do that, I find that really bothersome, because of the moving goal post. It's constantly moving."

"The whole idea that we are going to celebrate independence by essentially confirming everyone's dependence on the diktats of the government, there is that nonsensical element to it," added Szamuely.

Still, many Americans did not watch the primetime address, as they were too busy fixing dinner, helping kids with homework and getting ready for another work day. In this case, they may have missed both the speech's content and it's delivery.

Chris Barron summed up the mainstream media's misleading coverage of the event in his Friday column in the *Political Insider*, saying "Even by Biden standards the speech was dismal. Biden rambled, looked lost, and delivered cringe-worthy attempts at "showing emotion." It was more Saturday Night Live than Lincoln, but you wouldn't know that if you didn't watch the speech."

On the whole, the speech was derided as much for its tone as for its obvious inaccuracies. Months ago, on the debate stage, Americans saw two candidates. One, with an optimistic vision that the country was turning the corner against the virus, with bright days in our immediate future. The other warned of a dark winter, as we continue lockdowns, forsaking commerce, school and social relationships.

Joe Biden is delivering on his promises.

"He himself gave this very, very gloomy outlook, which is simply not borne out by the numbers. I mean, the numbers are falling drastically," Szamuely said. "It's a very, very peculiar lesson unless he's trying to use this, still, as a cudgel with which to beat Trump."

Lavelle wondered if millions of citizens will be punished for refusing to take the vaccine, saying he "read into it an implicit threat, because a vaccine can be available but jurists have talked about it. Should people be compelled to take it? There is an argument on both sides."

In both style and substance, all but the liberal stenographer-type media found so much lacking in the president's first chance to make a primetime impression.

March 22, 2021

A Call to Protect America

The spotlight has been activated, and there is nowhere to hide.

It is time for you to stand up and do the job America elected you to do.

This is the message from many in the media, as we reach the spring with the country's moral and economic degradation commencing at breakneck speed.

Over recent days, conservative media have ratcheted up calls for the Republican party to stand strong for America and against the leftward pull toward a borderless, socialist utopia. With the country's currency being debased at an unprecedented pace and a crisis being created at our borders, many in the media are calling on the only ones who can stop the socialist slide - Republicans.

During his opening monologue Friday on *The Chris Salcedo Show*, the Newsmax host blasted Democrats for their reliance on phony science. But first, he took aim at the Republican party for largely going along with such ridiculous initiatives.

"As the GOP's surrender caucus seems to be leading the Republicans off a cliff, holding hands with socialist Democrats every step of the way, the socialists are pushing America over that same cliff with their anti-American, anti-freedom policies," Salcedo began. "As we stated, virtually every problem in the United States can be traced back to socialists and their policies. But we now, we're sure that the moderate Republicans who are in charge are not the solutions to those problems. In fact, milquetoast Republicans seem intent to negotiate the speed of the fall of the United States, not prevent its happening."

This same criticism was lobbed at former House Speaker John Boehner and his Republican crew from 2008 to 2016, when they seemed happy to stand by and watch the last Democrat president attempt to bring an unjust America down a peg or two.

Salcedo pointed out that many Democrats remain silent today as seven accusers have come out and made allegations against New York Governor Andrew Cuomo. At the same time, these same Democrats purport to "stand for women," while also actively trying to expel two female Republicans from Congress. He also pointed out the mainstream media's double standard - praising Democrats for challenging an Iowa Congressional election, months after the fact, while demonizing conservative American voters who demanded transparency during the dubious mail-in presidential election debacle of November, 2020.

Fellow Newsmax host, Grant Stinchfield, called on Republicans to "stand firm" on Friday, opining that they are moving backwards and losing the game.

"Remember what the Make America Great Again movement is about. Embrace those principles and do not be ashamed of taking a hard line," Stinchfield implored Republicans. "When you bend, when you concede, you ultimately break. Look at the two latest amnesty bills that now move to the Senate. Thirty Republicans voted for the Farm Worker Modernization Act, giving amnesty to 1.5 million illegals. The number, I'm sure, is actually much higher. The so-called Dream and Promise Act provides a pathway to citizenship for 3 million illegals. Immigration is a winning issue for Republicans. Why fold on this? Why cower to Democrats?"

With the Democrat administration's rapid push to throw open the border floodgates, and their lustful rush toward economic slowdown and forced government dependence rather than growth, prosperity and self-reliance, Stinchfield says the time is now to stand up for hard-working citizens across the country.

"Stop acting weak," he challenged. "First and foremost, our nation's safety and security depends on Republicans' strength, now more than ever. Our political future depends on it too. President Trump taught you how to fight, how to win. So do it, please."

Time will tell if they stand up to heed the call.

Beware of the Climbing Stock Market

Spring is here and good economic times seem to be returning. More Americans are getting back to work as usual, many with newly-injected vaccines. The stock market is surging, with the Dow and S&P 500 rising to near all-time highs.

Some states that enforced the most strict lockdown regulations are now starting to allow citizens to return in larger numbers to restaurants, theatres and entertainment venues. Even in New York city, with some of the most draconian shut down rules in the country, it was announced last week that Broadway musicals may return as soon as this fall.

But with that backdrop, and with financial markets seemingly revving up, some in the media are urging caution, saying the underlying economic fundamentals could usher in a swift and forceful market correction.

"We have to remember that we saw technology peak in late February and then it dropped significantly. Some of them are negative year to date," said ER Shares CEO Eva Ados, during Friday's edition of *The Claman Countdown* on the Fox Business Network. "Value companies, we're seeing some of them trading at an all-time high, even though some of them might have bankruptcy risk and weak financial statements. So we have seen a reversion to the mean with overreactions in both growth and value. And investors have to be very careful, going back to traditional fundamental metrics."

Television pundits will tell you over and over that the stock market is not the only, or sometimes even the best, barometer with which to judge the economy. Thus it would be incorrect to point to a surging stock market as evidence the American economy has rebounded from the pandemic and, more accurately, many states' shutdown response.

These same hosts and analysts may differ on policy, but they cannot argue results. After a sluggish economic era for many years following the crash of 2008, employees saw rising paychecks and inflated 401k accounts during the last four years.

Now, many Americans are watching anxiously as the new Democratic administration plans massive tax hikes on individuals, families and businesses. Much of the market's success, or failure, could hinge on the deleterious effects of these policies if they are eventually rammed through.

"We think it's going to be detrimental for our economy, " Ados told Cheryl Casone. We all know that entrepreneurial companies are the ones that generate the most jobs, compared to the government, and if you tax them higher, you're taking away the incentive they have to create more jobs, invest more in research and development in the future of our economy, the growth of their company, property, plan and equipment."

With these possible punishments looming on the horizon, many businesses may already be eying the exits, in efforts to protect their companies, employees and future growth.

"We will also have more companies leaving the U.S. They'll have an incentive to move to tax havens, such as Bermuda, UAE, and this has a multi-layered effect," Ados said. "The more people you hire, the more money they have to spend in the U.S. economy, and now we are reversing it. We are going the opposite direction."

Ados boiled down her conversation to this one major risk that could cause the U.S. economy to take a quick turn for the worst.

She didn't hesitate in saying "certainly it's taxes. That's our main concern because the growth of this country is entrepreneurial companies, and without entrepreneurial companies keeping the talent here, keeping technology and growth, and supporting bureaucracy and regulation, unfortunately this is the biggest threat our economy can see."

Americans are welcoming spring with a feeling of economic optimism. Their hope is that the good times continue rolling, and that burdensome taxation doesn't crush the recovery just as it is getting started.

April 5, 2021

Today's News is So Cliche

The news can cause your blood pressure to skyrocket, in more ways than one. Especially if you are someone who values and cherishes precise use of the English language.
Like fingernails across a chalkboard, avid news consumers have become accustomed to, and increasingly annoyed by, the same old, worn-out cliches.

There is no doubt that you have heard these phrases and words used over and over. Probably a hundred times in the past week. In fact, they are so prevalent that you may not even notice their non-stop overuse by television and radio talking heads, analysts and guests.

If you are one of the lucky ones who never noticed the over-reliance on the following words, consider your days of naivete now permanently over.

Not that using these phrases and words make you a bad person, or even a subpar news broadcaster. It's just that your audience has been irked by them for far too long.
They may not be bothered enough to tune you out, although it now provides them a clarifying opportunity to separate the broadcasting wheat from the chaff.

So here is a list, albeit not a complete one, of some of the most bothersome, annoyingly-overused crutch words and cliches heard every day across the broadcast airwaves.

"Um", "ah", "you know" - These are the classic of all classic crutch words. Since the first time a mic was powered on, we've heard these words sprinkled into broadcasts, by talent across all levels. Non-discriminating and quick to jump out, these common culprits have stood the test of time.
"It was...*um*...quite a scene on 2nd Avenue today, when....*ah*....police cornered the armed suspect who, *you know*, was ready for a fight."

Essentially - Seemingly a favorite of the new woke, millennial crowd, this flavor of the week appears everywhere a host, guest or analyst wishes to instill a sense of his or her intelligence.
"Well Jim, *essentially* what this move does is put Tesla in a position of power. *Essentially* they are the leader in new technology, with Elon Musk *essentially* lighting the way across a new, *essentially* endless universe."

Yeah, no - It's difficult to know what this phrase actually means when it is used. Usually, a guest uses it to start a response to a question. The real question, though, is does in mean YES or does it mean NO? Or does it mean both? And if so, why combine both the positive and negative when simply one would do the trick?

"Isn't it true that this government spending has to stop, Joe?"

"*Yeah, no,* Sally, we're mortgaging our kids' future with every dollar we spend on social engineering garbage."

So.... - This one is straight forward. For some reason, may guests feel obligated to start their answer to a question with "So". It doesn't really fit at the beginning of a sentence, but this has been a common way of beginning an answer to a question for about five years, when it emerged as a top crutch word for champions in all walks of life. Most notably, this has become a go-to in the corporate world, making appearances in lectures, earnings calls, media programs and corporate gatherings.

"What is your biggest product development going to be this year?"

"*So....*we've got a truly deep and revolutionary pipeline....."

Right - This self-affirming word has been popping up on the air for about a half a decade now, and it still doesn't quite fit. It would be fitting to use this word as a questioning technique, at the end of a sentence. However, it is now interspersed in monologues, responses and commentary, seemingly adding nothing to the overall feel of the conversation. To many, the use of this word makes the speaker sound rather obnoxious.

"This is a big year for the party, *right.* They need to prove they can govern, *right,* rather than just be the opposition. Now is the time to put results or face the consequences, *right.*"

Literally - How many times do we hear this word used incorrectly? The word "literally" means to adhere to fact. So why, then, do we hear it used so often to hyperbolize a scenario? For example, "This will *literally* be the end of the Senate if the filibuster is abolished." In actuality, and in terms of adhering to fact, the Senate will still exist. Putting the policy argument aside, the Senate would indeed continue to exist. To use literally would mean there would, in fact, no longer be a Senate if the filibuster is abolished.

Super - This one added a little pizzazz to your commentary about a decade ago. If you said something was super-anything, it gave it a feel of extra intensity or importance. Now, however, the term is so overused, that it has gone the way of lazy cliche. You now stand out as unique and fresh only if you don't use it.

"He is a *super*-smart leader, and I am *super*-excited to have him on our team."

100 percent - At some point in the past bunch of years, this became a replacement for the word YES. Or a stand-in for the feeling of agreement. Regardless, it has become overused as a crutch word of choice.
"Isn't it true that raising taxes is equal to stealing from good, hard-working Americans?"
"*100 percent* Laura, that is exactly what it is."

Sort of / Kind of - These phrases have become filler material, much like white rice or dinner rolls. They don't give you anything of value, other than fill you up for the short term.
"The market is *sort of* like water or energy. Money *kind of* flows to the best projects, the best people and the best ideas. This is the way that we *sort of* define value and grow the economy based on *kind of* what actually helps our societies grow."

Like - In many areas of the media, and certainly the alternative, non-traditional media, this word still holds a high place of esteem. But to the traditional, trained ear, it rings of teenage, valley-girl hanging out at the mall. Especially to an older audience, using this word often during the broadcast makes one come across immediately as less intelligent or sophisticated.
"It was, *like*, a great day to be in New York. The parade was, *like*, an important moment for the city and, *like*, very inspirational."

Really - Another filler word, meant to imply a higher level of importance. It doesn't add anything precise.
"The governor initially took a *really* strong stand, and since then he has *really* stood even stronger on principle. This is *really* his best moment in office."

Look - This word is used when a guest, analyst or host begins to talk and his mouth hasn't yet caught up with his mind. This crutch word is used to help put his thoughts in place and begin the substantive portion of his commentary. If he needs a second or two to compile the perfect sentence, this word can give him the time he needs.
"Look, I wanted to get you all together today to discuss our 3rd quarter initiatives....."

So there is the list, right. It's kind of frustrating to hear these really annoying crutch words in, like, literally every news broadcast. Look, it's essentially a chore to listen to a broadcast where these words are sort of sprinkled everywhere. 100 percent.

Now get off my lawn, and enjoy the news!

April 12, 2021

Project Veritas Fights Back

James O'Keefe leads perhaps the most successful undercover journalism operation in the country today, Project Veritas. Time and time again, he and his group have done the job most in the media no longer want to do - holding those in power accountable and uncovering the truth that these entities hide from the public.

It is true that many Americans feel that today's mainstream media serves as little more than an advocacy appendage of the liberal left. O'Keefe and his supporters, meanwhile, believe it is his organization that does the job the media no longer cares to do.

Project Veritas filed a lawsuit against the New York Times late last year, and Sean Hannity invited O'Keefe on his Friday radio program to share the details of recent developments.

Last month, a New York judge refused to dismiss the suit, implying that it had "substantial basis in law to proceed." The move in no way foreshadows the suit's ultimate outcome, but it was such a big development in favor of Project Veritas that former president Donald Trump personally congratulated O'Keefe in a video recorded at Mar-a-Lago.

Fox News reported online in March that the *"judge denied the paper's motion to dismiss the suit by the right-wing guerilla news outlet over the Times' portrayal of Project Veritas' reporting on alleged voter fraud in the congressional district represented by Ilhan Omar, D-Minn. last fall. Times reporters Maggie Astor and Tiffany Hsu described Project Veritas' reporting as "deceptive," "false," and "with no verifiable evidence."* Fox News also quoted the judge as saying, *"The facts submitted by Veritas could indicate more than standard, garden variety media bias and support a plausible inference of actual malice."*

"James O'Keefe comes under constant, never-ending, non-stop fire. There have been more lawsuits, attempts to silence, cancel, shut down his operation," Sean Hannity pointed out on his radio program last week. "The untold story here is that every single time that these accusations are made against his organization, or they've tried to take Project Veritas to court, that's just another tactic of trying to silence people...they've won. They've never once lost a lawsuit against them."

Hannity also mentioned the high price O'Keefe has paid so far to fight back in this particular battle against the well known newspaper.

"Yes it costs a lot of money, it's cost us a quarter million dollars to get to this phase of the litigation," O'Keefe said. "We've taken on the New York Times and their army of lawyers and we've won this historic motion in the State of New York Supreme Court. This judge, Sean, this is like one of the first times ever, one of the few plaintiffs since the 1960's, unlike the Sarah Palin case, she sued the New York Times over the Op-Ed page. We sued the New York Times over a news article in the A Section, Sean, where they called our voter fraud videos deceptive. They said that we used unnamed sources, which we did not. They said we had no evidence. We did have evidence."

Hannity has long been a public supporter of Project Veritas, often promoting their work and sharing their reporting on both radio and television. A frequent critic of the mainstream media, for both their overt and covert liberal bias, Hannity offered O'Keefe a chance to air his side of this confrontation.

"The judge in this historic 16-page order has said that it was the New York Times that acted deceptively. That they used misinformation by putting their opinions in the news article." said O'Keefe.

Ironically, the decision in New York last month came the same week a federal judge said "we are very close to one-party control" of the media.

The lawsuit will now proceed with discovery and depositions, and time will tell where the facts lead.

Sean Hannity will undoubtedly keep us posted.

April 19, 2021

Woke Bullies Unmasked

Tucker Carlson recently began a segment of his Fox News television program, opening up about the current state of vaccines, masks and America beginning to stand up to the woke mob and the virtue-signaling media.

His focus was on the current mask culture, and the true benefits our society is currently receiving from the requirements. He also called to mind a fellow television host, who has been an outspoken advocate for forced mask wearing.

"Sometimes Chris Cuomo does get angry, pretty darn angry. And when he does, we pay attention, sometimes it's at us," Carlson began. "Recently, he was very angry at people who'd been vaccinated, or had the Coronavirus, who have antibodies, who are immune from getting it, apparently, and they're not wearing masks. And that infuriated Chris Cuomo."

Carlson then cut to a clip of Cuomo on his CNN show, saying "There's nothing wrong with wanting to know when this could all end, but it's hard to see how attacking Fauci helps. You know when it ends. It ends when we get our crap together, right. So that's why it is baffling when you have people like Senator Ted Cruz joining Rand Paul and ditching his mask as they walk the halls of Congress. And the current CDC guidelines state very clearly that if you're vaccinated, you gotta still keep taking precautions, like wearing a mask. You can still get sick. You won't be as sick, but you can give it to somebody else."

Carlson followed up, noting that the CDC has not clarified why citizens should still wear masks after being vaccinated, and what provable benefit may be gained by doing so. It has simply been an order. Do it because we say so.

At the same time, Carlson called out Cuomo for doing one thing while saying another.

"Wasn't it Chris Cuomo who had the Coronavirus, who was capable of transmitting it to other people, who was wandering around Long Island with no mask on?" Tucker asked. "Kind of Typhoid Mary of cable news."

Carlson brought in his guest, Matt Walsh, host of "The Matt Walsh Show," and asked when the we-know-best directives will end.

"Obviously the rank hypocrisy of anyone named Cuomo lecturing anyone about anything to do with Covid I think should be obvious to anybody," Walsh noted. "The idea that you have to mask after getting a vaccine is so fundamentally insane, it's hard to wrap your mind around. The CDC claims, what they say is that your chance of there being a breakthrough case, of you getting Covid after a vaccine, it's like .0008 percent or something. If your risk management philosophy is that you still have to mask even with that kind of risk, then how could you ever get behind the wheel of a car?"

Walsh pointed out the statistical risk of being injured in a car accident, or in fact being struck by lightning, would be equal or greater than that of getting sick from Covid after being vaccinated.

Which brought Carlson and Wash to the growing sentiments across the country.
What are the real reasons Americans are being forced to continue wearing masks, and when will the restrictions end?
Why aren't more states following the lead of those such as Florida and Texas, who have had outsized success against the virus, compared to some centrally-managed, restrictive, lockdown states.
Even with more citizens receiving vaccines, are these mask regulations going to stay in place forever?

"I guess that's the case because it's obvious now that masking is not about Covid, it hasn't been about Covid for a long time. It's really about, it's a badge of honor. It's kind of a signifier," Walsh said.

The comments also bring to mind the flood of social media posts, with people gleefully sharing pictures and stories about receiving their vaccination shots. Since when did it become "cool" to eagerly rush to social media to share the medical procedures and outcomes one has just undergone?

"Hey look, I just had my yearly blood work drawn!"
"Over here, pay attention! I just left my doctor where I had an allergy test!"
"Look at me, I just got that annoying rash checked out!"
"Aren't I so important, my doctor just told me to turn my head and cough!"

Carlson and Walsh wrapped up, with Walsh observing, "For the religion of the mask cultists, a mask is now an outward sign of their wokeness. It's like this religious symbol, which means that we're going to be wearing them forever, at least if they get their way."

"It's like a little obedience signifier, like Yes, I'm following the orders," Carlson quipped.

Much of America, including Tucker Carlson and his audience, are beginning to demand proof, evidence and reason to back up the orders. Time will tell if the data is forthcoming.

April 26, 2021

Leaders Say Time To Secure Voting Rights

American leaders of all backgrounds across the country are speaking out. Voting rights need to be protected for all citizens, and the reforms need to start in the states.

North Carolina Lieutenant Governor, Mark Robinson, appeared on the Sean Hannity Radio Show last week, to discuss new efforts across America to safeguard voting rights and protect free, open and fair elections. Robinson appeared before the U.S. House Judiciary Sub Committee last week to address claims by Democrats that these measures to require a free ID when voting is racist.

"How absolutely preposterous," Robinson, a Republican, scolded the committee. "Am I to believe that black Americans who have overcome the atrocities of slavery, who were victorious in the civil rights movement, and now sit in the highest levels of this government cannot figure out how to get a free ID to secure their votes? That they need to be coddled by politicians because they don't think we can figure out how to make our voices heard. Are you kidding me? The notion that black people must be protected from a free ID to secure their votes is not just insane, it is insulting!"

"I watched this moment and I was so grateful to you for sharing that," Hannity told Robinson, the first black Lieutenant Governor of North Carolina.

Hannity pointed out that the new voting laws making news out of Georgia are much less restrictive than those in New York or President Joe Biden's home state of Delaware. The host also pointed out that Biden latest incendiary statements comparing new voting requirements to "Jim Crow 2.0" are nothing new, being that Biden has made similar comments in the past and also partnered with a former clansman to stop the integration of schools. The President notably didn't want American schools to become "racial jungles."

"When you think of Joe Biden, when you think of the Left, one word comes to mind every time, and that is hypocrisy. They are experts on hypocrisy," Robinson said. "Whether it be the racial jungle comment or "they're gonna put y'all back in chains" or the "you ain't black" comment, Joe Biden's political career is wiped not just with making racist statements but fighting for racist policies. How dare this man now stand like he's forgotten that and claim to be this champion for racial justice. He is anything but and this needs to be pointed out."

Hannity called out the Washington swamp, pointing out the double standard between what they say they will do and what they actually end up doing once they feel the pull of power. In a land of double-talk, Hannity praised Robinson for being a courageous leader "coming in and telling the truth, whether they want to hear it or not."

"These guys that go to Washington, D.C., and I told them this yesterday, they sit up high and they look low and they think they know better than us. They think they know what's right for the states, what's right for the people, and it is time for us to stand up and push back against the Federal government," Robinson said. "The Federal government has stepped out of its bounds. It did it decades ago and it continues to do it at an increasingly alarming rate."

Robinson compared the federal government to the annoying co-worker who cannot seem to do his job competently, but who continuously butts in and tells you how to do yours. He specifically pointed to education and voting rights as two areas that should be left to the states to carry out.

"Are there national voting laws that we need to have? Absolutely, there should be. But we should not be allowing the federal government to reach in and dictate a partisan wish list upon the states for the purposes of trying to keep one party in power," Robinson stated.

The two discussed Hannity's four common sense pillars for secure, open and fair elections - picture ID, signature verification, a rigid standard for ballot chain-of-custody and partisan observers to watch vote counting.

Hannity concluded the conversation, noting that Robinson's political future may indeed be just beginning, and imploring the Lieutenant Governor of North Carolina to consider higher office, perhaps even a run for the U.S. Senate.

On that topic, Robinson seemed to leave the door slightly ajar.

"I"ve already publicly said no to the Senate, but with God anything's possible."

May 3, 2021

Liberal Backlash Begins in Liberal Bastions

America is appalled at the direction Joe Biden and the left wing extremists are pulling the country, and the odds of a swelling reprisal are rising rapidly.

Many across the nation feel we are starting to feel the rumblings of a backlash against emerging liberal policies being pushed by Democrats at a breakneck pace. And ironically, many think the pushback is emanating not from America's heartland, but rather from inner cities and Democrat party strongholds.

Last week, a nationwide poll from Rasmussen Reports showed that only 36% of likely voters feel Biden's first 100 days have been a success. The survey also reports that "many still doubt that Biden won last year's election fairly."

One of radio's newest talk voices has been tapped into this growing trend, and he's making this connection in one of the nation's bluest cities.

Since beginning his mid-day talk radio program on WABC Radio in New York City earlier this spring, Greg Kelly has been a breath of fresh air for listeners searching for a daily dose of reality. A former vet turned radio and television and radio personality, Kelly shoots straight and appeals to traditional, rational Americans. With no pretense, Kelly espouses common sense views that hit home to most normal Americans.

Where Rush Limbaugh was the daytime talk leader of the American conservative movement, Kelly is more of a common man on the street, focusing less on politics and parties and more on principled stands on issues. Not that he and Rush wouldn't agree on most issues - certainly they would, as common sense and conservatism share a natural brotherhood. Kelly simply approaches issues and conversations from a mostly non-political lens. More right and wrong than a focus on party.

On Friday, Kelly welcomed pollster John McLaughlin onto his radio show, where the two talked about the current woke culture and it's coming effects across America. McLaughlin, coming more from the political angle than Kelly, believes there is an approaching backlash against the country's radical liberal left.

"We're seeing the numbers, because in spite of all the talk about unity and positive coverage, you see this surreal State of the Union with Joe Biden. A lot of people didn't watch it," McLaughlin began. "Less than half of the viewers that President Trump used to get. But here he is with a moment where he could thank Trump for the growing economy, he could thank Trump for the vaccines that he was left so we could reopen. And he could do some unifying there. Instead, they're sticking it to us and they're saying that they're going to pass a voter law to override the voter ID and state laws in a lot of places. They start talking about division, and it's sad."

McLaughlin alluded to Senator Tim Scott's rebuttal to Biden's address. Scott, a black Republican, and possible 2024 presidential hopeful, spoke conversely of unifying the country across racial divides. The uplifting tone was met immediately with bigoted and racially-charged attacks by Democrats across social media platforms.

"He gives the rebuttal, does a great job, says we're not racist, we're all Americans. And he gets slammed the next day in the media as 'Uncle Tim' and the social media right after it, they're making fun of the guy." McLaughlin said.

Senator Scott followed up his speech by telling Fox News host Sean Hannity this week, "In my opinion, what they're fueling is a backlash. I don't know if they realize it or not, but at some point people get sick and tired of being sick and tired and they start reacting as opposed to responding to the criticism and the negativity."

McLaughlin insists that Democrats are on the wrong side of public opinion also in terms of Republican efforts to strengthen and protect voting rights. He says his polling shows that only 45% of respondents support Biden and the Democrats in opposing Georgia's new voting laws, which include voter ID. Democrats successfully pressured Major League Baseball to move this year's All-Star Game out of Georgia, a move that McLauglin says only 42% of national voters support.

"I get the sense, even in this liberal, woke city (New York), that this woke movement is going too far and it's starting to spook some people on the left. Some people who are woke, who see themselves as enlightened," Kelly pointed out.

McLaughlin said New York Democrats doing an about-face and now calling for more police shows how the left's anti-police rhetoric is no longer resonating, even with the woke base.

"When they don't like de Blasio, they see the businesses and jobs leaving, but more important, they see the drug dealers and the gangs and the guns back in their neighborhood, then people are saying it's time for some common sense," McLaughlin said. "It's time to get more police here and let them protect us again."

Time will tell if America truly stages a comeback against the radicalism of recent months. One thing is for sure, however. If the early stages of discontentment are being felt in the bluest of the blue areas across the country, a large-scale boomerang may not be far off.

May 10, 2021

Could This Be Our Next President?

Could this guy actually become our next president?

He's not a politician. He is adored by some, despised by others. His popularity is at an all-time high, as he often takes the contrarian view. But above all, he stands for the people, against the swamp of both parties.

We're not talking about our last president. Rather, we are making these considerations regarding, perhaps, our next one - Tucker Carlson.

This past week has fanned the "Carlson-for-president" flames to their hottest levels yet.

The discussions began after Carlson reported on his Fox News program that Republican House Minority Leader, Kevin McCarthy, currently rents a Washington, D.C. penthouse from pollster Frank Luntz. While many saw the revelation as another example of political swampiness, Luntz deflected the attention to focus back on Carlson.

"Tucker realizes that he can make any accusation he wants to make, and that cadre, because he's very popular among a certain segment of conservatism," Luntz told the New York Times "Sway" podcast. "I think Tucker is running for president. And I think that's what he's going to do. And I think he's going to try to demonize and destroy anyone who might stand up against him. And that's all that this is."

Conservative pundit, Erick Erickson, offered his thoughts on the attention being turned toward Carlson. He penned an article last week entitled, *The Media's Tucker Carlson Obsession*. In the article, Erickson opines that *former President Donald Trump has gone mostly silent. Instead, the media is attempting to use Carlson as its proxy for Trump and is trying to define Carlson as the new "big bad guy" the media needs for its antagonist and narrative.*

For his part, Carlson has ridden the attention wave and remained coy about a possible run for office. In 2019 he said he would never run. But some think the landscape has moved in his direction in recent years.

"He's a talented communicator with a massive platform. I think if he runs he'd be formidable," Luke Thompson, a Republican strategist who worked for Jeb Bush's super PAC in 2016, told Politico last year.

But would Tucker actually run for president, and could he win? It may depend on the conditions over the next couple years.

The country is clearly recoiling from the extremism and economic destruction during the start of 2021. Last week's horrific jobs report put Democrat economic policies in the spotlight, with many, even on the left, claiming disbelief with how bad the report was. American taxpayers are already feeling the economic tailspin at the kitchen table, as inflation drives up expenses and liberal policies remain slow to re-open state economies to 100%. Under these conditions, which show no signs of letting up, any 2024 challenger to the "status-quo" may be in the driver's seat.

Even more so as he dominoes have started to fall in Georgia, Florida and other states, with legislatures acting to protect fair, transparent and secure voting rights for all legal citizens.

There is no question Tucker Carlson has captured this current mood in the country, harnessing the anti-establishment mantle left vacant, for the time being, by former president Donald Trump. Americans are sick of wearing masks, especially in the outdoors after being vaccinated. The country is pushing back against the slew of liberal wish-list items, ranging from a crackdown on how many hamburgers one can eat to how far one can travel without getting a government-forced shot. No host has tapped into prevailing sentiments like Carlson, and the ratings prove his success.

CNN's Oliver Darcy put forth an article in recent days with the headline *Sean Hannity used to rule Fox. But in the post-Trump era, Tucker Carlson is king.* The story points out data showing that, while both programs have lost viewership this year, Carlson has now pulled ahead of Hannity as Fox's primetime ratings leader.

But do broadcast ratings and popularity translate into electoral success? Could Carlson indeed run and win the Republican nomination? After all, he doesn't come from the same background as most recent presidential nominees. He's never been a governor, senator or community agitator. He hasn't run a city, state or government entity.

And the biggest elephant in the room is former President Trump. Should he decide to run in 2024 for a third presidential victory, he'd undoubtedly become the party's nominee. Florida's successful governor, Ron DeSantis, seems to be the strongest, yet far-trailing, second choice.

So could a non-politician, smooth-talking outsider like Carlson actually run, and perhaps win, the Republican nomination and presidency? Like Trump, the thought seems far fetched, if not outlandish at first. With so many "experienced" and "competent" leaders to choose from, why would the nation pick a talk-show host?

But is it really outlandish to imagine? One could certainly envision the left selecting a daytime talk-host such as Oprah, if only she would agree. And in the current social media world, where popularity and persona carry increasing significance, one would be well served to take her chances seriously. And if Oprah, why not Tucker?

If the last decade has taught us anything, it is that we can never say never. What seems outlandish and outside the realm of possibility today may seem entirely plausible, or dare we say probable, with the passing of time.

The worse things get, the wider we should leave the door for the unexpected.

May 17, 2021

Cable networks highlight split on "global warming"

They sit curled up in the corner, shaking and cowering, terrified of the impending doom about to befall our country and planet.

They believe the earth is just days or weeks from annihilation, due to man-made global warming.

Interestingly, new data links this level of fear to the specific news media these viewers consume.

A new poll conducted by the Heartland Institute and Rasmussen Reports showed that viewers of leftward networks, such as MSNBC and CNN, believe the world is doomed by global warming. Newsmax reported that the study found non-cable news watchers, or those who tune into networks like Newsmax, Fox, the Blaze, "were more likely to correctly estimate the amount of warming that has occurred since the late 1800s."

The poll says that 54% of MSNBC viewers and 53% of CNN viewers believe humans will be extinct within 100 years at the hands of global warming. Meanwhile, only 25% of Fox News viewers feel the same.

Global warming alarmists, just 20 or 30 years ago, were lecturing Americans about the danger of global *cooling*. They have shrieked that the world would be obliterated by the year 2000, or even that we only have a dozen years left. Kids in school are bombarded by images of polar bears stranded on small, melting chunks of ice or depictions of Manhattan submerged, with streets flooded by rising tides.

The facts, however, say the earth has warmed slightly over the last 200 years. The National Oceanic and Atmospheric Administration says this warming has been about 2.1 degrees Fahrenheit since the 1800s.

In this poll, only 37% of voters correctly answered that the impact of global warming is between 1 and 3 degrees Fahrenheit. Almost as many, 27%, overestimated it was between 3 and 5 degrees Fahrenheit. More extreme yet, another 14% estimated it was between 5 and 10 degrees Fahrenheit. Another 8% said temperatures rose more than 10 degrees since the 1800s.

The key finding is this - while most Americans don't follow the year-by-year temperature fluctuations, Fox News viewers had much more accurate responses regarding the actual data and facts than MSNBC and CNN viewers. Fox News viewers choose the correct range of historical global warming 41% of the time, compared to only 30% of MSNBC and CNN viewers.

Most rational Americans want a clean world, with drinkable water and breathable air. There are good people on both sides of the issue, watching varying cable networks, with sincere concern for our care of the planet. In fact, many cite the Biblical roots of man's stewardship of the earth and its environment. Most agree those littering or polluting indiscriminately should be punished. People and corporations should be held accountable to their communities, based on guidelines influenced by an informed citizenry. However, Americans can sense the politicization of the issue.

30 years ago, the tag phrase was global cooling. Then, when political goals are not achieved, it shifts to global warming. Eventually, it became the all-encompassing "climate change." Regardless, the solution from the left is always a bigger government to crack down on the freedoms of an uncaring and pollution-intent population who is destroying the planet. Unsurprisingly, the regulations consistently take aim at America and it's enduring way of life.

Many scientists and experts note that even if the earth is warming, it is indeed questionable whether man's actions are the cause. The late Rush Limbaugh was fond of saying, "Ok, if man is the cause of the weather, then man should be able to fix it. So go ahead, fix the weather. Cool the temperature. Of course, man can't change it. So it should also be assumed he isn't the cause." Limbaugh also doubted that God would create man to yearn for more, strive, innovate and advance, while at the same time allowing this advancement to cause the earth's demise as its byproduct.

On man's contribution to global warming or cooling, there is certainly no consensus. Scientists argue from both sides, and the Founder of The Weather Channel, John Coleman, called global warming "the greatest scam in history." Still, study and discussion about how to leave a cleaner and healthier planet to future generations is a worthwhile endeavor. The question is, what gains are possible, and at what cost.

On his Fox News television program, Sean Hannity recently summed up his perspective, calling out the Biden administration for the surge in gas prices caused by the new administration's policies.

"They put new restrictions on fracking, sought to artificially reduce oil and gas supply. Supply, demand, criss-cross equals the price. Limited supply, higher prices, all in the name of socialist climate change and the new definition of infrastructure," Hannity said during a monologue last week. "And now Americans, you, the American people, you will pay the price. Gas prices are at a 7 year high and they are climbing fast. And the east coast of the U.S. is likely now more reliant on Russian oil than ever before."

This new poll shows that, unsurprisingly, those watching left-leaning cable television networks have one view of global warming, and those watching right-leaning networks share the opposing view.

The media's real question - is it the chicken or the egg? Are the networks creating their audience's bias, or reflecting it?

We'll probably shudder and shake in the corner until we figure out the answer to that one.

May 24, 2021

Prepare For the Bubble to Burst

The Baby Boomers are about to go Baby Bust, along with the rest of the United States asset market. That was the warning on the recent episode of the Rich Dad Radio Show with Robert Kiyosaki. Guest and author, Harry Dent, updated his recent predictions and foreshadowed an impending event that will shake the country's economic markets to their core.

Financial news click bait, or sound fundamental forecasting?
You be the judge.

Harry Dent, known for his reliance on demographic trends, has for months been calling for a massive market collapse.....in April. The spring came and went, with markets still standing.

Now Dent, the author of many books predicting booms and busts, has updated his prediction. He told Kiyosaki he is now eying June as the month the asset bubble will burst, leaving Americans high and dry.

Skeptics point to unending inflow of new money into the system, through stimulus, money printing and fiat debasement, as the way the United States will inflate its way out of an economic collapse. The current administration seems hell-bent on opening the money spigots, a skill honed by both political parties of the past decade. However, Dent isn't so sure the "money printer go Brrrrr" method will work this time.

"The reason we have non-stop money printing is to offset the decline of the Baby Boom generation," Dent said. "And this is the worst policies ever in history. And these central bankers are first of all going to be destroyed by the internet, blockchain technologies number one. And number two, by being the dumbest asses in history, to think you can offset a downturn, printing money out of thin air, and thinking it will go away."

Dent clearly doesn't think continued money printing will lead to a prosperous middle class, and he also feels the economy peaked in 2007. Also, he's not too fond of those currently putting the money printer in overdrive, particularly Janet Yellen. Dent asks, "How does she become the Treasury Secretary after the Fed Chairman? How did this happen? She's never done anything, EVER, in history! An academic researcher. This is insanity!"

Kiyosaki, and his wife Kim, pressed Dent on the future of blockchain technology. Dent not only believes in the future of Bitcoin, but he also doubts the government's ultimate ability to control or stop it. In fact, he sees blockchain monetary technology as the best way to democratize finance and lift the poorest Americans into the middle class, through it's "bottoms-up" network.

Mr. Kiyosaki is also not a fan of where the Democrat administration is taking the country.

"I was talking to my accountant, and he's looking at the new tax changes coming up," Kiyosaki mentioned. "His belief is they want to shut down small entrepreneurs, because they threaten them."

"That's not good policy. I agree with you on that," Dent responded. "The truth is, the only way you grow long term is to encourage entrepreneurs and entrepreneurial investment."

Dent believes the combination of demographics and continued poor governmental economic policy has the nation's asset markets at the breaking point. He has predicted some past economic downturns correctly, however he originally called for this massive correcting to take place by April. Now he says June.

"The demographics already peaked in 2007, but they've pumped it up into now," Dent said, offering his most concrete evidence of an impending collapse. "I mean, all artificial, so this bubble is worse. I think it normally would be like the '29 to '32 crash, 80 to 90-percent. I see the Dow as low as 5000, and at best 12 to 13,000 in a couple years from now. That's going to wipe out a lot of wealth."

Harry Dent's crystal ball has had a mixed record over the past 20 years, but both he and Robert Kiyosaki believe the can has been kicked down the road past the point of return. They say this one will be the big one.

If things take the disastrous turn these two are predicting in the near future, it will be unmistakable. Time will tell if Dent's latest prediction hits the mark.

May 31, 2021

Why is Cleaning Up Our Financial Act a Bad Thing?

Americans are apparently improving their financial situations, but don't think this is considered good news by everyone.

A major national talk show host is congratulating everyday people who are getting their financial houses in order, and he's also calling out the entities and individuals who seem dismayed by this display of financial responsibility.

Dave Ramsey doesn't mince words, and recently he took the big banks and credit card companies to task for openly showing their disappointment in the fact that Americans have recently paid off large amounts of consumer debt. Ramsey and co-host, John Delony, last week discussed an article from the Wall Street Journal entitled *Credit Card Debt Keeps Falling. Banks on Edge.*

The article says Americans are paying down debt at levels not seen in years - good news to everyone except credit card issuers. Overall balances are falling, which brings down the amount of interest credit card companies are collecting from borrowers. As a result, some lending companies are planning to loosen underwriting requirements, as well as pour more money into marketing.

"If people don't keep on screwing up, we're going to make less money guys," Delony said on this episode of *The Ramsey Show*, "Here's what's going to happen. You're going to start getting these emails and cards in the mail saying "Hey, we miss you guys." Here's some more money you can go spend."

The article said that Discover has seen the share of card balances that were paid off at the end of the first quarter rise to the highest level since 2000. Perhaps due to rounds of government largess, Capital One said nearly half of the credit card balances that it had at the beginning of March were paid off by the end of the month. Store card balances were also down considerably in the first quarter this year.

Delony and Ramsey pointed to the months-long pandemic as having re-focused consumers on proper financial management. In other words, many families were caught off guard and now want to be better prepared in the future.

"I don't want to be the little pig in the straw house any more. I'm going to get my crap together. I'm going to get out of debt and have an emergency fund," Ramsey said. "I'm going to be the little pig in the brick house so when the wolf comes and blows, I don't have credit card debt, I don't have student loan debt, I don't have car payments. I'm under control and I got a pile of money."

Some economists and politicians, perhaps those steeped in Keynesian economics or Modern Monetary Theory, also believe these trends are harmful to the economy's ability to continue it's recovery. Ramsey said this belief is nonsense.

"If you get completely out of debt, thus you have your entire income to work with, and you have money saved for emergencies and saved to buy things - do people then spend less over the next decade following that, or more?" Ramsey asked.

The answer for most, according to the hosts, is more.

"This idea that debt drives the economy is not true," Ramsey added. "Now consumption does drive the economy, but consumption increases when people aren't broke."

In Ramsey's opinion, and according to his decades of financial teaching, financially strong families combine to form a financially strong economy.

"The idea that getting rid of debt in America and getting rid of this burden on the back of everyone is somehow going to cause the American capitalistic system to completely fail is asinine," he said. "Because the reality is that when people get out of debt and have money, they spend more money. Now they spend it differently, more intentionally, more wisely. But it's not less dollars being spent on big screens."

For decades, Dave Ramsey has been a media voice helping listeners get out of debt and build a solid financial future. He'll be pleased if recent trends continue, both for individuals and families, and for what it could mean for the country as a whole.

Remembering America's Greatness

Since the day of its birth, America has been a symbol for liberty and freedom across the world. But while the political party currently in power too often seems intent on bringing the country down a peg or two, one radio talk host believes the American public is correct to remain prideful in our great nation.

In fact, he wouldn't have it any other way.

Mark Levin took to his national radio airwaves Friday to commemorate the June 6th anniversary of D-Day, when Allied forces invaded France via the beaches at Normandy in 1944. Levin began by playing remarks from former President Donald Trump, who two years ago stood on that sacred location and delivered a stirring speech, recognizing the 75th anniversary of the invasion.

"They battled not for control and domination, but for liberty, democracy and self-rule," Trump said on June 6, 2019. "They pressed on for love and home and country. The main streets, the school yards, the churches, the neighbors, the families and communities that gave us men such as these. They were sustained by the confidence that America can do anything because we are a noble nation with a virtuous people, praying to a righteous God. Their exceptional might came from a truly exceptional spirit."

"God do I miss that man," Levin commented. "He was a great president. Despite all that's been said about him and written about him, by the same forces we confront today."

Levin drew the distinction between the unifying words of Trump, and Reagan before him, praising the courage and goodness of America, juxtaposed against the division fomented by the modern day Left and their media. Levin harkened back to the not-so-distant past, when both political parties held America in the highest esteem and proudly lifted it up as the best example for liberty and freedom ever created by man.

"Joe Biden is like an ambulance-chaser, trying to find historical events, run to those historical events, to tear this country apart in a thousand different ways," Levin noted. "He's a street-hack politician, Joe Biden. He's not a leader and he's not a statesman."

The comments from the fiery Levin were directed mostly at Democrats, who he feels have relished the art of creating victims, stirring hate and pitting Americans against each other. However, his words Friday were aimed at a wider-reaching cohort than just the Left. He referred to former House Speaker, Paul Ryan, and the establishment Republicans, who fought side by side with Democrats to "defeat" Trump last November.

"We don't need to remake the Republican party into what it was before Reagan, or before Trump. And I say with the deepest respect, you need to open your eyes and your mind, as do your compatriots. That the great things these men did for this country, and to the terrible things that are being done to our country today," Levin said. "Terrible, and you should be focused like a laser on confronting those who seek to overturn the most fantastic and fabulous nation mankind has ever established."

For years, Levin has preached the dangers of socialism, and in his opinion, Americans are now understanding his point clearly for themselves. Rapid inflation and money printing, a degradation of the country's moral underpinnings and a rise in violence and division have forced citizens to take notice. His comments also played off of an earlier segment of his show, where he featured Tatiana Ibrahim, a mother who's passionate comments against the radicalism indoctrinating children in public schools recently went viral.

"The American Marxists have finally exposed themselves. They used to just trash the country, and I would tell you when you trash a country, you're trashing its people," Levin pointed out. "They used to deny that...just attacking the history. Now they're attacking America's people. They're attacking you. Now they're in our classrooms. They're in our televisions. They're in our books. They get to decide what we read, what we see, what we hear. They get to decide what monuments stand and what monuments don't. They get to define morality in a thousand different ways."

For decades, through his work on radio, television and in print, Mark Levin has been a staunch supporter of America. Today, the pro-America movement may not have the support of some in the highest echelons of national power. Regardless, this media voice and stalwart for liberty continues his daily duties - illuminating and calling attention to America's enduring greatness.

June 14, 2021

Bypassing the Media, Right to the People

There is a reason the term *journalist* commands such little respect these days. Normal Americans have caught on to the game and realize that, unless otherwise noted, the term simply implies *radical liberal party activist*.

Take just a few examples from this week, where Americans learned what they probably knew all along - that the media blatantly and purposefully lied about key developments during President Donald Trump's first term.

Remember when Trump touted the possible pandemic-fighting benefits of Hydroxychloroquine? They said he was an unstable nut. However, as reported this week, Trump was right. A study shows using the drug plus zinc increases survival of the virus by three times.

Remember when they said Trump cleared out Lafayette Park across from the White House, shooting "peaceful protesters" with rubber bullets and bombarding them with pepper spray, all so he could have a photo opp in front of church? Well, it turns out he didn't order the clearing of the protesters. The plan had been made days earlier, to build a fence to protect police officers.

And the worst part, the media knew the truth all along, yet declined to share it with the public.

How about the cringe-worthy moment from a recent White House press briefing, where a breathless reporter asked subserviently, "as we are covering the Biden White House, what are we getting wrong?"

And these are just a few of the purposeful media deceptions from this week alone, designed to influence and convert the citizenry, rather than inform it.

The good news for truth-seekers, however, is that the real story is soon coming right to the people. The people will soon hear directly from the source.

Veteran broadcaster Bill O'Reilly is launching an upcoming *Trump History Tour*, where he will interview the President during a series of fireside-talk themed events at the end of the year. O'Reilly joined Glenn Beck's radio program this week to explain the concept.

"The approach here of the president, sitting and talking and having someone like you, who can rope him in in a fun way, I think is going to be extraordinarily effective," Beck began.

"Here's how it all came about," O'Reilly said. "So I'm watching the inauguration of Joe Biden, and I'm taking notes. In the back of my mind, I'm going...I don't know what happened in the last four years inside the White House, I don't know anything. Because all the reportage was we hate Trump and want to destroy him, or we love Trump and want him to be emperor forever. The basic history arc was empty."

O'Reilly says he wants to cut through the personality-driven hype and the leftist media hate to get to the facts.

"How on earth did the United States get a vaccine to defeat a pandemic in seven months? That seems to be a miracle," he pointed out. "How did that happen...nuts and bolts. What did you do, Mr. President? Who did you speak to? How much money changed hands, and all that. Now these are essential, important questions for every American to know, particularly now when we've entered another era of chaos, absolute chaos is happening in Washington, D.C."

O'Reilly notes that it took some arm-twisting to get Trump to agree to the series of discussions.

"You're not going to be able to recover your political profile, if you don't put things on the record for history," O'Reilly recalls telling Trump about the importance of bypassing the liberal media. "You must tell the American people how you did what you did. And you cannot get a fair shake."

For his part, Beck wants to know how Trump consistently taps into the instincts of Americans, saying "he has the best gut I've ever seen."

Certainly, Mr. Trump has been known to embellish or hyperbolize at times, a tactic that many think is warranted, considering the culture of hatred pushed by Democrats and their media.

"This is not going to be a debate," O'Reilly noted. "I'm going to ask the questions. If he doesn't answer them I'll point it out to him and there will be seven thousand people looking at us. It's not going to be a rally, no MAGA hats on stage, we're not going to do any of that. It's all going to be history."

Ultimately, it came down to Trump agreeing with O'Reilly that citizens deserve the truth the extremist liberal media consistently hides from them.

"The clincher for President Trump was, I said the American people have been deprived, and they have been deprived on purpose, of information about their country which affects them directly. I was looking at him in the eye when I said this. I said that these people, even the people that voted against you, and don't like you, they have no blanking clue what you actually did, because the corporate media assembled to destroy you. And so anything that you did that was positive, including the vax, they were not going to report it accurately if it helped you. And it's the same thing going on now. If it hurts Joe Biden, they're going to black it out."

Tickets for the upcoming *Trump History Tour* with Trump and O'Reilly are widely available starting today.

June 21, 2021

Biden Already Polling Poorly

Most of the media wants you to believe that the country is unified in support of the job Joe Biden is doing as president.

As usual, don't believe the nonsense.

Biden's honeymoon is already over, if any such thing still exists. From day one, regardless of how the country felt about the legitimacy of his "win," voters had already dug in their heels. And the results are quite alarming - both for Biden and for supporters of his extreme policy agenda.

On last week's episode of *What are the Odds*, pollster and media personality, Richard Baris, shared some topline numbers on his recent national polling. The overall trend is that as the pandemic recedes, so does Biden's job approval rating. The data indicates his fate may be tied to this one fading issue. A mere six months into his presidency, his approval numbers are already nearing dangerous territory for Democrats hoping to have an enduring electoral impact.

Overall, Baris has Biden at 51 percent approve, 46 percent disapprove. Approval is trending down, with disapproval on the upswing. But he notes that without the reliably leftward-leaning northeast states, Biden would "be in deep, deep, deep trouble with his approval rating." Voters seem keenly attuned to the rapid downturn in conditions, as they watch rising inflation, increasing food costs, gas shortages, cyberattacks, violence in the Middle East, etc.

Biden's relatively high early disapproval is clearly linked to the continuing election investigations ongoing in numerous states. Increasingly, these recounts and audits are turning up multiple inconsistencies, adding more doubt in voters' minds.

"Whether the media or social media want to admit it, there are a lot of people who question the legitimacy of Joe Biden's win. That's a reality, whether you want to agree with it or not. That's irrelevant, it's what the country thinks," Baris said.

Biden saw an uptick in approval over the spring, a trend Baris attributes to the distribution of the vaccine rushed to completion and handed to him by President Donald Trump.

"How do we know?" Baris asked rhetorically. "Because we asked about the other issues and you saw it. He was underwater on immigration, badly. He was underwater on the economy, a couple of points. He's underwater on US/China relations. He's underwater on foreign policy." And this was before last week's disastrously weak showing at the G7 meetings for Biden.

Many Americans are finding it hard to believe the country's fortune has changed for the worst so quickly. And remember, these polling results were captured by Baris, one of the best in the business, whose work has been extremely accurate over the past decade. His polling in 2020 was very close to the election's final outcome.

"It's a general feeling of, what a minute, what the hell is going on?" Baris said. "None of this was happening under Donald Trump. Why is the world falling apart now? And the media wants to hide that, that's fine. But it's happening. The blue checks on Twitter want to ignore it, that's fine. But it's happening. The fake poll readers who think they are gauges of pollsters in their ratings of accuracy and trustworthiness, fine. But it's happening!."

And Baris's numbers might be some of the best for Biden, as a similar Monmouth poll has the president sitting at only 48% approval.

Some of the other notable takeaways from Baris's polling, which seem to show the Democrats increasingly out of step with mainstream American sentiment.....

56% of the country feels that social media bans are too often used to crush dissenting views and represent a grave threat to free speech rights. Only 23% disagree.

Americans do not support the Democrats' Critical Race Theory teachings in schools. By a spread of 67-21 respondents said children should be taught to be merit based, racially color blind and capable of being whomever if they work hard, not that they are disadvantaged based on the color of their skin.

63% of all Americans support the 2nd Amendment, but only 47% of Democrats support it.

China is viewed to be the biggest threat to the United States, by a commanding 42% to 22% margin ahead of Russia. Among Democrats, Russia was the top choice at 36%.

Most voters side with Israel over the Palestinians, 34%-13%, while Democrats favor Palestinians 21%-18%. 26% of all respondents support Palestinian statehood, 24% do not. Half of Americans are unsure or don't care.

86% of voters agree (with Trump) that policy should put the needs of U.S. citizens ahead of U.S. allies and the global community.

58% of Americans said they would much rather have a leader who always keeps their promises and shares their views, even if they have perceived moral flaws.

25% of respondents do not intend to get vaccinated for COVID-19. 45% of Democrats have a great deal of trust in the vaccine, while only 24% of Republicans do.

Things don't look great right now for Biden or his policies. Baris summed up his current polling, saying "This is the weakest margin since he put his hand on the Bible and took the oath of office, so it's safe to say the honeymoon period is now over."

June 28, 2021

Faking the News Without Worry

Much of the United States' mainstream media have made an art of lying, distorting, omitting and purposely misleading the masses. They also continue to give the matter not a single worry, even though media consumers are clearly tuned in to their deceptive ways.

A new poll released last week shows that Americans are not only distrustful of the corporate, establishment media, but also that the lack of trust is tops in the world.

The poll, sponsored by Oxford University's Reuters Institute, and conducted by YouGov, surveyed 46 media markets across six continents. The survey questioned more than 90,000 people, and the United States media won first place, as its viewers expressed the least amount of trust in the validity of their reporting.

Trust in the United States mainstream media stands at just 29%.

At the same time, the survey shows that across the world, "trust in the news has grown, on average, by six percentage points in the wake of the coronavirus pandemic - with 44% of our total sampling saying they trust most news most of the time," says Nic Newman, a senior research associate at the Reuters Institute.

Finland has the highest levels of trust, at 65%, more than double the United States' 29%.

As many U.S. consumers continue to catch on and lose faith in the media, some have tuned out altogether. Interest in the news across America has dropped 11% since the still-questioned election. Only 55% of American respondents say they are interested in the news. Newman notes that this shift is most pronounced among right-leaning groups, with Newman adding, "our data show signs that many former Trump supporters may be switching away from news altogether. Almost all of this fall in interest came from those on the political right." He also points out that many Americans, "especially with younger people and those with lower levels of education," are riding the technological wave and gravitating to non-traditional sources of news.

The poll, conducted between January and February of this year, would naturally act as a wake-up call to any news outlet actually interested in presenting fairly-reported news to consumers, rather than in shaping narratives. For the few still steeped in the idealistic, traditional view of "journalism," Newman says there is true cause for concern.

"Our findings that both political partisans and young people feel unfairly represented will be especially troubling for media companies looking to build engagement both across political divides and with the next generation," Newman said.

His conclusion makes the assumption that mainstream American journalists share, deep in their hearts, these lofty heights at which to aim. Based on the daily evidence and years of breathtaking duplicity, American consumers are clearly not ready to extend their mainstream, corporate media the courtesy of that assumption.

Overall, the poll still sheds a bit of bright news for the U.S. media establishment. If they wish to turn back to noble roots, some consumers may still afford them the chance. If not, at least their diligent work has them standing proud and tall, finally first in the world at something.

July 5, 2021

Reveling in CNN's Ratings Demise

Much of America is relishing this year's ratings collapse of the once once-mighty, once-balanced CNN news network. And while many are not surprised by the drop itself - with its main target of derision currently out of the White House - many of the network's detractors are surprised at the speed of the downfall.

In a recently-penned article at Townhall.com entitled *CNN"s Ratings Collapse: It Couldn't Happen to Nicer People,* Derek Hunter basks gleefully in CNN's rapid ratings decline.

He begins, "To paraphrase the old saying, when your opponent is destroying himself...let him. There are few things I enjoy more than bad things happening to bad people, and the news about the collapse of CNN's ratings falls nicely into that category. It couldn't happen to nicer people. So let's revel a little in the historic 70 percent ratings collapse of the Cable 'News' Network."

The numbers tell the story. FoxNews.com reports that in the 2nd quarter of 2021, CNN averaged 654,000 viewers. Fox News averaged 1.2 million viewers. CNN's most popular program was "Cuomo Prime Time," which finished behind 14 different Fox News shows and seven MSNBC shows.

Former President Donald Trump also offered his thoughts, lumping the top three cable news networks together in a statement that read, "CNN ratings are down 70%. MSDNC is also way down. Actually, they are ALL way down. They say the news is "boring" since I left D.C. Morning Joe, Joy Reid (whoever that is?), Nicole Wallace, Jake Tapper, and even Chris Wallace, at Fox, in a free fall. A wonderful thing to see!"

After this, Joseph Wulfsohn said on Fox News.com that "CNN personalities are getting defensive after former President Trump mocked the liberal network's dramatics ratings free fall." He highlighted CNN's head of strategic communications, Matt Dornic, who "appeared to celebrate President Biden's administration" when he tweeted, "Imagine that. People are vaccinated, no longer terrified, and out enjoying their lives. If the trade-off is that every news net's ratings are down, I'll take it."

In his Townhall piece, Hunter goes on to say "the primetime line-up of CNN is a joke. How can a network in literally every home with cable, which is almost all of them, draw fewer than a million viewers nightly?"

Hunter goes on to opine that "CNN's biggest problem is the people who are supposed to be the "faces of the network" are simultaneously the face of the Democrat Party and, unfortunately for them, they're also wrong as often, if not more so, than the party itself. People can be forgiving about wrong, they can't forgive being unrepentant about it."

CNN clearly made their bed, as was their prerogative, when they swerved unabashedly leftward sometime around the time President Trump came down the escalator to announce his candidacy. Upon retrospect, it was undoubtedly much earlier than that when the network made a deliberate choice to throw in with the Left.

But again, no freedom-loving American doubts their right to nurture an editorial style. Let the free market decide, with viewers voting with their time and attention. Most viewers would simply prefer an honest and open elucidation of the network's philosophical bent. What viewers reject more than anything is the guise of objectivity, camouflaging a biased liberal agenda. The majority of viewers see the battle lines and have chosen accordingly. But as the political winds shift, those lines in the sand can cut into the most important line of all - the one sitting at the bottom.

"CNN is in the midst of a ratings free-fall, and it couldn't happen to a nicer, more deserving group of people," Hunter sums up. "The network's only redeeming quality is the thoroughness with which they demonstrate the fact that they have no redeeming qualities. That's something, I guess."

July 12, 2021

You Don't Have to Be a Jerk

"Can I be successful without being a jerk?"

The question was raised recently in the context of excelling in the business world, however it can similarly be asked in the realm of news media.

Dan Miller, the author of the highly-acclaimed job and career book, *48 Days to the Work You Love,* fields weekly questions and offers advice gained from years working in the personal development and career growth field. He fielded the following question recently on his highly-regarded online radio show.

"Can a naturally shy person, who might not fit the profile for your typical leader, truly lead from a loving and caring attitude? I sometimes feel like I'm not the business owner potential because I don't have that corporate America attitude. I want to help others and I think I can be a great leader, but I don't have such a dominant personality."

In a world where business owners and leaders are often portrayed as obnoxious, forceful brutes, a la Cornelius Vanderbilt or Biff Tannen, this question is a common one. Popular culture and media often amplify this caricature, and many feel that you have to be a strong willed, outgoing personality to succeed in business, or similarly in media.

Miller began his answer by referring to the DISC personality profile system, which many companies and organizations utilize to analyze their employees and teams.
D - Dominant, forceful
I - Influencing, outgoing
S - Steady, even-tempered
C - Compliant, analytical

"You can be that person, absolutely," Miller told his audience, "The question is not do you have to remake how God has made you in order to be successful. No, the question is, can you shape your business so it fits what you know about yourself?"

For decades, Miller has focused on self-knowledge and introspection as the foundation of any job or career decision. He has helped thousands, if not millions, by coaching job-seekers to find the perfect career. His analogies are tailored for employees and entrepreneurs, but the same correlations can be carried over to the media world.

If one is an introvert, perhaps an S or C on the DISC profile, he may not want to build a career as a dominant business owner. In media, Alex Jones, Bill O'Reilly or Dave Ramsey might fit that personality style. It doesn't infer a positive or negative about their style, but simply that their personalities are naturally more forceful and outwardly opinionated than others. Meanwhile, examples of S or C type personalities would be, perhaps, Stuart Varney, Brett Baier and Dan Miller, himself.

"That's why we promote the profile so much, so you know about yourself," Miller said. "Once you know about yourself, then you know exactly how to focus the business that you want to have."

In other words, start with your personality profile, traits and skills and work outward from there. Build the business, or media career, that fits you, rather than the other way around.

"Knowing what you know about yourself, now you are 80% there," Miller concluded. "Because now you know how to shape a business, how to find a business, that does fit you."

Dan Miller's wisdom provides an interesting way to take his advice, transfer it across industries, and analyze the foundation of a media career.

July 19, 2021

More Please, Sugar Daddy

The money printer chugs along. Rampant Inflation devalues each dollar hard-working Americans earn every day. And the bill for this party will eventually come due, in the form of dramatic financial pain forced on children and grandchildren by current generations.

Senator Ron Johnson of Wisconsin joined radio talk host Andrew Wilkow on Friday to discuss the consequences of the current administration's money printing and the possible consequences of a bipartisan infrastructure spending deal. The host began the conversation by wondering out loud if the Democrat president and Congress' goal is to give out enough goodies to cajole, coax and sweet-talk voting majorities in 2022.

"They will spend as much as they can get away with," Johnson replied. "What I don't want to see is Republicans complicit in it. First of all, everybody realizes we need to spend money on infrastructure. And in normal times I actually would support deficit spending on infrastructure, true infrastructure, things that last 20, 30, 40, 50 years. It would make sense to borrow money. But we just spent, basically, five, six trillion dollars of money we don't have."

Johnson proposed that the Republican position on infrastructure should be to take the $700 billion in Covid relief that isn't spent fully until 2028 and repurpose it for infrastructure. Johnson believes any bi-partisan deal would simply lead to more Democrat-devised entitlement programs.

"Here's the really nasty thing. What they're going to do is put forth a new entitlement," Johnson predicted. "They'll say it will sunset in three or four years, to get a decent score. But we all know entitlements never end, so this will be way more expensive than what the bumper sticker amount that is going to be passed by the budget committee."

Although it has ramped up considerably in the past six months, the printing didn't begin when the tax-and-spend Democrats took over and began pushing high-spending, socialist policies. While he never took action on the matter, President Donald Trump talked often about a large infrastructure spending plan that, in the end, did not materialize during his first term. Spending has been ramping up to out-of-control levels for years, if not decades, through the actions of both parties.

Wilkow, as has been his philosophical bent, questioned the need for the Federal Government to tackle needs in individual states, such as high-speed broadband access in rural communities.

"This is what I don't understand. When we talk about infrastructure, tell me if I'm crazy, we're no longer separating federal infrastructure from state and local," Wilkow said. "So if you're talking the federal highway system, you're talking about ports, or military bases or any of the things that fall under the guise of the Federal Government, that I get. But all of this other stuff is state-based stuff. Why should states have to wait for a bipartisan agreement to do state-based things? And this idea that if the states put all their money in a big pot somehow the sum is greater than the parts, that's not true. The only reason we're doing this, it sounds like, is because the states cannot run up debt like the Federal Government."

Johnson continued, saying that our nation's Founding Fathers would be apoplectic with the country's ever-growing and powerful national government dwarfing states with irresponsible, massive money printing and control. Long gone is the country's initial design for strong local and state governments, held closely accountable by the smaller communities they represent. Today, rather, the nation's original intent and design has been turned on its head.

"Through the generosity - and I say that statement cynically - of the Federal Government, spending money that they don't have and further mortgaging our kids' future, we have pumped hundreds of billions of dollars into state and local governments and they don't even know what to do with it," Johnson said. "There are literally cities and municipalities that have gotten so much money that they're dreaming up things to spend this money on. But everybody wants more. The Federal Government is the sugar daddy."

Politicians have always offered "ice cream for votes," as Wilkow puts it. And now Americans may be force-fed another heaping scoop or two if an infrastructure deal is ultimately finalized.

July 26, 2021

Media Forced to Cover the News

They say the key to effective humor is making sure the joke contains at least a little bit of truth. You get right up to the line and then hit the punch line, leaving your audience wondering exactly where the truth ended and the ridicule began.

Of this, Fox's Greg Gutfeld is a master.

The comedian/television talk show host has a knack for hitting home with real people, by feeling what they feel and expressing those thoughts in a cogent, funny and often irreverent manner.

Last week, Gutfeld penned an opinion piece on FoxNews.com, in which he took aim at the mainstream liberal media, specifically CNN. The title of his piece was *Greg Gutfeld: The crime problem the media pretends doesn't exist actually found them at a baseball game.*

In the piece, the Fox News talk host opinied that Big Media was forced to cover the scourge of inner-city violence epidemic after a recent shooting outside a baseball game at Nationals Park in Washington, D.C. Many fault the corporate media for downplaying the escalating violence and rioting in Democrat-controlled inner cities in recent years.
Gutfeld, co-host of the networks *The Five*, and host of *Gutfeld!*, says the recent incident forced their hand and made them discuss the issue.

"Now obviously CNN covered the shooting, doing live shots outside the center field gate," Gutfeld wrote on FoxNews.com. "Why is that important? Because it was refreshing to finally see CNN cover a crime story. For once. If you watched their network you were told crime was largely made up hysteria. Just an idea, but nothing real."

In reading Gutfield's comments, one can recall the infamous clip of the reporter standing in front of fire-filled riots last year, telling viewers it was a "largely peaceful protest."

Gutfeld had previously commented that the only way big, corporate media would cover crime is if they were impacted. This game, he said, forced them to face the issue and report the facts that have been affecting much of America, outside the media bubble.

"For a brief moment that bubble popped Saturday night at a baseball game - where the true reality of our crime epidemic hit home, or rather home plate," Gutfeld wrote. "They got a taste of how the rest of DC lives. Where policies the media supports have turned their neighborhoods into a John Wick movie."

Gutfeld will continue to be irreverent, as he has been since he joined the network in 2007. He'll surely continue to deride and mock the Left and their establishment media elite, right up to the line.

He summed up his piece, writing, "So will they learn any lessons from this? Will they reexamine their news coverage, especially regarding crime, and how they dropped that ball when it should have been a routine catch? Of course not. They'll forget about it by tonight. And say the game was postponed due to climate change."

August 2, 2021

Planning for the Next Generation of Financial Talk Radio

For decades, the Dave Ramsey show has talked the talk and walked the walk. Over the past year, the home of EntreLeadership has unveiled the path toward their next stage of financial and business leadership.

Since its inception, *The Dave Ramsey Show* has focused almost entirely on the opinions and advice of one man alone, Dave Ramsey. Over the past couple years, however, the radio show - and the brand itself - has expanded to include new personalities, new voices and a new way of looking at the company's future.

The most formal transition points were the name changes. Changes from the *Dave* Ramsey Show to the Ramsey Show and Ramsey Solutions were signals of the shift toward the future. The baton hasn't been passed yet, but the team is gearing up.

On any given day, listeners and viewers can tune in to hear the show's namesake joined by fresh, new, up-and-coming voices, such as Ken Coleman, Rachel Cruze, Christy Wright, Anthony O'Neal and John Delony. Changing the name of the show and including new members of the on-air team hasn't been without challenges, however, as on any given day you may hear Ramsey mistakenly introduce the show as the *Dave* Ramsey Show. Decades-long routines are difficult to break.

The introduction of new voices apparently signaled a realization by the company that it needed to expand in a younger, more diverse direction that would outlast any one person. Again, a common theme in terms of small business growth and transition discussions. Each voice brings a specific focus to the team, and many host individual podcasts as well on the Ramsey Network.

In Ken Coleman, the company has an experienced, values-based broadcaster who focuses on career and job advice. Rachel Cruze connects with younger generations to help them "win with money and live a life they love." Christy Wright brings strong Christian wisdom to topics such as personal and professional development, goal setting, life balance and business. Anthony ONeal hits home with the youth, teaching them about planning for college and their financial future. John Delony brings his two PhDs to the areas of relationship and emotional wellness.

Together, the group puts forth a well-balanced array of viewpoints to tackle varying areas of financial and business discussions. Some days we hear Dave Ramsey, while other days feature the new personalities with, or without, Ramsey himself. Some listeners may feel that individual programs may lack a little luster without Ramsey. However, the audience is gradually seeing greater value in the Ramsey team as a whole, and the company has clearly broadened its base with the refreshed lineup of new personalities.

The company's look ahead shouldn't be a surprise, being that succession plans and seeing down the road have been common themes of the Ramsey brand, and more specifically their small-business-focused business unit, EntreLeadership.

"The best succession plans are thoroughly laid out and very, very gradual," Ramsey said, talking about family business transitioning on a recent episode of the EntreLeadership podcast. "Too many people in family businesses grab their chest having a heart attack as they fall back in the grave, toss the next generation the keys and go, Good Luck I'm done."

Through their radio programs, live events, books and other materials, the company has always "talked the talk" regarding planning for the future, especially in a small business eying an eventual transition. Now they are "walking the walk" live on the air.

"More is caught than taught," Dave Ramsey, and other Ramsey personalities have said more than once over the years. They are growing and planning for the future in real time, and listeners are taking notice.

August 9, 2021

The Impeachment Boomerang?

With the word "impeachment" making a resounding comeback in recent years, many conservative voices are now sounding the alarm and making a new call for that rare solution. This time, they say, it's use would actually be warranted and legally sound.

Talk show host and legal scholar Mark Levin is one of many labeling the actions of President Joe Biden as impeachable offenses. As usual, "The Great One" didn't mince words during his appearance on *Hannity* last week, offering his opinion about the Democrat president's recent moves.

"Joe Biden is the most disastrous president in modern American history," Levin began, calling out Biden for reports of floods of Covid-positive illegal aliens streaming across the country's unguarded border. "I don't care if it's by design or by the fact that he's dimwitted, it doesn't much matter to me. It would be like a president when we have a polio vaccine, telling everybody to get vaccinated but inviting people into the country who he knows has polio. No president has ever done this to his own people."

The fiery Levin continued, saying "This guy is a coward. He buckles to the radical left in his party. He's a fool. The idea that people who are vaccinated are the people who are going to be punished is like the gun owners who are law-abiding are the ones that are going to be punished. It's like the successful people in this country, they're the ones they intend to punish with the tax code. Is there anything going right in this country?"

Levin, who has already sold more than 750,000 copies of his latest book, *American Marxism*, drew the straight line between the president's new policies and the economic pain being felt by Americans.

"Gasoline prices going up, food prices going up. Anything going right in this country?" he asked. "The border wide open. You're going to have people flooding into our school districts , flooding into our hospitals. Law enforcement is overwhelmed. Towns are overwhelmed."

Levin has never been shy about stating his opinions. In fact, he may be one of the most forthright voices on the right willing to literally shout his opinions to anyone that will listen. In his view, the current policies are but a means to an end.

"Let's be blunt, he wants to turn Texas blue. He wants to turn Arizona blue," Levin said. "This street politician from Wilmington, Delaware. The dumbest man to ever serve in the Senate. The dumbest man to ever be vice president is now the dumbest man to ever be president. He's got a massive ego, he's a narcissist. He wants to go down in history as the greatest president. He's going to go down in history as the greatest disaster."

Levin then honed in on the CDC's recent extension of the eviction moratorium, a specific move Levin says is illegal. Traditionally, elections have served as the remedy for similar disagreements. However, based on recent precedent, political battles now quickly transition to calls for a different solution.

"He's just defied a federal statute, a Supreme Court decision. He knows that the CDC doesn't have the power to extend these moratoriums on rent. He says, we're going to do it anyway!" Levin stressed. "He's just violated the federal Constitution. Now let me say this, I brought this up on my radio show last week. Republicans, have you ever heard of the word impeachment? Are you just going to go down to the border and whine yourselves to death? I know you're not in the majority, but you need to start explaining to the American people - this man just violated a Supreme Court decision. This man has the border wide open in violation of our immigration laws. I mean, you impeached Donald Trump when he's out of office because of a letter. You set up a phony incitement insurrection. This man is doing enormous damage to this country!"

The "impeachment" genie was brought forth and trumpeted by Democrats in recent years, and there appears to be little hope of putting that boomerang back in the bottle.

Media Cheap Shot Over Bitcoin

Taking a cheap shot for clicks is a tried and true strategy for many online broadcasters. But when the bomb is lobbed by a classy, respected voice it comes across as even more shocking.

Last week, one of the world's leading voices on Bitcoin and Digital Assets took aim at financial education powerhouse, Dave Ramsey. On an episode of his twice-daily stream, George from *Cryptos R Us*, titled his episode *Sorry Dave But You Were Wrong About Bitcoin.*

George led off the episode by explaining how a major financial voice, Suze Orman, now recommends that investors include Bitcoin in their long-term investing strategy.

The episode then transitioned into George playing a 2014 clip of Ramsey, where he disparaged Bitcoin holders and casted doubt on the future of the asset.

"Bitcoin is the Iraqi Dinar of the internet," Ramsey said in the 2014 clip. "And I know intelligent people, who while they are intelligent are not wise, that have put a bunch of money in Bitcoin. But it's a really good way to turn a million dollars into nothing. To play in unstable currencies. Let me tell you what Bitcoin is… it is W, W, W. Wild Wild West. You're back to the western banking system, because all of the sudden, one of these computer nerds just flips a switch, the whole freaking thing's gone. It has no value. They just got completely ripped off and it took them down. And so the little hipster techie guys are sitting in front of the building with a sign that says, "Where's my money?." Well honey, you never had any. It's not real money, because it's not a stable currency that has any kind of a system that backs it, that has any kind of a system that protects it."

"This was just really, really bad advice," George said after the clip. "This advice probably cost a lot of people millions upon millions of dollars."

Obviously, in the year 2021, with massive worldwide Bitcoin adoption now underway - from hedge funds, sovereign countries, large companies, family offices, financial institutions and major retail expansion - the comments from 2014 sound completely off base. In truth, it wasn't until recent years, or months, that the worldwide financial system began understanding, and accepting, Bitcoin en mass. Ramsey shouldn't be faulted for holding his opinion in 2014. Very few saw Bitcoin as digital gold, as it is generally considered today. And through decades of live on-air work, any broadcaster would occasionally share an opinion that turns out to be off the mark in hindsight. Plucking a comment from nearly a decade ago seems unfair in most any context.

However, regarding Bitcoin's historic performance - averaging roughly 200% gains per year over the past decade - George certainly is correct.
Seven years ago, when Ramsey made the comments, each Bitcoin was valued at a mere $225.
Today each Bitcoin is worth roughly $47,000.
That is roughly 208X in about 7 years, compared to the S&P, which did a little more than a 2X in that same timeframe.

The fact that Ramsey was incorrect - in 2014 - belies the fact that he has, in some ways, moderated and come around to accepting Bitcoin's value today. Yes, Ramsey has voiced on-air doubts over the past decade, but his discussions about Bitcoin these days often includes the fact that he knows many people who have made a ton of money holding the digital gold. He no longer seems to dispel it out of hand as a ponzi scheme or scam. Rather, he still feels that more traditional assets such as mutual funds and real estate are more secure ways of holding value and growing one's net worth.

"Bitcoin's hot. Crypto's hot. A lot of people making a lot of money on it right now," Ramsey said on his radio show just two months ago. "It falls for me, an old guy, under the heading of getting rich quick, and I have not found many people that get rich quick."
He continued, saying of Bitcoin, "at a minimum it's speculating, not investing."

George has been involved with Bitcoin since roughly 2014, and he has seen both the booms and the busts in the years since. His *Cryptos R Us* streams and website have become trusted sources for his 430,000-plus YouTube subscribers. In a space where many hosts get audiences riled up with pie-in-the-sky predictions and hype, George delivers information and opinion from an informed and educated perspective.

"I'm George, we are all George," he begins each broadcast. Similar to Ramsey, he is a broadcaster who has built a niche with normal, everyday people.

Which makes the hit against Ramsey all the more surprising.

In fact, George is clearly a fan of Ramsey and the fact that he has helped more people get out of debt and onto solid financial footing than, most likely, anyone in history. Both men hit a chord with a non-pretentious audience searching for solid information from a trustworthy source.

"If you listen to him, he really does help people who are in financial situations," George said of Ramsey last week. "Especially the ones that are financially illiterate. The ones who can't control themselves. The ones that have hundreds of thousands of personal debt, credit card debt. And Dave really helps them get out of that situation. But when it comes to investments like Bitcoin, Dave is just - No, No, No - this is not his wheelhouse."

Perhaps in the future, these two "champions of the little guy" can get together and hash out some of these ideas over the air, in a discussion that would benefit viewers and expand knowledge of the booming Bitcoin ecosystem.

Both men will undoubtedly continue to have a positive impact in their lanes of the financial media landscape, and they'll also continue to have more in common than not.

Maddow Wins Big

Rachel Maddow was on the verge of being on the outside looking in, and it would have been her decision that put her there.

That was all before a pile of money was thrown her way last week. And perhaps more importantly, some flexibility and runway for growth that came with it.

The Daily Beast reported two weeks ago that Maddow was considering her options as she heads into the final year of her current contract with MSNBC. The Beast's Lachlan Cartwright joined CNN's *Reliable Sources* at that time to share his reporting on the possible break up.

"This isn't about the money for her, this is about a change in lifestyle," Cartwright said about the motives of the whip-smart Maddow. "This is about a more balanced lifestyle. She's had talks about starting her own thing that would involve podcasts and streaming and potentially newsletters."

Cartwright currently reports that Maddow's new deal is for $30 million per year, and includes a large downsizing of her workload. He says her nightly show will end in 2022, with her transitioning to weekly contributions through the 2024 election. The plan is for her weekly show to air for roughly 30 weeks out of the year.

A staunch liberal, Maddow studied at Oxford as a Rhodes scholar, and then began her media career at a small Massachusetts radio station before joining Air America, and later MSNBC.

Some believed that the public negotiations of recent weeks was simply a tactic to ramp up pressure on NBC to keep her. Even before the deal was struck, Cartwright's knowledge of the situation told him otherwise.

"This is deadly serious. This wasn't a plant from her representatives. In fact, I think they would have preferred if we didn't write about it," he told Brian Stelter a couple weeks ago. "This isn't a bargaining chip or a negotiating tactic. She is deadly serious about potentially leaving and that has NBC Universal scrambling. Their talks have become very heated, I'm told. And they're going to have to throw a bucket load of cash at her and make some concessions on her workload if they want to keep her."

In Cartwright's accurate estimation, NBC was between a rock and a hard place. How could they possibly thrive in the years to come without their number one host?

"They have to keep her, Brian, because they have no succession planning, and without her it will be diabolical for MSNBC," he said at the time.

Before the deal, *TV Insider* also added that Endeavor Co. president Mark Shapiro, who represents Maddow, felt "Rachel has an excellent relationship with them (NBC)."

Maddow began her MSNBC primetime program in 2008, and has since been the network's premier personality. Just last month, her show averaged a robust 2.29 million viewers, and the news of a possible breakup has the television news industry abuzz.

"I was chasing this story, and my sense is the same as yours" Stelter concluded two weeks ago. "This was not an intentional leak by her side to try to get more money. This is something she's really thinking about, and we'll see if she does it."

Some media insiders have said that no television personality represents a network's brand more than Maddow does for MSNBC. That includes anyone on CNN or Fox News. NBC Universal apparently felt the same, and backed up the truck to keep their number one star on the team.

It seems that Maddow and NBC have planned a thoughtful pullback in workload, with a boatload of cash to go with it. A deal that works well for everyone involved.

America Aghast Over Biden's Early Results

Well that was quick.

Less than a year into his presidential term, Joe Biden's approval numbers have tanked faster than a Major League Baseball franchise "building for the future."

Shannon Bream covered the developing story on Friday's edition of *Fox News @ Night,* where she set the table with the week's abhorrent job numbers and ghastly Afghanistan horror.

"Some tough polling out for the president today in numerous different outlets," Bream began. "The *Federalist* says this… President Joe Biden's approval rating following his handling of the Afghanistan disaster is tanking, a new poll from ABC News and the Washington Post indicates 57 percent of independents are increasingly frustrated with Biden's tenure in the White House, a 14-point increase since the 43 percent disapproval rate measured in June."

"President Biden is tanking. Kamala Harris, the Vice President, was tanking before the Afghanistan tragedy, and so you see this whole entire administration tanking in support because there are so many crises," RNC National Spokesperson, Paris Dennard, responded. "If you are an American who cares about safety and security, there's been no movement on the border. If you care about safety and security, there's been no movement when it comes to police reform. There's been no movement when it comes to stopping the defund-the-police issue. If you're a family that is concerned about your pocket book, you go to the grocery store and you see food inflation. You see gas prices increasing. And now, you look at the jobs report that was so terrible, especially for black Americans."

Dennard went on to chide the president for inflicting additional pain and suffering on the country, and to Gold Star Families specifically, for leaving Americans stranded in Afghanistan and for his words surrounding the debacle.

These shockingly-poor numbers align with last week's Zogby poll, which showed that 20% of Biden voters regret pulling the lever for him. This rapid swoon also comes against the backdrop of his already historically thin victory, where he lost 18 of the 19 swing counties that have a solid record of predicting the presidential election winner.

Bream noted that "a lot of Republicans are already going to be on board with what Paris has to say, but it's about the independents. We keep seeing that in these different polling apparatus. NPR, talking about that, says that a majority of independents now disapprove of his performance is bad news for Biden and Democrats. They're a key swing group, one Biden won in 2020 but who now think he's off track. Are you worried about the implications for 2022?"

"Yeah, absolutely Shannon," Democratic strategist Kevin Walling answered. "To your point, independents are key to the president's victory obviously in 2020, to Democrats taking back the House of Representatives in 2018 against Donald Trump. And certainly it's been a difficult couple of weeks obviously, with the news of Covid increasing across the board with the Delta variant, and obviously with the situation, tragic situation, coming out of Afghanistan with our troops, 13, losing them on the ground in Kabul. But I'm an eternal optimist. I'm a happy warrior."

Walling believes that shifting the focus and pushing toward a new trillion-dollar spending bill will be exactly the thing to get the liberal policy agenda back on track.

"Obviously, I'm not going to sugar coat this, the president is down in numbers from what we've seen," Walling added. "But we have plenty of time to turn those numbers around, I think 430 days out from 2022, the original point."

In politics, 430 days is a lifetime, and there is no way to accurately forecast the complete list of events that will transpire to influence public opinion heading into next year's midterm elections. While daunting, the nation's overwhelming disapproval of his job performance today is in no way written in stone.

For that, the president and his party should be extremely grateful.

Janice Dean, America's Storm Chaser

Last week Janice Dean pinned a tweet to her profile. It read,

The Devil Whispered in My Ear, "You're not strong enough to withstand the storm."
Today I whispered in the Devil's ear, "I am the storm."

A fitting tweet from the Fox News Senior Meteorologist, who, over the past two years, led the crusade to oust Democratic New York Governor, Andrew Cuomo.

Dean lost both her parents-in-law to Covid-19 while they were confined to long term care facilities in New York. Almost immediately, she embarked on the personal mission - searching for accountability from the former Governor over his Covid-related policies.

"I blame our governor for being reckless and irresponsible for the deaths of thousands of seniors in New York," Dean wrote in her April piece on Fox News.com. "He celebrated himself, with the help of complacent media, selling a $4 million memoir to the highest bidder filled with lies and inaccuracies. High-profile news anchors and hosts fawned over him, never asking about his tragic decisions, and whispered about him as a future president all while we were unable to see our loved ones before they died and have wakes or funeral afterward to help us get through the grief."

When many moved on from the Cuomo nursing home story, Dean remained laser-focused, intent on pinning blame where she felt it belonged.
This summer, she saw the fruits of her toils, as the Democratic governor resigned amid sexual harassment allegations.

On August 10th, Dean tweeted, "He. Is. Out. God bless America."

She followed up with an opinion piece titled, "Cuomo, the monster, is finally leaving. I thank God for the angels who gave us strength."

For her efforts over the past two years, Dean has received praise, accolades and public support.

In recent days, Dean announced that she started a new Multiple Sclerosis therapy. She posted on Twitter that she was nervous about the potential side effects of the new medication.

Almost immediately, the responses came flooding in. A tidal wave of well-wishes to a leader making another personal journey through a different type of monsoon.

"I hope all went well," read one tweet.

"Praying for You and Yours Janice"

"I think it's the Multiple Sclerosis that should be nervous."

"Good luck my friend."

"Prayers!"

"You are as strong as they get, @JaniceDean. But, still, we hold you in our thoughts and pray for it to be the best therapy yet for you."

Dean later posted an update, thanking everyone for the support and reporting that the new therapy went well.

Janie Dean has been very public over the past two years - about her grief, anger and determination. She has learned to face down cyclones in full view of anyone wishing to watch, or to join in.

On Dean's wall reads another quote.

"And once the storm is over you won't remember how you made it through, how you managed to survive. You won't even be sure, in fact, whether the storm is really over. But one thing is certain. When you come out of the storm you won't be the same person who walked in. That's what the storm's all about."
- Haruki Murakami, "Kafka on the Shore"

Janice Dean has built a career on chasing storms. She studies them, she predicts them and she follows them to their conclusion.

And when she does battle with them, she wins.

Democrats Fret Over Their Divide-and-Conquer Strategy

Chirp, chirp.

Those are the ever-increasing sounds of the "canary in the coal mine," foreshadowing the ongoing shift of Hispanic Americans away from identity pandering and toward the Republican party.

A few days ago, radio talk-show host Erick Erickson discussed this phenomena on his program, detailing the shift that began being noticed a few years ago and continues in full force.

"*Texas Monthly* did a big story, and it turns out that Hispanic voters in south Texas, if you force them to identify as a race, as opposed to an ethnicity, they identify as white," Erickson began. "And they're embracing what the media views as "whiteness," which is they're voting Republican."

Erickson details how the increase in Hispanic voters is, contrary to Democrat predictions, making Texas, among other states, more Republican.

"Now there's this, from of all places, NBC News. Here's the headline… *Democrats Warn of Canary in the Coal Mine for Latino Voters in California Recall*," he quoted. "Here's the subtitle… While California voters voted to keep Governor Gavin Newsom in office, they did so by a smaller margin than Democrats have won in the past."

Erickson continued to quote the story, saying "Donald Trump got a historic number of Latino votes in 2020, and you can claim it was because of this or because of that, but it's not like Larry Elder broke through for these folks. There is something else going on," said Michael Trujillo, a Democratic strategist based in Los Angeles, referring to the leading Republican candidate in the failed recall attempt."

The article from NBC reported that California voters sided with Newsom and against the recall 60-40. This is a slightly smaller margin than Newsom and California democrats have enjoyed in the past, as Newsom won 64% in his previous election. In contrast, black voters broke 83-17 for Newsom, while Asian voters picked Newsom by a spread of 64-36.

"It looks like Latino voters, even in California, are drifting away from the Democrats," Erickson noted. "Now, not at such an alarming rate as they are in places such as Colorado, and in Texas, and in Florida, but they are. And it presents a problem for the Democrats."

Erickson says his theory is different from what the media is pushing as the reason for this shift. His belief is that "Latino voters are historically immigrants to this country, surprise. And as immigrants to the United States, they are focused on America and being an American. So when you have Democratic candidates who try to treat them as Latino voters, you are treating them as something other than an American voter."

As he continued, Erickson detailed how this covert racism against Hispanic Americans is creating a boomerang effect from the very people the Democratic party has been talking down to.

"They want desperately to have the American dream. Here come Democrats, telling them that they are oppressed by white people and they can't have the American dream," Erickson opined. "Meanwhile, the Latino voters are thinking, I can have the American dream."

Erickson says Hispanic voters want politicians to pay attention to them not as hispanic voters, but as Americans. At the same time, he believes the Republican party has often erred with phony outreach toward the Hispanic American community.

"It's some white dude in his 20's, who learned Spanish from Rosetta Stone and shows up and says "Hola Mi Amigos." Nobody wants to pay attention to that guy. Just treat them like Americans," he said.

Erickson, backed by the data from recent elections, pointed out that the right approach is by talking to all groups simply as Americans, based on shared concerns and common sense solutions.

"That was the secret of what Donald Trump did," the one-time "Never-Trumper" pointed out, citing Trump's ability to improve conditions for all Americans, rather than cherry picking based on race, gender or ethnicity. "Donald Trump did not go talk to Hispanic voters as Hispanic voters. He didn't even talk to them in Spanish. By and large, Donald Trump just talked to these people as Americans. As people who were hard workers. As people who needed a job. As people who saw loved ones go to jail. And it worked for him."

Erickson summed up by saying the constant efforts by Democrats to divide Americans by race and ethnicity is clearly coming back to bite them at the ballot box.

"So keep on playing identity politics, Democrats," Erickson concluded. "It's amazing what happens when you divide up people by the color of their skin. They think you're racist and don't like you."

September 27, 2021

Another Mark Levin Masterpiece

Another book, another runaway success.

Mark Levin pumps out books, radio programs and television content at a pace rarely seen in modern mass media. And once again, he is firmly entrenched atop the charts.

As much as it pains the liberal mass media, Mark Levin's most recent book, *American Marxism*, is already a runaway hit among scholars, Constitutionalists and traditional readers across the nation. The book recently surpassed a million copies sold, while also remaining as the country's top-selling book on the *New York Times'* nonfiction list for more than 10 weeks straight. In fact, when it was released this summer, the book sold a staggering 700,000 copies in the first three weeks alone.

And it's not like this one is a fluke. All 8 of Levin's previous books have been bestsellers, evidence of his impact on wide swaths of the American reading public. This includes the highly-regarded 2007 title, *Rescuing Sprite*, which took an emotional look at his family's special relationship with a remarkable rescue dog.

This year's release from Levin, *American Marxism,* follows up on his runaway 2009 hit, *Liberty and Tyranny*, in which he detailed the radical leftward turn taken by Barack Obama and the Democrats. In his new book, Levin argues how liberal Democrats have largely won in solidifying their extreme policies and Marxist ideals into all areas of American life. Levin, as always, defends traditional American Constitution-based values and writes "The counter-revolution to the American Revolution is in full force. And it can no longer be dismissed or ignored for it is devouring our society and culture, swirling around our everyday lives, and ubiquitous in our politics, schools, media, and entertainment."

Levin says exposing this philosophy and its deleterious effects is key for the 2022 elections and for keeping America as a strong, prosperous force for good in the world.

"We're running out of time. You know, there are tens of millions of people in this country who have no voice in academia, the media, Big Tech, even in politics. And we're not going to roll over and play dead," Levin said in Paul Bedard's *Washington Secrets* column on Thursday.

Bedard wrote that the book tackles the Left's attempt to rewrite U.S. history, take over American institutions, and erase conservatism.

In July, on his Fox News program, *Life, Liberty and Levin*, Levin placed stacks of books on his desk, telling his audience they were just a small fraction of the books available "about what's going on in our classrooms, in our colleges and universities," but about which "we haven't been paying attention."

"Throughout our culture, whether it's newsrooms, whether it's entertainment, whether it's academia, the Democrat party, this ideology, what I call American Marxism, has been spawned from Marxism. It has been Americanized," Levin said. "It has been used to try and use our differences , our imperfections, to exploit them to drive this ideology."

As he's done on television and radio for years, Levin then followed with an exhaustive list of examples of "American Marxism" in modern-day America. And as always, he believes the solutions for most of the country's problems can be found in re-orienting around our founding principles and once-uniting values.

Levin's recent chapter of publishing success comes as he announced last week that he recently received a cardiac stent in his ongoing battle with heart disease. But the 64-year-old says his health will not stand in the way of him continuing to fight for America against Marxist policies forced on citizens by Democrats.

"All of this, all of a sudden is appearing, but the foundation for these movements, these American Marxist movements, these offshoots from Marxism, they've been in place for decades," he said in July. "It's just that they are appearing now in a big way."

Glenn Beck's American Optimism

It's only a matter of time before the pro-freedom, conservative movement triumphs against the radical Left currently governing the country.

Glenn Beck took to the radio airwaves last week to voice that opinion and lay out the evidence.

Beck quoted from a recent opinion piece by D Parker in the NOQ Report, titled *The Case for Optimism: 10 More Reasons Why the Pro-freedom Right Will Defeat the Anti-Liberty Left.*

He began by quoting the article, saying "Many of these reasons for optimism of the pro-freedom right are because they are directly contrasted with the negative characteristics of the anti-liberty left. While it may seem they have the upper hand at the moment, it is only a temporary condition." Beck reminded his listeners about some of his radio and television discussions regarding Dr. Martin Luther King Jr. over the past decade and a half.

"Once you have the images that people can contrast, between good and evil, people will always pick good. Americans will," he said, referring to Dr. King's peaceful, righteous example. "That is true as long as our Judeo-Christian values are still alive in our heart. That's why we try so hard to keep our hearts soft."

Glenn Beck has been at the forefront of this battle against the extreme Left, specifically during his television days, broadcasting in his weekday Fox News 5pm slot. Last week, he harkened back to the Obama era, and the infamous Newsweek 2009 cover saying, "We Are All Socialists Now." He cited the time period as a key awakening, clearly laying out the contrast against which Americans would eventually push back.

"Now they're coming out and they're embracing Marxism," he said of the Democrats currently in control of government. "They want to tell you exactly what they're doing. But they can't, because the minute they do, you're onto them and you're saying that's not me."

Beck laid out examples, where American citizens are watching this year's results with disgust, saying "That's not us." In one illustration, he points to Afghanistan, where "Joe Biden failed miserably and then claimed it to be a victory."

As the segment continued, Beck referred to Parker's ten reasons, starting with bullet point number one.

"We are on the side of freedom, the anti-liberty left is on the side of authoritarianism," he quoted. "This is becoming more and more clear." He continued, discussing a recent television appearance by notable Democrat, Noam Chomsky, who suggested that Amercians choosing not to receive a Covid vaccination should be shunned and isolated, to the point of not having basic necessities, such as food.

"So, who is on the side of people, and who is on the side of authoritarianism?" Beck asked, pushing back against the blatant discrimination. "It is becoming clear that the Left is authoritarianism. And not because we say it, but because their actions are now showing it."

Beck continued on to Parker's second reason for optimism.

"We have timeless advantages, the anti-liberty left has short-term tactics and tricks," he quoted. As an example, he pointed out the changing numbers being offered when answering how many Americans remain trapped and abandoned in Afghanistan. "Nobody really knows, but when we said that, we were called conspiracy theorists, we were called all kinds of names, unreliable," Beck said. "It's becoming apparent that their short term tactics and their tricks don't work."

He then added another current example, citing Democrats' insistence that today's historic monetary inflation, resulting from their policies, is "just transitory."

"Have you checked what you're paying for meat? Have you checked what you're paying for gas?" Beck asked, rhetorically. "Have you noticed how expensive almost everything is? Did you know that this Thanksgiving, the meal that you put down, the traditional Thanksgiving meal here in America, will cost you more than it ever has in the history of our country. That's saying something."

He continued, saying the tactics and tricks of the Left no longer work in the face of tangible results Americans can see for themselves.

Glenn Beck summed up the segment, pointing to hope, optimism and brighter days ahead, as America eventually pulls itself out of the current Democrat-created, media-supported, malaise. In his opinion, the current policy positions of the Left are far out on the fringe of current American values.

"They are overplaying their hand, and they are exposing themselves, and exposing Conservatives as the ones that had it right the whole time," he said.

Many in Media Support Aaron Rodgers

"I'm in the crosshairs of the woke mob right now, so before the final nail gets put in my cancel culture casket, I think I'd like to set the record straight."

Aaron Rodgers acknowledged the obvious last week, after being diagnosed with Covid-19.

"I am somebody who's a critical thinker," Rodgers added during an appearance on *"The Pat McAfee Show,"* while explaining his decision not to get vaccinated. "I believe strongly in bodily autonomy and the ability to make choices for your body. Not to have to acquiesce to some woke culture or crazed group of individuals who say you have to do something."

On Friday evening's episode of *"The Five"* on Fox News, the panel discussed the McAfee interview and, like the country as a whole, most agreed with Rodgers.

"If you watch this interview, it's really thoughtful," Pete Hegseth began. "He breaks down the research that he did, what he knew about the vaccines, allergies that he had, reasons that he didn't want to take it. He went through what he called an immunization protocol, which he didn't really get into the details of what that meant, and said he talked to the league and the Packers about it. So he's not someone that just dismissed the whole thing."

Hegseth opined that Rodgers has often sided with the NFL's woke, "social justice" initiatives. He also pointed out a few similar instances of NBA stars speaking out and taking courageous stands against the extremism from the authoritarian mob.

Perhaps elucidated by last week's blowout, pro-America, pro-Republican electoral results, the country's awakening could be very much in line with Rodgers'. Enough may finally be enough.

"I'm no Rodgers fan, I think he's a jerk," co-host Lawrence Jones said, also referring to Nets' star Kyrie Irving in the same light. "But you need the jerks to win this battle right here. And Pete is right that they have touted the social justice agenda and they have been comfortable going with the mob. But I think this is an awakening period. They are understanding now what government will do." He also pointed out that Rodgers had been tested every single day, and the belief is that "someone that was vaccinated gave it to Rodgers, is what they're saying."

"I encourage everyone to watch every word of this interview because he really goes through all of the conflicting information that has been fed to the American people over and over again," Dagen McDowell said. "Fomenting fear, Biden and Harris did when it benefited them on the campaign trail. And then when they turn around and get the jab, now they're fomenting fear over and over again that the vaccinated should be afraid of the unvaccinated."

Rodgers, as one of football's pre-eminent stars, has felt free to speak out, while most other athletes, and Americans, remain silent for fears of bullying and retaliation from Democrats and the Left. McDowell added that Rodgers recalled the Packers sending in a "stooge" during training camp, to tell the team that they were 19th in the league in terms of vaccination totals. Rodgers said he challenged some of the representative's assertions and added that many of his teammates quietly thanked him for standing up when they couldn't.

Rodgers also made the point that vaccines have become about much more than health.

"When Trump in 2020 was championing these vaccines that were coming so quick, what did the Left say?" Rodgers asked. "And I'm talking about every member of the Left. Don't trust the vaccine. Don't get the vaccine. You're going to die from the vaccine. And then what happened? Biden wins, and everything flips."

Co-host Jessica Tarlov took the opposite tact from the majority of the panel, calling out Rodgers for initially saying he had indeed been vaccinated.

"No one has mentioned the critical component in this, which is that Aaron Rodgers lied," Tarlov said. "And if Aaron Rodgers had answered the direct question, "Are you vaccinated?" with "No I am not, I follow the protocols that have been laid out, I get tested every day," and admitted that he breaks masking protocols that the NFL has sent down, he'd be in a much better position now." For Tarlov, Rodgers' main infraction was that he lied.

"And so did the Democrats during the presidential campaign, saying they shouldn't trust the vaccine," Jones quipped. "So there are a lot of liars."

"People who are unvaccinated can get Covid from the vaccinated," McDowell noted. "And there's no evidence that people are dying who are vaccinated because they were in contact with the unvaccinated. This has got to end, and there's got to be a lot more discussion like this around the country."

November 15, 2021

Media Fanning the Flames of Hate

While most Americans thought "hate had no home here," many are now calling out the mainstream, liberal media, as they continue their pattern of stoking division across the nation.

Newsmax host Eric Bolling began his Friday evening program, "*The Balance*," by chiding many of his media colleagues.

"To paraphrase the patriot Paul Revere, the woke mob is coming, the woke mob is coming!" Bolling warned. "Folks, this is not a drill. America is bracing itself for yet another wave of riots. The woke mob is threatening violence and mobilizing. The trial of Kyle Rittenhouse isn't even over yet, but it's looking more likely that the defendant could be found not guilty, and that does not sit well with the woke mob or the Leftist media."

Bolling then cut to a clip of MSNBC host, Joy Reid.

"If you want to know why Critical Race Theory exists, the actual law school theory that emphasized that supposedly colorblind laws in America often still have racially discriminatory outcomes, then look no further than the trial of Kyle Rittenhouse," Reid said.

"They have made this trial about race, isn't that right, Don Lemon?" Bolling asked, then playing a clip of CNN's Lemon calling former President Donald Trump racist numerous times.

"Nine times in two minutes," Bolling continued. "They love calling people racists. The Left makes everything about race, even when it comes to a court case where no one involved is black."

He then cut to these mainstream media headlines from the past week.

A sobbing Kyle Rittenhouse already won - even before his trial is over.
- NBC Think

Kyle Rittenhouse deserves an award for his melodramatic performance on the witness stand. - USA Today

White Judge refuses to allow Black Lives Matter protesters killed by Kyle Rittenhouse to be called victims in court. - Black Enterprise

146

"The judge is white, and bad. Rittenhouse is acting," Bolling continued, paraphrasing the media's overarching message. "Is it me, or are these media outlets writing their headlines to make it sound like this court case is fraudulent?"

Viewers then saw another clip of Lemon on CNN from last week, where the host shared his opinion about the trial's judge.

"His demeanor, the way he refers to the prosecution, the way he looks at Kyle Rittenhouse like it's his grandson. I mean, come on America," Lemon said. "I mean for me, I don't know how they look at it legally, but for me that's cause for a mistrial."

The program then played a cut of MSNBC host Joe Scarborough, adding his view of the televised trial.

"This judge is an absolute joke. He's been a joke from the very beginning," Scarborough commented. "It's absolutely disgusting the way he's conducting himself on the stand there. He's obviously playing for the audience, a certain audience."

"Did you hear all that they are literally saying the judge is intentionally trying to give Kyle Rittenhouse every chance possible to get off," Bolling followed up. "Listen, for better or worse, our justice system is based on innocent until proven guilty. You should get every chance to prove your innocence. But not to Liberals. To them, you're guilty even if you're innocent because the media's pushing this insane notion that this court system is rigged because of racism."

Time will tell if Bolling's accusations against the media continue to hold true. And due to it's television coverage and transparent viewing options, citizens can judge the merits of the case for themselves.

As for the media's intentions, they'll be able to make up their minds on that account as well.

November 22, 2021

Punishing Americans By Design

With Americans becoming increasingly frustrated with high food prices, high gas prices, high energy prices and higher everything prices, they are also becoming increasingly bewildered.

Since everyone can clearly see the policies that are leading to the current pain and misery, why won't our leaders change course? Why are they continuing to needlessly inflict pain on American citizens?

On the heels of the U.S. House approving the $2 Trillion Democrat "Build Back Better" Bill, commentator Bill O'Reilly joined radio host Glenn Beck last week to discuss the trajectory of the American economy and what may lie ahead.

"Over 40 percent of all the money the federal government hopes to spend in the next ten years goes to green stuff," O'Reilly began. "Now I don't have any objection to research and development. I think that's good, that if you want to get electric cars that people can afford, and work, okay. And solar panels and windmills, ok. As long as it works, as long as it's affordable for the folks. But to just dump money into theoretical, well we're going to clean up the planet and save everybody, is just garbage."

O'Reilly pointed out that not one Republican supported this House bill, and that there are very few oversights to keep track of where the "Build Back Better" money actually goes. In his opinion, the entire slush fund is ripe for corruption, waste and fraud.

"This is wildly unpopular in West Virginia," Beck said. "It goes to the Senate next. Manchin and Sinema are the only ones that are a chance of voting against it."

O'Reilly predicted that the only two centrist Democrats remaining in the Senate - Joe Manchin of West Virginia and Arizona's Kyrsten Sinema - will try to whittle the bill's price tag down 25% to $1.5 Trillion and then claim victory.

"But Bill, as you know it's not the money, as much as it is, this is a software bill," Beck interjected. "This has all of the tools they need to shut down the oil and gas and coal industry. It has everything."

O'Reilly believes the two Senators will make a political calculation that they can claim victory by approving a bill that spends less money overall. But O'Reilly believes that Manchin, who has been rumored to be eying a run at the Governorship in Republican-leaning West Virginia, has a better option.

"If I were him, here's what I would do. I would jump parties right now, and I'd vote against that bill," O'Reilly said. "This overarch bill changes the government forever and we become a nanny state, which is what the progressives want. You can revoke part of it next year when Americans will be suffering terribly economically, this time next year. And they'll throw the Democrats out in a lot of places. But the nanny state with all of this money is now going to be so firmly entrenched, telling you what to do, when to do it. And then for a large part of the population, giving them money, buying their votes, so they don't have to go out and really be self-reliant at all."

Next, Beck implied that the overall plan to get voters hooked and dependent on government handouts, while at the same time providing a political battle line. In his opinion, Democrats want to give a bunch of money and goodies to certain voting blocks, before challenging Republicans to run on taking those entitlements away next year.

"They want to take away your childcare. They want to take away your subsidies. They want to take away all of these things that you need now more than ever. And I think they'll get a lot of people to vote that way," Beck said.

Even while agreeing, O'Reilly said he believes that most Amercians want to "earn their own way," without government coercion and entitlement handouts, because "they see this is not good for them or their families.". But on the Democrats' intent, he concurred with Beck, because "when people suffer, all the other theoretical garbage goes out the window."

He predicted that the continued punishment of the working class in America, in addition to upcoming tax increases, will continue to stifle economic growth and further crush American families.

"You're going to have a triple whip on people," O'Reilly forecast. "You're going to have inflation, which you have now. Then you're going to have higher pricing on top of the inflation, because corporations are going to pass it along. And then you're going to have fewer jobs."

O'Reilly believes the financial pain being inflicted on Americans by Democrats is not accidental.

"This is by design," O'Reilly concluded. "Progressive economists know this. They want to run the economy from Washington. The entire economy. If you break down the capitalistic system and people are desperate, that's how that can be accomplished. It's the only way it can be accomplished."

November 29, 2021

America's E-Bike Future

If only they'd give them a try, Americans would fall in love with E-Bikes.

That is the opinion of MSNBC's Chris Hayes, who last week on his *All In with Chris Hayes* program discussed his newfound joy of commuting via an electric bike. He has had a great experience with his futuristic commuting method, and he believes that most Americans would feel the same.

"Last fall it was still Covid and there was no vaccine, and I started to have to come into the studio to do the show," Hayes began. "I had a little bit of a commuting problem. I didn't really want to start taking the subway at that point. I think there's some of it that suggests that masking is pretty fine, but I was like ehh, I wasn't that psyched about it. But I had to get from Brooklyn to Midtown, it's about nine miles, and I had to do without the subway. I didn't want to take a car everyday. I came up with the ultimate solution - a foldable E-Bike."

Hayes said he started to use the foldable e-Bike to make the 9-mile commute to the MSNBC Studios and then stored it in his office. Among it's benefits, according to Hayes, was that he got to enjoy the sights of New York City, while not arriving hot, sweaty and disheveled for his television duties.

"Changed my life, best commute I have ever had in my life," Hayes said, noting that he arrived each day "cool and clean."

Hayes welcomed New York Times writer Jay Caspian Kang, who last week penned an Op-Ed titled *Free E-Bikes for Everyone!* Kang pointed out that his E-Bike conversion was much the same as Hayes', and that his daughter now enjoys being brought to school on the bike. Kang said the bike has given him a liberated feeling, being able to travel New York City after the past couple years of Covid-related lockdowns.

"First of all it's a very cool feeling because you feel like a superhero. It's like the vision I had as a kid of having a cyber-suit where you are like Ironman. It's you, but you're stronger," Hayes said. "So when you're pushing the pedals there's like this extra oomph, so you can put kids on it. You can run errands on it. It also means you're not sweating in the same way. And it also just replaces a lot of car trips, I think that's a key thing to think about."

The MSNBC Segment by Hayes was titled "The Case For Giving Every American a Free E-Bike."

In his Times piece, Kang concurred, saying *"City governments should purchase an electronic bicycle for every resident over the age of 15 who wants one. They should also shut down a significant number of streets. Shutting down some streets for bikes is not only for safety, but also because the more inconvenient driving becomes, the more people start to consider other options."*

Some may see a similarity in this approach by Kang to the current president and administration increasing gasoline prices and the costs of many other goods. Administration officials have made clear that one clear benefit and objective of these rising costs will be a change in citizens' behavior, similar to the change Kang hopes to see if New York were to use tax dollars to give bikes to New Yorkers.

"We have to get cars off the street somehow," Kang said. "We have to get cars off the road somehow for every reason. Pedestrian safety, bike safety. But mostly because of climate change and the carbon that they emit. So I don't know, I think you need to come up with some kind of drastic measure that also incentivizes people. And I think that we've been waiting around for some sort of solution to this. I don't know, I think every single person that I talk to who has ridden an E-Bike, and who has sort of committed to it in a way, has said it has replaced tons of their car trips."

Kang said the only problem with having more people adopt the emerging technology is the expense, citing the high cost per E-Bike. (A quick internet search finds many E-Bikes priced near $1500 apiece.) Kang opined that only by "giving them away for free" could the plan be brought to fruition.

"If you're going to get cars off the road, you're going to need something to replace that," Kang said. "People are still going to want some sort of speed, they're still going to want some sort of convenience. E-Bikes are the way right now."

Hayes wrapped up the segment, saying that the key is for planners to think ahead and assess what cities, and suburban areas, would need as they move into the future. And as the holiday approached, he said he would soon be heading out on his E-Bike to pick up his Thanksgiving pies.

The Art of the Interview

The Larry King-style interview set the standard and set the stage for all others who have followed in recent decades.

But this approach often seems to be fading into extinction. Nearly gone, with flickers of life emerging only so often.

One of the most important attributes of a great interviewer is getting the guest to open up. Allowing him to answer questions and offer his insight and unique perspective.

The reason this approach is so rare in news media, and its implementation so difficult, is that it requires something antithetical to most modern-day news personalities. It demands the host, or *interviewer*, simply keep quiet and let the *interviewee* speak.

As Marty Glickman used to say in the sports realm, "people tune in to hear the game."

Similarly, during a television news media interview, viewers mostly tune in to hear the guest. Otherwise, they'd have ditched the segment and headed elsewhere for content or entertainment.

In a world of larger-than-life egos, fighting endlessly for "hot takes," attention and clicks, a host clamming up and letting the guest steal the show is truly rare indeed.

On that note, it was hard not to notice the epic interview last week between Fox News' Tucker Carlson and Michael Saylor, the pioneering CEO of Microstrategy.

Saylor, arguably the largest Bitcoin holder in the world, and one of the asset's biggest proponents, joined Carlson's *Tucker Carlson Today* weekend program last week. A shortened version of the conversation then aired during Carlson's weeknight primetime program.

Carlson set the table by admitting to be a Bitcoin neophyte, before asking the Bitcoin guru to explain the technology and why it is valuable.

"Bitcoin is the first engineered monetary system in the history of the human race," the forward-thinking Saylor began. "The first question is, what's money. The second question is, what's the problem? And the third question is, what's the solution?"

Over the next hour, Saylor explained why he and the company he runs started accumulating Bitcoin in March of 2020. Saylor also discussed the role of money, the risks of inflation, Bitcoin as digital gold, the value of the asset for citizens worldwide, among many other angles related to the digital asset. Carlson nodded often and occasionally commented briefly, as the technology genius laid out his case.

"The point of Bitcoin is to fix the money. And money is energy, and energy is life. And if I keep sucking the energy out of the economy, I'm sucking the oxygen out of your system," Saylor said. "Under the best case, you perform poorly. Under the worst case, I suffocate you to death or freeze you to death. That's the problem. That's why empires collapse."

"You spoke on and off for about 50 minutes," Carlson pointed out. "That was amazing. That was one of the most unbelievable things I've ever heard. You've made the most compelling case I've ever heard for the need for something like Bitcoin."

True indeed, but only because Carlson did his job as an interviewer. The marvelous *content* was only the result of, and specifically derived from, Carlson's wonderful *approach*.

Fascinating enough, another talk host also discussed this very same facet of communication last week. On the December 2nd episode of his *Daily Hope* podcast, entitled *Learning to Live Wisely,* Pastor Rick Warren explicitly discussed the role of a host when conducting an interview with a guest.

"One of the keys is listening. If you don't listen, then you're not going to grow," Warren began his monologue. "I have never learned anything while I'm talking. If my mouth is moving, I'm not learning. I'm only learning when I'm listening. You don't learn when you're talking. You learn when you're listening, so you gotta learn to listen."

In other words, your *audience* only learns if *you listen*.

"I've done an awful lot of interviews. ABC, CBS, NBC, PBS, BBC, CNN, on and on and on," Warren, the author of *The Purpose Driven Life*, explained. "What I've noticed is that the interview shows have changed. They're no longer about the guest. They're about the interviewer. And the whole goal is, the interviewer wants to draw attention to himself. The interviewer wants to explain his or her opinions, and you're just the foil."

Marty Glickman got it. Tucker Carlson gets it. And Rick Warren gets it. Many others do as well, albeit far fewer than we'd hope.

"I long for the old Larry King days," Warren said. "You know what I liked about Larry King? He would ask a question and then he'd let you talk. And he realized that the interview, people weren't going to listen to Larry King. They were going to listen to all of the fascinating guests that he had, and learning from them."

Warren quoted the late King as saying "in an interview show, if the host is talking 50 percent of the time, something is terribly wrong. The host *listens* the most. The host *talks* the least. The host sets up the question and then just listens. That's what a good TV host does."

Completely different realms - Glickman, Carlson and Warren - yet each one, in their own way, acknowledging one of the keys to effective communication (and media success).

December 13, 2021

Grocery Store Cashier Headed to the Moon

"Sometimes you need to see how someone else forged a path, to give you courage so you can do the same."

These were the opening words offered by host Liz Claman, during her weekly *Everyone Talks to Liz Claman* podcast. During her recent episode, the Fox Business host talked with Carl "The Moon" Runefelt, who discussed his meteoric rise from grocery store cashier to crypto millionaire and YouTube influencer.

As is her style, Claman was warm and direct with Runefelt. Did he ever, in his wildest dreams, think he'd one day transition from an hourly-wage job to being a well-known, highly-respected multi-millionaire?

"This specifically I did not imagine, that's for sure, but I did imagine a future full of wealth and success and that's actually, I think, the whole reason why I reached my success," Carl explained. "When I was in the grocery store, I was doing all these classical grocery store things. Stacking bananas, normal job. But I started to think like a successful person. I started to try to feel like a successful person. And I started to visualize and see myself being happy, rich, traveling the world in private jets, drinking champagne on yachts in Monaco. I was trying to see myself as that person way before I actually was this person. I tried to act as if I was already this successful." ·

Runefelt said he began reading books and watching material online, "looking for clues" about how to become successful. He continued learning about dream achievement and began a growth program that continues today.

"Long story short, things started to change after a few months, I think. To make it quite simple, I found out about Bitcoin and I became a complete nerd," Carl said. "I found it so interesting. I started to research every single day, hours and hours. It's a complete rabbit hole, the whole crypto space. I just became completely consumed by the crypto space and I started my YouTube channel and I started all of the businesses that I'm involved in today."

Carl "The Moon" said it took only about two years before he was on his way, making ten thousand dollars a month, and turning his dreams into reality.

These days, Carl is one of the most well-respected online crypto experts, providing daily market updates, technical analysis and fundamental insight to more than half a million subscribers. He also makes frequent appearances with other leaders within the space, such as BitBoy Crypto, perhaps the biggest and most influential Crypto-related YouTuber today.

"This,to me, sounds like the grain of the power of positive thinking, visualization and if you can dream it, you can do it," Claman said, referencing her own dreamer days, reporting overnights in Columbus, Ohio. "I used to sit there and think, I'm going to get there, I'm going to get to the network, I'm going to do this. I understood there were thousands and thousands of local news reporters in the world who were trying to do the same thing I was doing, or at least aiming for. But it's a big leap to go from visualizing to taking the first crucial step."

"Some people think you just visualize and everything is just going to happen for you," Carl added. "I think it's more like, you visualize and then you have to take the first step out to kind of let the universe meet you halfway. It's not about visualizing and then sitting down on your sofa."

Claman added another piece of wisdom, saying "never hope for it more than you work for it. The two have to go hand in hand."

She also asked Runefelt how it felt to spend a million dollars on a CryptoPunks NFT (non fungible token) earlier this year.

"I wish I had a very, very good answer to that," Runefelt said. "Some people called me crazy. Some people called me a genius. I think I'm more crazy than a genius." He went on to say how he feels NFTs are only just beginning to take over and are destined to become much bigger in the future. In his opinion, buying the million-dollar NFT was a great way to gain exposure to that side of the crypto market. It didn't turn out to be the wonderful purchase he envisioned, however. Carl intended to buy the NFT as an online representation of himself. To his dismay, and only after making the purchase, he realized he had bought a *female* NFT!

"It was a funny mistake and people thought it was very funny, so actually I think it's fine," he said.

One of Claman's distinguishing factors is that, on one hand, she can talk stocks and bonds with traditional Wall Street investors, such as Charlie Munger or Warren Buffett, while at the same time having a solid grasp of new, emerging digital assets. Predictably, she transitioned the conversation to Bitcoin.

"I think people need to understand that Bitcoin is the most important crypto. Bitcoin is the king, as I usually say very often on my Twitter. Bitcoin was the first cryptocurrency. It was the first blockchain," Carl said, referencing the tens-of-thousands of other altcoins. "It is the most decentralized and most secure and most liquid form of cryptocurrency out there. There is never going to be a crypto that is ever going to be able to replace Bitcoin."

Carl advises that all crypto investors hold at least 70% of their portfolio in Bitcoin, which he refers to as "digital gold." In Runefelt's option, security, network effect and trust are the keys to Bitcoin's success.

"Crypto will take over the whole world," Runefelt concluded, in response to the naysayers. "It's already successfully taking over the whole world."

Claman hosts *The Claman Countdown* of Fox Business weekdays from 3pm-4pm. She has been with the network since 2007. Her podcast "presents motivational stories about some of today's most successful entrepreneurs and business leaders....which provide feel-good accounts that will leave the listener feeling inspired and moved."

Carl is no longer stocking bananas, and he sees his life trajectory catapulting him straight to the moon.

December 20, 2021

Silver Lining in Media's Self-Serving Behavior

Over 75% of Americans Say Media's Primary Goal is Advancing Own Political Agenda

That headline hung over an article on NeonNettle.com on Friday. The piece, written by Jack Murphy, included the subtitle, *Advance their own opinions on public.*

At first glance, one might feel duped, bamboozled or slighted. How could the media have a side agenda they feel is more important than informing me, the viewer? Isn't informing the public their job?

But on second thought, with a more nuanced eye, one could easily view this poll, and the public opinion it shares, as a positive step in the right direction.

The article quotes a new poll from the Trafalgar Group and Convention of States Action. As a reference, Trafalgar has been one of the most accurate political pollsters in recent years, along with Richard Baris of People Pundit Daily and the Big Data Poll, among a few others.

The poll states that "76.3% of Americans now believe the establishment media's primary goal is to push its own political agenda."

Going deeper into the poll, 62.7% of Democrats believe "the primary focus of the mainstream media's coverage of current events is to advance their own opinions or political agenda." 37.3% believe "finding and reporting the facts" is their main objective.

90.3% of Republicans agree with that assessment in the poll, along with 76.1% of Independents.

So in an age of record-high polarization, and unlike anything any modern-era politician has been able to do, this issue brings together voters from all sides.

It seems that citizens widely agree - from those that don't quite like the country and want to radically alter it, to those that drape themselves in the American flag - that the media's main focus is pushing their own agenda.

How is that for national unity! Hope and change making America great again.

Further in the article on NeonNettle, President of Convention of States Action, Mark Meckler, commented on the poll.

"Thanks to the decentralization of the news through the internet and social media, the mainstream press outlets no longer have a monopoly on controlling the news," he said. "Unfortunately, the mainstream media has been slow to adjust to this reality and don't seem to realize that the average American can now see in real-time the difference between the actual facts of a story versus what the mainstream media says."

So if American's of all stripes have come to the same conclusion, how then should we judge that reality?

Most of us now understand that most of the personalities we see on nightly cable news television are not objective sources. They are opinion-laden partisans. They come with a worldview and shape their programs to match. And viewers are also beginning to make this distinction with the "straight news" anchors, hosting nightly news programs. They too have become subject to, and tools of, the controlling corporate bosses with philosophical agendas.

But the good news - the truly positive, eye-opening, foundational news - is that we all seem to *get it*. Our eyes are clear. We *understand*, which is the first step to moving forward.

If your worldview comes from the left, you'll gravitate to Don Lemon or George Stephanopolous. On the right, it's Sean Hannity or Greg Kelly. That is the essence of free-market options offering abundant choices.

So if we now understand that many "straight-news" anchors are truly nothing of the sort, the ruse has lost its effect. Excellent!

For a liberal slant on the day's events, you've got Lester Holt and most others. For the conservative take, Brett Baier might be your choice.

But either way, viewers have seemingly come to the realization that true objectivity can only be found within the individual, if they indeed aim for that goal at all.

"People are realizing the open bias and partisanship of the press," Meckler said in the article. "It is making them increasingly cynical."

And increasingly awake.

December 27, 2021

Who is Really to Blame for Inflation?

Reckless government spending and careless government policies aren't causing prices to go up. The real cause of the pain being inflicted on American families is the pandemic.

This is the message from a current CNN video, titled *"Prices are going up on almost everything. Here's why."*

The brief two-minute video on CNN.com begins, "One of the unique features of the COVID crisis is the speed at which the demand for goods really rebounded." The world's rebound from pandemic lockdowns has created shortages and skyrocketing prices for most goods Americans purchase every day.

"That has led to unprecedented rapid rises in the prices of certain goods," continued Gregory Daco, Chief U.S. Economist for Oxford Economics. "We've seen a rise in food prices whereby we saw the vegetable sector as well as the meat sector see increase in inflation generally reflective of supply disruptions, but also the fact that we've seen strong demand and strong consumption from eating away from home to eating at home and perhaps in some cases even consuming more than people were consuming before the COVID crisis."

Although consumers have always eaten vegetables and meat, the abrupt shutdown and subsequent reopening has induced them to *really* eat vegetables and meat now. They used to nibble, but now they are truly gorging.

The piece then noted the increased spending focus on products such as sporting goods and beauty products. Casual observation leads one to believe these trends. After staring at themselves on video call screens for a year, many Americans were finally motivated to purchase that treadmill or straighten their teeth. Especially now that we are piling on the calories from unruly, never-before-seen amounts of vegetables and meat.

Passengers have returned to air travel, the story points out, and they are nearly back to 2019 levels. The airline industry is still playing catchup, however, creating "a mismatch between the availability of flights and the number of passengers that are willing and wanting to travel."

Other areas of personal transportation are mentioned in the piece, as the video points out that people are travelling more by car, leading to "increased gasoline demand… and higher energy price inflation."

Were people not eating, traveling and driving before March of 2020? 2021 levels are much higher than 2020 numbers, but could this shock be quantified as simply as reversion to pre-pandemic norms?

Summing up, Daco notes that "this has occurred in an environment in which labor supply remains fairly constrained and so that's leading to higher labor input costs that have passed on to consumers."

Nowhere in the CNN video was the mention of out-of-control money printing as a catalyst toward record modern-day inflation? Perhaps THE main catalyst.

As for the cause of the "constrained" labor supply, how about government policy of paying workers more NOT to work than to work in lower-paying jobs? Have increased government handouts, funded by taxpayers, led to apathy by a segment of the workforce? Might that be the reason why some employees are not turning up for previously-desired hourly work?

The video includes no mention of exploding bipartisan political spending, as politicians attempt to out-do the other to buy votes, continue the gravy train and remain in power. No mention of central banks flooding the financial system with fiat currency. No mention of the last-ditch effort by the United States, and others, to print our way out of unmanageable debt.

More than a year ago, financial talk show host Dave Ramsey pointed out that the pandemic did not cause economic hardship. It was the *reaction* to the pandemic, he said, in the form of lockdowns and business cessation, that directly led to the economic hardship many Americans have yet to rebound from.

Today we feel the pain of escalating prices affecting the goods and services we purchase every day.

The question remains - who really bears the blame?

January 3, 2022

Your Pension May Not Save Your Golden Years

On last week's Rich Dad Radio Show, host Robert Kiyosaki opened up with the financial calamity he sees coming for retirees counting on government-backed pensions to fund their golden years.

"The reason I'm so hot on this is that my old man, Poor Dad, lost his pension, and he didn't know he was poor until he lost his pension," Kiyosaki began. "He lost it because he ran for Lieutenant Governor as a Republican, which is an idiotic thing to do with the communist republic of Hawaii."

Kiyosaki, author of the decades-old smash hit, *Rich Dad, Poor Dad,* has occasionally criticized the California Public Employees' Retirement System. During this episode, he provided some opening thoughts about the fund giant recently voting to use borrowed money and alternative assets to meet its investment return target.

"The dominos are falling. This is the retirement fund giant CALPERS, I think it's the biggest pension fund in America. It's going broke," Kiyosaki said. "Now that means firefighters, school teachers, public servants. They're all toast just like my poor Dad. They're going to find out that the government screwed them."

Kiyosaki predicted the looming pension system collapse will be the "biggest bust in the history of America."

Ted Siedle, former SEC attorney and Kiyosaki's co-author of *Who Stole My Pension,* agreed with Kiyosaki that the threat is real for unknowing Americans.

"These pensions, these state and local pensions are refusing to give the participants in the fund and the taxpayers prospectuses on what they're investing," Siedle said. "Every regulator in the world says read the prospectus before you invest. Well, these pensions refuse to give the prospectuses to state workers and taxpayers who are contributing, so nobody knows where the money is."

John MacGregor, Financial Planner and author of the book *The Top 10 Reasons the Rich Go Broke,* said he's seen many experienced employees who trusted their employers' pension plans, only to be disappointed in the end.

"I've been in the industry for over, gosh going on 27 years now, working with I estimate over 5000 people, all walks of life, all demographics - rich, poor, women, men, etcetera, and I've never seen it this bad, "MacGregor said. "Public pensions, they've seen their liabilities grow over the last 20 years, but particularly since COVID. These plans are now facing increasing pressure to generate performance, and now they're reaching and they're using risky investments to do so."

MacGregor specifically brought up the individual states, saying they are the most at risk.

"Nearly every state in America is facing a pension shortfall," he said. "States have a combined $4.2 Trillion in pension liabilities but less than $3 Trillion set aside for the pensions. And the typical state has about 70% of their fund is funded. And with this funding shortfall, we've got ten thousand people hitting 65, which is retirement, every single day. These states are headed for a pension crisis."

Kiyosaki has been sounding the alarm regarding public pensions for years. His newest book highlights the issue, and he will undoubtedly continue to discuss the issue on *The Rich Dad Radio Show.*

An Insider's View of the Media Game

It is one thing for an outsider to critique the media for its lack of honesty or intellectual curiosity. After all, polling consistently shows that Americans are steadily losing trust in the legacy, corporate media.

It is quite another thing, however, for a true insider to reveal what she saw inside the belly of the beast.

Last week, former co-host of *The View*, Jedediah Bila, joined radio host Glenn Beck to discuss the recent years of her career inside the mainstream media.

"We are truly in two different countries now," Beck said. "I've never felt that about America, but we are. I don't even understand the thinking of people. With Rittenhouse, what people said after the trail. Watch the trial. What happened with Jussie Smollett. MSNBC didn't even report on that in primetime, at all. That creates two Americas - one where there are facts and one where there's just this fantasy fact."

"I actually got into this business years ago, I wasn't someone who grew up in a political family. I wasn't someone who worked in Washington, D.C. I didn't want to work in Washington, D.C. But I was interested because I watched Sarah Palin. I didn't know who she was at the time. She came on the scene and she was immediately attacked," Bila remembered. "You had media that landed in Wasilla, Alaska and decided they were going to do oppo research on her. So I immediately said to myself - oh, I need to find out what she's done right because she's angered all the right people, so let's look at her record."

Bila, who spent time as the lone conservative voice on *The View*, said that was her first real inkling that the media was "very powerful and very destructive."

"The second moment I had where I said to myself, wow this is insanity, was the Kavanaugh hearings," she explained. "When you saw what happened there, this guy, they were destroying him, there was no evidence that he had done any of these things. They made a decision that they were going to make this about politics, and the media gathered together and decided he was guilty. There was no evidence being presented."

The two noted that to this day, based on this baseless media spin, many people still believe Justice Kavanaugh is guilty. Beck also pointed out that many also believe the same evidence-free media tale of "Russian collusion."

"How do you survive that?" Beck asked.

"I think what you are saying about two countries, there are people who care about facts. They're all over the country and they are sprouting up, not on mainstream media outlets, but you are seeing them on alternative media outlets," Bila said. "That's why you see them in podcasting, you see them in Substack. You see them all over Twitter saying, wait a second I'm not affiliated with corporate media but I'm going to tell you the truth. And more and more people are flocking to them."

To Bila, who has worked in different areas of the country, and for various media organizations, the threat is much bigger and overarching than any one outlet or news source.

"The problem arises that you have collusion here," Bila opined. "You have Big Tech, which has a narrative. You have Big Media, which has a narrative. You have Big Politics, right now, meaning Democrat politics. It's all the same narrative, and they've all come together and decided, we're going to make what's untrue true, at all costs."

Bila believes it takes much more effort these days to determine what is fact and what is political propaganda, and citizen journalists have often been on the forefront of ferreting out the truth. But in her estimation, non-traditional media has already been successful in exposing this media corruption and purposeful deception.

"People start to say, I'm being manipulated by the media," Bila said. "This is a game, and I'm being played. So see the game or be played by the game."

Dave Ramsey and Those Evil Millionaires

Readers got another strong shot of common sense for their dollars and cents last week, from the radio host known for delivering it in daily doses over the years.

During last week's launch week for his new book, *Baby Steps Millionaires: How Ordinary People Built Extraordinary Wealth - and How You Can Too*, author and radio host, Dave Ramsey, took to the airwaves to share the underlying philosophy of his newest hit.

"We launched this book in the middle of a society where a portion of the people are out there, I call them the hope stealers. Their job is to steal your hope," Ramsey began. "Their job is to tell you that the society, the culture, the country that we live in is so broken that the little man can't get ahead. You stand no chance unless you inherit it from a rich uncle. You can't make it, we need socialism. We need wealth redistribution. Wealthy people are evil anyway, and so they should be punished."

Ramsey spent some time discussing a recent New York Times article, which was pushing the moral need to "abolish millionaires." To Ramsey, this is anathema. After all, the radio host has made a name for himself, as well as created thousands of jobs through his multi-million dollar business, by becoming the financial voice for the "little man." He began small, became a millionaire, lost it all through bankruptcy and then prospered much more than before through the reliance on true, Biblical financial principles.

"A billion dollars is wildly more than anyone needs, even accounting for life's most excessive lavishes," Ramsey quoted the story. "It's far more than anyone might reasonably claim to deserve, however much he believes he has contributed to society. Billionaires should not exist. When American capitalism sends us its billionaires, it's not sending us its best. It's sending us people who have lots of problems, and they're bringing their problems with them. They're bringing inequality."

Ramsey pointed out the obvious case of jealousy and envy.

"Two evil character traits of anyone who is one with money. Money is evil, money is bad. If you get money you are evil and you are bad," Ramsey said. "You should have it taken away from you and given to someone else....so that they are evil and bad, I guess. I never thought about that part. If we give it out, is it not a problem for the poor people that get it. I mean, if it's bad, maybe we should just centralize it with a few people and destroy them, instead of giving it to other people. That's kind of illogical. The critical thinking breaks down on this, doesn't it?"

And as usual, Ramsey didn't hold back what he really thinks. As he has said countless times, he's an "expert on his own opinion."

"I'm old. When I was young, we called those communists," he said. "This is straight-up Marxism." He then referenced Democratic politician Alexandria Ocasio-Cortez's policy adviser, who said "every billionaire we have is because of a policy failure" and that "a moral society needs guardrails against it."

Co-host John Delony, questioning the logic of the extreme leftist logic Ramsey was referencing, asked a real-world question to test the veracity of the socialist theory.

"I'm just thinking of the first guy that popped into my head, everybody's favorite target - Elon Musk comes up with a cool computer program and sells it for a lot of money. Helps a lot of people do a lot of things. Then he develops a car and a battery. What's the inherent evil there? I'm perplexed by the argument," Delony said.

"It's not logical, it's not critical thinking skills. Marxism never is," Ramsey answered, cutting through the propaganda. "What ends up happening is that the whole thing is about vilifying wealth and the wealthy, so that we can do a power grab and move the money around and get credit for it. It's a power grab thing. That's generally what's at the core of Marxism or these kinds of things all along."

As Ramsey has been saying for years, and as studies clearly support, the wealthy lead all income earners in consistent giving.

"In the real world, the most generous people on the planet are the wealthy," Ramsey noted. "This is actual data, not theory, not political rhetoric that's trying to beat a drum. But the actual data says that wealthy people feed more starving children than not-wealthy people."

"88 percent gave to a charity in 2020," Delony pointed out, referencing a survey of 1626 households with a net worth of at least a million dollars.

"Millionaires, there they are again!" Ramsey chimed.

January 24, 2022

Entrepreneur Literally Saves the Children

For most parents, there are few thoughts that evoke the fear and terror of a choking child. The panic, with time stopping still, each moment pulsing that horrifying, helpless feeling.

On Friday's Greg Kelly Show, the radio host took a brief respite from plummeting Presidential poll numbers, skyrocketing inflation and other news of the day to discuss this type of traumatizing event with a special guest.

Arthur Lih, the inventor of the anti-choking device, LifeVac, began by explaining how he invented the device in his garage. Like so many great American success stories, it began with taking a calculated risk to fill a perceived need.

"Well, I'm blessed, my Dad was an engineer, worked on the space program. My sister's a doctor, so I grew up kind of learning and fixing, you know the old school America," Lih began. "I had an inkling of how to build things and I heard of a seven year old - my daughter was seven - that choked to death. Procedures didn't work, and I was scared."

Lih told Kelly he used this unique engineering and medical background as a foundation, once he became aware of the severe and immediate danger for choking children. He felt parents needed something that would be quick and easy to use, especially in the moment when they are paralyzed with fear.

"I pursued to find something super-simple, because I knew I'd be scared," Lih said during the half-conversation, half-advertisement. "I came up with a little plunger with a little valve. You place it, you push it, you pull it, and sucks out the obstruction. We've saved over 170 kids now."

The device is very similar to a mini sink plunger, however the difference is in the reverse engineering. When pushed down, the air vents out to create a suction. Then, when pulled, it attempts to pop the object out.

Lih implored Kelly that the secret for parents is being prepared, when data shows that one child dies from choking every five days.

Eventually, the discussion during the quasi-infomercial turned to current events, specifically the detrimental effects of the nation's economic and national condition. Lih told Kelly that both the pandemic and the porous border have created conditions for similar "knock-off" products to pour into the country and undercut his business and quality. He says these after-market replicas may let down parents when they need them the most.

"In a general scope, but an American-made medical product, particularly at this time," Lih said. "Do your research, buy America. It will be regulated and it will be safe."

Kelly and Lih discussed online sellers who hawk non-regulated devices and products, and the pair ultimately urged consumers to buy directly from reputable manufacturers and businesses.

In wrapping up, the inventor said the greatness of America played a large part in helping him come up with this life-saving device.

"The reason LifeVac lasts forever, the reason it has a ball valve, the reason the vent system is so detailed is because of my Dad," Lih concluded. "He was part of the generation that put a man on the moon, that tried to do things we've never done. And in many scope he lives on today with me because I made it last forever. You're not supposed to do that because you want to sell one every year. I made it for everyone. I made it inexpensive. And I made it in America and today is the one year anniversary of him leaving, and me and you are talking, so that's pretty cool"

The Golden Era of Media Just Beginning

Perhaps we've been wrong about this all along.

We think, and the data shows, that common sense is no longer all that common. In fact, our country and our world remain extremely divided.

The data also shows that, quite possibly, our biggest deficiency is this - trust. Trust in an objective truth. Highlighted by a lack of trust in the media.

But perhaps we've been wrongly thinking of this as a shortcoming, when in reality it is a budding attribute. Not a flaw, but rather a virtue.

A feature, not a bug.

In fact, as citizens lose trust in mass corporate media and embrace alternative sources, does this not show a willingness to think for oneself? Does it not show initiative to knock on doors and search for truth. Are we not asking, with the hope that we will find the truth?

Not *"their"* truth, but *"the"* truth, as there is only ever really one. Perspectives shift, but truth stands solid as a rock.

So in this era of declining trust in media, is it possible that we are creating a stronger, more engaged populus taking a more active, involved citizenry?

Last week, Rasmussen Reports released new survey results showing how American voters feel about the following statement.

"Do you agree or disagree with this statement: The media are truly the enemy of the people?"

58% of all voters agreed.
(56% of white voters, 63% of black voters, 76% of Republican voters, 61% of Independent voters, 37% of Democrat voters)

Now keep in mind, these are "likely voters," rather than simply registered voters or, even more broadly, adults en masse. In other words, this sample is already the most engaged and up-to-date among us. These are the people who generally follow the news, understand the issues and hold strong opinions on policy. Generally speaking.

So if these are the most engaged among our peers, and they clearly don't trust the mass media, where are they getting their information? And where are they prothletising, sharing and spreading those opinions?

It is reasonable to conclude that social media and our intertwined networks of the new century have, in essence, become our media. Newspapers have morphed into tweets, posts, shares and likes.

We no longer *rely* on the media. We *are* the media.

And isn't this what the Founding Fathers envisioned in the first place? Did they not urge the American citizenry to remain awake and aware? Did they not clearly expect and demand that citizens become their own watchdogs?

As America broke away from English rule, it took many of the latter's philosophies to this newly burgeoning land. Among these was the role of citizens in overseeing their ruling elites.

As David Hume wrote in 1742, and is quoted at ColonialWilliamsburg.org, *"Nothing is more apt to surprise a foreigner than the extreme liberty which we enjoy in this country of communicating whatever we please to the public and of openly censuring every measure entered into by the king or his ministers."*

Benjamin Franklin bought and became the publisher of the Pennsylvania Gazette, to educate, share the news of the day and keep the controlling aristocracy in check.

Today, we do much the same with a Facebook post or Instagram story.

In a 2017 piece in *National Affairs*, author Arthur Milikh summed it up, saying *"the press is meant to serve both intellectual and political liberty. Yet, on the other hand, few citizens directly experience this idealism, feeling instead the press's forcefulness, flattery, vehemence, and sometimes fanaticism — often akin to warfare directed at their minds and sentiments."*

In other words, we are all very much aware that most mainstream media shoves opinion down our throats, disguised as objective "news."

He quotes Thomas Jefferson, highlighting the fact that Jefferson and his fellow founders, as they often did, put the responsibility on the people.

"No experiment can be more interesting than that we are now trying, and which we trust will end in establishing the fact, that man may be governed by reason and truth," Jefferson wrote. "Our first object should therefore be, to leave open to him all the avenues to truth. The most effectual hitherto found, is the freedom of the press."

All avenues of truth.

Not all avenues of *my* truth, or *your* truth. But all avenues of *one*, objective truth.

Avenues such as Twitter, YouTube, Rumble, Locals and Substack.

As with most questions, we don't all agree. We don't all agree that power to, and through, the masses is a positive aim in and of itself. In a 2018 article in *Axios*, author Ina Fried quoted constitutional scholar, Jeff Rosen, as saying *"the filter bubbles of social media are exacerbating the fact that Americans are already pretty divided along geographic lines."* He is correct. We are undoubtedly divided and splintered into our own camps.

Rosen referred to James Madison's quote from Number 55 of the Federalist Papers, where Madison stated, *"In all very numerous assemblies, of whatever character composed, passion never fails to wrest the sceptre from reason. Had every Athenian citizen been a Socrates, every Athenian assembly would still have been a mob."*

Most would agree with Madison, and Rosen, in that mob rule - based on mob emotion, rather than deliberated reason - would, and arguably has at times, lead us toward ever- hardening factions.

One could argue, however, that those balkanizations have always existed, ever concealed, and that the current period of mass awakening is leading to gradual, unexpected shifts.

Only through social media and large-scale opinion sharing could you imagine a time where influential "thought leaders," such as Elon Musk, Joe Rogan, Robert F. Kennedy Jr., Russel Brand, Kyrie Irving and John Stockton are being pulled in directions few expected.

New opinions, shared by our "new media," lead to new and unexpected shifts.
We are awake, alert and seemingly receptive, willing to re-evaluate the truth and organize accordingly. We are constantly learning, and (God forbid!) growing.

Our Founders envisioned a nation engaged, connected and aware. And regardless of our opinions, differences and squabbles, we may be satisfying that requirement like never before.

February 7, 2022

Bitcoin's Call Option on Morality

It has been called "Digital Gold, the "currency of the internet," and even "rat poison."

But one Bitcoin thought leader recently went in a different direction, saying adoption of the asset may actually lead to a higher level of morality among its holders.

Robert Breedlove, founder and CEO of Parallax Digital recently joined host Michelle Makori on Kitco News. During the YouTube presentation, the "Bitcoin Professor" shared many other eye-raising and thought-provoking ideas regarding Bitcoin and the digital property's role in restoring the world to monetary and moral responsibility.

"We've been trying to bootstrap ourselves out of economic scarcity or depravity for as long as we've been around," Breedlove said, in his measured and thoughtful style. "Only in the past few hundred years, though, did we really figure out capitalism. This idea of trading with one another, that is this positive-sum game that increases wealth for everyone. And the results have been absolutely spectacular."

He pointed out that even though poverty exists in our country and in the world, the numbers of people suffering from starvation for purely market-driven reasons have consistently declined. Even so, he told Makori that over time, world leaders have become corrupted by, and often because of, the fiat money system. In this system, dollars or other forms of currency are created out of thin air by fiat, or dictat. One of the results of these actions is exploding inflation, such as that the United States is currently experiencing.

And as he sees it, that's where Bitcoin comes in.

"This is a very interesting angle. It's been written about in a great book titled, "*Honest Money,*" by Gary North." Breedlove said. He explained that the higher "time preference" you are, the shorter-term thinking you do. And the lower "time preference," the longer-term you think and plan. This theory is also dissected at length in "*The Bitcoin Standard,*" by Saifedean Ammous.

"If your money is depreciating rapidly, as fiat currency does, you are directly financially incentivized to think shorter-term. You want to get out of cash savings and into any other asset just to protect your purchasing power," Breedlove explained. "Because if you just hold cash, if you hold U.S. dollars for instance, you are getting significantly debased in the medium to long-term. Whereas if you have something more like physical gold or Bitcoin, a money that no one can arbitrarily debase, you can now accumulate purchasing power safely, without counterparty risk, such that you can have a much longer time horizon for planning, and thinking and considering life. And that turns out to be directly related to morality."

Breedlove surmised that if one were a caveman with high time preference, simply concerned about where his next meal would come from, he could be more likely to "club anyone over the head" if need be, just to get that meal.

"But if I'm a long-term thinking person, I live in civilization, there's a lot of capital stocks, I'm trading with people...I'm much more likely to value a virtue like honesty, for instance. I'm not thinking about just my pure, short-term immediate gain," the erudite Breedlove said. "I'm considering my life, my trading relationships, my reputation on a much larger and longer time scale. So you can say that as we consider broader scope of time, our morality actually increases in tandem."

"You, as well as several other Bitcoin maximalists as well, have been saying that Bitcoin will truly, truly take off when a leading central bank buys Bitcoin," Makori said. "That will create a chain reaction, game theory, FOMO of other central banks."

"If you're a central bank and you determine that any of this Bitcoin thesis is even marginally possible, even just a 1 percent chance, for instance, of Bitcoin succeeding in the way that Bitcoin maximalists envision it, then the calculus for a central bank is quite straightforward," Breedlove said. "It's like, ok, there's a one in a hundred chance of this thing destroying my business model. What can I do to hedge myself? What can I do to hedge my business model against its success? And a very straightforward, pragmatic answer would be just allocate one percent of your assets into Bitcoin as an insurance policy against its success."

And that could start the bigger dominoes falling.

Breedlove also didn't shy away from giving Makori what many Bitcoiners really want - a price prediction. He said his target is for Bitcoin to be worth around $307,000 by the end of 2023. If that weren't enough to excite the Bitcoin community, last year he said he expects the asset to be worth around $13 million per coin in a decade.

If the Bitcoin Professor is correct, those millions of investors will be extremely rich and, quite possibly, highly moral as well.

March 7, 2022

BSM Summit Unmasks the Secret for a Successful Media Career

Last week's Barrett Sports Media Summit in the heart of New York City served as a shining example of how to build a successful sports, or news, media career.

And although there was plenty of insider information discussed, perhaps the event's biggest secret wasn't hidden at all. It weaved its way seamlessly throughout the days' captivating content, for all who were adroit enough to spot it.

The secret was hidden in plain sight.

From their seats in the Anne Bernstein Theater, attendees soaked in two days worth of knowledge and expertise, shared by some of the best and brightest in the sports media industry. The yearly event provides a candid industry introspection that is unparalleled across the country, and guests heard the unabashed truth from power players who earn their living by making things happen in, and around, the airwaves.

As the conference unfolded, however, it was interesting to hear so many of the speakers and panelists, from all areas of the industry, referring back to a bedrock principle for success in the business.

For aspiring professionals to experienced executives, the days' panel of guests repeatedly came back to this one common theme - some by plainly calling it out and others in less overt ways.

They all seemed to agree - the media business is *all about relationships.*

During the two days, guests heard from media managers discussing how they handle talent. They heard talent talk about dealing with heavy-handed Program Directors and awkwardly-aligned broadcast partners. They heard executives discuss the future of online gambling as well as creative innovators discuss the art of storytelling. They heard millennials and Gen Zers bantering about social media strategy and the ever-expanding digital marketplace. They even heard talent agents talking about challenging contract talks with tough-minded media executives, including two professionals together on a panel who reminisced about their real-world negotiation sessions.

In other words, the gathering was a priceless immersion into all areas of the sports media business. And again, the experts continued to return to the ultimate key to a lasting and successful media career - relationships.

The executive talked about how important it is to build relationships with the next generation of leaders as an organization develops it's growth plan.

The agent talked about how integrity and maintaining relationships helps him build and preserve his reputation as someone worth working with, and more importantly, as someone worth trusting.

The afternoon-drive star discussed intimate conversations with his Program Director, who urged him to heal his personal demons fully before resuming his career's second act.

The social media guru spoke eloquently about building a relationship with your audience, for only through that relationship can you truly know what will resonate with the audience and allow you to better deliver for them.

The media managers discussed the importance of relational intelligence when building teams to distribute content in new and innovative ways.

The former President of a worldwide media company talked about how crucial relationships were as he changed the culture of his company, and how those inter-organizational bonds were stronger because of that evolution. Disagreements and fractures occurred, but the relational glue proved, in many instances, enough to maintain connections.

Legendary sports talk pioneers collaborated on stage to share the secrets of their often-tumultuous on and off-air marriage, including the interpersonal decisions that ultimately helped them succeed to unmatched levels of industry acclaim.

As Summit guests entered the venue, they were greeted warmly by either Barrett Sports Media's President, the company's Director of Strategic Partnerships or it's Assistant Content Director. An immediate reinforcement of the connections that have helped the yearly event grow to serve countless industry professionals. The company has been built through, and sustained by, years of mutually-beneficial industry connections.

The warm and welcoming greetings were not for show; they were real and reciprocated.

As Summit guests departed after the 2-day affair, they were sent warmly on their way with hugs and handshakes from the company's numerous team members. And as you watched the host's son interact in such a classy and professional way with countless guests and attendees, you could literally feel the family-type rapport being built across the industry by this groundbreaking company. Existing relationships strengthened, new ones created.

The event was about sharing actionable knowledge and expertise to help grow the industry as a whole. Attendees were able to gather more than 16 hours of invaluable content on which to cement the foundation of a lasting career, and the company succeeded tremendously in achieving this goal.

But they also learned that whether sports or news, it's about relationships.

In front of the camera, or behind the scenes, it's about relationships.

From the newsroom to the boardroom, it's about relationships.

The Barrett Sports Media Summit - while providing 2 complete days worth of nuts-and-bolts, real-world sports media content - provided perhaps their biggest lesson without even trying.

March 14, 2022

Doug McKelway's Change of Pace

A change of scenery is often good for the soul.
And possibly quite literally, in the case of television news broadcaster Doug McKelway.

Axios reported last week that McKelway has been tapped by the Christian Trinity Broadcasting Network to anchor its new program, "Centerpoint."

The program is expected to cover the news of the day and other stories, presumably through a Christian, conservative lens. It will air weekdays at 7:30pm, with a rebroadcast later in the evening.

The fit may prove to be a comfortable one for McKelway, who retired from Fox News in September of 2020 with what the Washington Post called an "eyebrow-raising video." The video, posted on his Facebook page, featured McKelway praising specific Fox News executives, including the late Roger Ailes, as well as offering advice for aspiring television news on-air talent.

"You make a deal with the devil when you work in television news," McKelway said in the 2020 video. "You make a Faustian bargain. You got hired in part because of your looks, and that's the Faustian bargain. Over time, you start to age. You don't look as well as you did. And there's another crop of young, good-looking, talented people who are making their own Faustian bargain."

In the video, he then went on to share how Ailes, upon meeting McKelway, told him he was good looking but "no Megyn Kelly."

"When that day comes for you to leave, a piece of advice....don't leave embittered. Don't leave feeling like a victim," he said before taking a swig of what he said was Winston Churchill's favorite champagne. "Leave with your head held high, and with graciousness. With grace."

As McKelway becomes the face of "Centerpoint" for TBN, he joins producer Michael Clemente, former Newsmax CEO and Fox News EVP of News. TBN VP of Marketing, Nate Daniels, told Axios the network's goal is to create a "Christian lifestyle brand," rather than just a network known for "preaching and teaching."

TBN was founded in 1973 and now spans 175 countries. In recent years, the network has moved further in the direction of news and political programming. They welcomed Former Arkansas Governor and Republican Presidential candidate, Mike Huckabee, as a talk show host in 2017. Late last year, actor and Christian evangelist, Kirk Cameron, took the hosting reins of his own program, "Takeaways." The network is also expected to launch a new program in May, featuring hosts Mike Rowe and Matt Crouch, the network's President.

McKelway indeed has deep journalistic roots. His grandfather was the Editor of the Washington Star newspaper and President of the Associated Press. During a 2021 conversation about Big Tech censorship with Tony Perkins, McKelway referred to his grandfather as "a powerful defender of the First Amendment during the Cold War years."

"He wrote that it's incumbent upon publications, upon newspapers, and now of course moving into the digital age which did not exist back then, incumbent upon individual publishers to exercise their rights responsibly," McKelway told Perkins last year. "And there's a message in that for today's digital age. A lot of these guys are not being responsible overseers of their technology. And algorithms won't do it. Algorithms cannot have the kind of judgment that individual human beings who are morally grounded have. And that's what seems to be lacking here."

McKelways seems to be well-positioned for the move to TBN. Morality and responsibility, two strongly-rooted themes of Christianity.

Logistically, the move should provide additional comfort for McKelway. He reunites with producer Clemente, whom McKelway, in his aforementioned retirement video, thanked for helping him get hired at Fox News back in 2010.

McKelway, who also spent time as a correspondent for the Washington Examiner, has publicly chided the current Administration, tweeting on March 10th that "a statement from this Biden Administration should not be taken at face value, nor as the gospel truth." In an April, 2021 piece for the Examiner, he detailed "A Dangerous World: Biden Foreign Policy." In the video piece - well before the United States' horrendous withdrawal from Afghanistan and today's current list of world crises - McKelway foreshadowed how Biden's approach could lead to destructive consequences.

He also drew the ire of many in the mainstream media for leaked emails from his time at Fox News, when he defended President Trump. However, many polls estimate the former President garnering roughly 80% support among the Evangelical community.

McKelway's Twitter profile reads," Blissfully retired. I speak for no one but myself."

In the days to come, he will speak to, and perhaps *for*, many Christian viewers as TBN expands its programming offerings.

March 21, 2022

The Problem with Television News in America

"The shitty model of news that we are fed is based on an antiquated system that is not reflective of who's watching it."

Jon Stewart offered the insight during last week's opening moments of his Apple TV program, "The Problem." The program offered a critical look at television news - its goals, its methods and the product it offers up every day to millions of eager eyeballs.

Many have grown accustomed to hearing news critiques from more conservative American enclaves. But to come from the liberal side of the spectrum was both refreshing and, as Stewart himself predicted might happen, just the match to ignite a blowback from inside the industry.

"Generally, our news media has been collected into two major categories, for the most part. You got your, what they call the mainstream, liberal corporate media. And then you got your right-wing, also mainstream, corporate media," Stewart said, "One side of this media equation believes they are purveyors of truth and justice. The guardians of our democratic republic. The other side is effective."

Stewart did not hold back during the program, stating that television news has largely become a vessel to deliver ratings-tested material to willing and eager viewers. In his opinion, the industry focus is now on delivering what the viewer wants, rather than on what the journalist believes is worthy of time or trust. He feels a journalist's job should be to lay out the facts and truth as he sees it, and let the chips fall where they may.

The host didn't hide the fact that his bias may lead him to see a specific tilt to a story. His main point, however, is that television news should provide what the journalist believes to be true, rather than offering up what they think will simply be popular or agreed with by their audience.

Stewart zoned in on the issue of "Critical Race Theory," offering up a montage of conservative media opinion, referring to CRT as "poison," "marxist," "communist," and "racist." He blamed the conservative media for creating the issue and "lighting the fire" of outrage across America.

"The right-wing media, working seamlessly with their political arm, made that happen," Stewart said. "That's how fucking good these guys are. If you're going to battle this coordinated effort - political and media together - we're gonna need a hero." Stewart feels that this narrative was born not from truth, but rather from the corporate media's effort to create the hullabaloo only to exploit it to the max.

"Unfortunately, if they are the one thing that stands between America and chaos, we are in trouble. Because rarely has there been an institution that has such a distance between its aspirations and its execution," Steward said. "The media keeps informing us how incredibly important they are to our survival, because knowing keeps us free. But when given crucial informational tasks, they instead build us prisons of what the fuck are you people talking about?"

The program then moved on, with its host saying the media was correct in its initial pursuit of the Trump "Russia conspiracy." However, he said they quickly descended into absurdity, hurting their credibility in the process. Stewart played montage after montage, featuring mainstream media claims of "bombshells" about President Trump, and featuring the qualifier, "if true." Most of these "bombshells" turned out to be either untrue or far different than what had been portrayed. Try as they did, the media's claims of "walls closing in" on the former president turned out to be nothing more than false promises to their eager audiences.

"The media is such an important part of a democracy's immune system, but can the saviors of our democracy be saved themselves," Stewart asked.

"The problem is that we've become moral imbeciles, as we are being spoon-fed little pieces of outrage day by day, no, stay with the story, stay with the story. You can't lose any number. The death knell is if your numbers go down," said Chris Stirewalt, former Politics Editor at Fox News. "That's why we only get one story at a time. Producers know that that will work and that will rate, so we're going to stick with the thing that people are expecting and that they know, because if you take it away from them, they may get mad, the number may go down and they may go someplace else to get it."

During his time at Fox, Stirewalt was known for his wit, political expertise and, when the situation dictated, for offering less-than-popular opinion.

"I think what people don't realize is that it's a ratings-driven business, but it's also driven by meetings. People have meetings and make decisions every day that affect the tone, tenor and direction of coverage," Stewart said. The panel added that producers are guided by ratings showing minute-by-minute audience reactions, a trend that allows decision-makers to remain focused on the stories and angles that attract and keep the most eyeballs.

The table is set, giving the audience what the networks feel they want and will pay for, regardless of what many of the producers and journalists feel are, in actuality, the most important and relevant stories or angles of the day.

"There are meetings that set the agenda for the network, that set the agenda for the morning shows, that are gonna set the evening show agendas. You have to divy up who's gonna have which guests, because you can't have everybody shared on every single show," former CNN anchor Soledad O'Brien said. "And then the shows themselves have specific meetings. What are we gonna start with? What are we gonna end with? Who's the guest? How long do they get? I think this idea of, hey we just report the news, is ridiculous, because of course it's a zero-sum game. If you're covering something, then that means you're not giving coverage to something else."

In addition, social media is now the shiny new object attracting news producers, and compelling them to chase left and right. The excitable cat trying to land his paw on the laser pointer.

"You can see a television news story in which people are like, this idiot said this about this idiot on Twitter, and they treat it like it's a whole new story," Stirewalt said. "So it has permeated the thinking in very profound ways and it's made us dumber." Stirewalt said in the ten years he was at Fox, he saw the business change from keeping away from ratings talk, to relying on it before all else.

Stewart added that when he started the Daily Show at the age of 35, he led with what he believed in, hoping it would attract an audience, rather than starting with what he thought the audience would want and "backing into it." In his words, this purity of intention led to a more honestly-rooted journalistic effort.

"I think what this is really about is a lack of courage of changing the model," Sean McLaughlin, V.P. of News at E.W. Scripps said. "The part about the minute-by-minutes, you're looking at data that is already incredibly flawed from the beginning." He explained that today's hyper-fragmentation makes the Nielsen-collected data much less reliable than in years past. And even then, many have felt that the reliance on a relatively small set of households recording their viewing patterns was an already-skewed method to begin with. "At some point, you just start realizing, I wonder if what we're looking at is any degree of realism at all," McLauglin added.

O'Brien said most newsrooms now perform under essentially the same set of unwritten rules.

"I think for most of the journalists working there when I was there, they loved journalism, as I did, and I do. But I think the mission was to do the best job you could do, and win," O'Brien said. "Win as in the ratings. Win is making sure that you're getting picked up by the New York Times. Win is not about educating the public. It's not so complicated."

The prevailing theme of this episode of "The Problem" was that television news has become an all-too-tailored production. Especially in cable news, the product has become opinion-driven entertainment.

"What differentiates news from entertainment is that sometimes we have to tell you what you don't want to hear," Stirewalt summed up. "We are supposed to be the vegetables. We are supposed to be the nutrient-giving portion of the plate. Not dessert. What cable news has tried to do, and what local news sometimes does, is get the green beans in the shortbread, and you've got now you've turned the news into entertainment and you're treating entertainment like news. Both of those are bad things. News should be news, entertainment should be entertainment."

The episode concluded with a conversation between Stewart and former Walt Disney CEO Robert Iger. Iger felt news organizations may currently be on the defensive because they feel they've been under the microscope like never before.

"My advice to them was to not hear the noise as much, to continue doing the job that we've entrusted them to do," Iger said about his 30-plus years overseeing ABC News. "Which is to tell the truth, to state the facts. To present the news in an accurate and a fair and a timely basis. But we never sought to drive ratings or even bottom-line success at the sacrifice of what we consider to be quality. It wasn't part of our discussion."

Jon Stewart and the rest of America wait patiently, hoping this once again becomes the norm in newsrooms across the country.

March 28, 2022

Ramsey Solutions' Lesson on Legacy

Investing in your people is the surest way to ensure your brand's legacy.

In business or media, securing the next generation of leaders is not simply a crucial step for healthy corporate succession. It is a crucial process for any media company's long-term growth, stability and future.

No company walks the legacy-planning journey like Ramsey Solutions, the company led by financial talk-show host Dave Ramsey. In fact, one of Ramsey's lesser-known yet highly influential books, *"The Legacy Journey,"* teaches individuals to think financially past today and build something lasting for the future.

And in terms of building a legacy of financial media, Ramsey has always had an eye on the future.

Take, for example, talented host Anthony O'Neal, who for years with Ramsey Solutions helped spearhead the company's effort to help college students emerge from school without burdensome student loans. With Ramsey's leadership, O'Neal went into communities to share the truth about the predatory student loan industry, educating and imploring students and families that there are alternatives to the traditional model involving the financial handcuffs of college loans.

O'Neal, a black American, helped Ramsey extend his reach to a more diverse audience, one that was also younger and more rooted in popular culture. For O'Neal, it was a chance to speak to audiences across the country, both in person, through books, and on Ramsey's nationally-syndicated radio program. A true win-win, until O'Neal left Ramsey Solutions late last year to continue building his platform on his own.

Contrary to first thought, however, the change was welcomed and perhaps planned-for by both parties. No drama and no hard feelings, at least publicly.

Across the media industry, grooming the next generation of leaders is more difficult than ever before. And it's not unique to Ramsey and O'Neal. It holds true for on-air talent, to production crews, to editorial staff and the corporate boardroom. In all cases, a proactive approach helps develop the next batch of professionals to grow a brand or sprout the branches of a company's ministry into the future.

"A lot of these pathways into becoming the Program Director or the brand manager just don't exist anymore," said Jeff Sottolano of Audacy, at the recent Barrett Sports Media Summit in New York City. "The college internship, the Promotions Director, the APD in some instances. We've made very specific and intentional investments in restoring some of those positions, and making sure we've got a pathway inside of our organization to grow and develop the next major-market brand manager, maybe in a secondary role in another market."

So it becomes a two-part framework - invest into your future stars and , if necessary, help them spread their wings and fly. For O'Neal, the timing of his move was a welcomed one, both for himself and the Ramsey organization.

"Me and Dave recognized that my brand was going in a different direction than what we saw it was going while I was at Ramsey. And so we both just agreed that it's time for you to just step out on your own," O'Neal said on the Nicky and Moose YouTube show last month. "It was such a smooth transition to where this guy was so into it. He said we love you, we want to support the route that you're going when it comes to really serving that market that you want to go after. And it wasn't like this was a better situation, or this was a bad situation. It was like, hey Anthony go do your thing. I said yeah, I'm going to go do my thing. It's so funny, because when people see people separate, they automatically think it's drama. And I'm like, no, there's no drama there. That was a season. I'm a Christian man and God just shifted the season."

And when it comes to investing in future leaders, Dave Ramsey puts his money where his mouth is, often without much fanfare.

"Because I honor Dave, because I honor that place, I'm going to love that place. Dave was one hundred percent supportive of it," O'Neal said. "I'm going to be real with you all. He even gave me some money to go out. It was like a church plan, we're gonna go allow Anthony to do what he was called to do."

But that's not to say it's been all rainbows and lollipops for Ramsey when team members have departed. Over the years, there have been others who, through their actions or the company's philosophical approach, left under much less amicable circumstances. Sometimes it just isn't the right fit any longer. Sometimes the investment doesn't pan out for either side. And sometimes, as Ramsey's "Entreleadership" hosts have said over the years, the loving and caring thing to do is to push a team member to their next challenge, recognizing that their success is limited, or has ended, in your organization.

Many listeners and industry insiders might be shocked at Ramsey's approach to help grow and build an on-air personality's brand, only to help him take off on his own. But that may be one of the true secrets to the company's success - truly investing in people who will give their all to your brand and spread your message. There is an integrity to the approach, which helps attract the best and help them fulfill their potential, both for your organization and, ultimately, for themself.

But it starts with the right person, with the right attitude. And with Ramsey, O'Neal was the right fit. A person of integrity who had the qualities any successful team would desire.

"First and foremost, you want self-starters. Anybody that sits across my desk talking with me about a job, the first thing I say is, you better believe in you before you ask me to," said Don Martin of Fox Sports Radio during the Summit, while talking about grooming the next generation of media executives. "I mean, bring the game. If you walk into that room and you don't have passion for this game and you don't have enthusiasm then don't come in the door. At the end of the day, it's not up to us to make them care and make them want. We want hungry people. We need young people and as society life has changed."

For Ramsey, O'Neal embodied those attributes - a ceaseless passion that connected with a new, younger and more diverse audience. O'Neal's addition brought years of energy to the network; a benefit to both the organization and the talent. Dave Ramsey and his leadership team presumably saw what they lacked and sought out a professional who could fill in a weak spot. Their self-awareness and humility allowed them to chart the path toward company growth, seeing an addition rather than a threat.

"Your team needs to have someone on it that can replace you," Sottolano said about running a sports media organization. "We've got to be more judicious about, when we have those spots, whether it's the late-night host in terms of talent development, or its in the programming ranks, we've got to be invested in people that demonstrate potential. And not be afraid of someone who's going to challenge us in that seat. I'm not afraid of somebody challenging me in my seat. That makes me better, that makes me better, that makes the organization better."

And when this is your approach, you cultivate not only strong, talented leaders and talent for your team, but also raving fans and advocates of your mission and brand. These people emerged from inside your four walls and can't wait to share the truth about your wonderful company culture.

"I am so grateful. So grateful to the team behind the camera, to the team in this building, to Dave Ramsey, to the board, the leadership, to every single person who has poured into me and loved me, and truly shaped me into who I am, even as I leave this season and enter the next season," said fellow Ramsey personality, Christy Wright, who joined the company in 2009, and announced earlier this year that she, too, was stepping out on her own. "The gifts and skills that I've cultivated in this place are unbelievable, more than anything that I could ever ask or imagine. I've learned from the best of the best."

That is the power of a brand that does what it preaches. That is the power of legacy.
For Anthony O'Neal, for Christy Wright and for Dave Ramsey.

And also for media organizations who care enough about their team and their audience, to build the next generation of voices and leaders while living their mission today.

April 4, 2022

Surprising Delivery for New York Employees

While some Americans celebrate their 2-day shipments of specialty shampoo, softball cleats or that new spring shirt, many others are excited about an altogether different delivery within Amazon world last week.

Thousands of New York employees are celebrating after last week's surprising development - a vote to unionize an Amazon warehouse in Staten Island. And in their estimation, it was a case of 8000-plus employees banding together to fight the corporation, with little or no help from local or national politicians.

MSNBC's *The Beat, with Ari Melber* characterized the development with the title, *Billionaire 'Goliath' Bezos loses to 'David' organizers in huge labor upset at Amazon.*

On Friday evening's program, Melber welcomed former United States Labor Secretary under President Bill Clinton, Robert Reich, along with former Amazon employee, Christian Smalls, who led the effort to unionize.

"I'm with the people, I couldn't have gotten to this point without them," Smalls said, recapping the historic effort. "I've been fired from Amazon for two years now, and I'm still unemployed as we speak, even as the interim president. But I couldn't have done it without the support of my supporting cast, my comrades, these workers that I've organized with every single day, the workers that have been with me even before. Without their support, without their dedication and sacrifice, none of this would have been possible."

Melber pointed out some of the factors being considered by the employees in the warehouse, as well as what went into their thought process.

"When workers have to make these decisions, there's many pressures on it, which I've covered," Melber said. "People have the right to decide to join, they have the right not to join. That's how it's supposed to be."

The host probed deeper to find out the level of opposition faced by the organizers.

"Did you find that this was a debate at the warehouse that was on the level?" he asked Smalls. "Or do you think Amazon, and effectively Jeff Bezos, if we're going to talk specifically, were funding and interfering in a way that made it not a free and open debate?"

"Of course it wasn't fair, Amazon spends millions of dollars," Smalls responded. "There's already been reports that came out of how much money they've spent on us, and that's just the surface level."

"Overall, labor participation has crashed to nearly an all-time low in the United States, down to about one out of ten employees. It used to be much higher," Melber said, turning to Reich.

"This is the biggest labor victory in the last thirty years," Reich commented. "I want to congratulate Christian Smalls and all of the workers at the Amazon warehouse, but it goes far beyond the Amazon warehouse. We are seeing the beginnings of a revival of American labor organization in America, such as we have not seen. And it's about time. Workers need and deserve higher wages, better working conditions, safer working conditions."

"We've seen more Democratic politicians engage this labor debate," Melber said, cutting to a clip of Senator Bernie Sanders, touting the need for better working conditions at another Amazon location.

The Twitterverse has been ablaze over the weekend, with political opinions and public posturing aplenty. The actual impact made by politicians on the final outcome, however, has been a source of debate.

"You did this through organizing, we showed that. Are there any leaders, local or in Congress, who have been helpful?" Melber asked Smalls. "Was Senator Sanders, or AOC, where there's been some discussion, were those individuals helpful to you, or neutral, or not helpful?"

"Unfortunately, I would love to give them credit but that hasn't been the case," Smalls said, pointing out that the effort was pulled forth by the employees themselves, with little or no help from Democratic politicians. "We haven't had any support since we started. I tried to invite them, I tried to reach out. I did the best I could. I met with the, AOC personally. She said that she was going to come, and then she canceled on me the day before. But we didn't hold any grudges"

"That's interesting, she had posted today that in her view she was trying to be helpful, but that's not your view," Melber asked.

"I don't know what she's talking about," Smalls responded. "All I can say is it's unfortunate because I saw a tweet that she said this was not in her district. And I just think that's a terrible response because there's absolutely workers that live in her district that travel and commute to Staten Island every day that I know personally. It's disheartening to them, these are her constituents."

As Melber highlighted, labor reporter Steven Greenhouse tweeted that the development represented "by far the biggest, beating-the-odds David versus Goliath unionization win I've seen."

For this group of New Yorkers, last week's victory represents something much bigger, and something they hope is much more lasting, than getting that timely delivery of T.P. or those new sneakers.

April 11, 2022

A New Media Face for Bitcoin

Sometimes a wonderful message is lost because of the messenger.

Perhaps the messenger lacks knowledge. Maybe the communication skills are missing. Possibly, the messenger lacks vision or a channel to deliver the message. Or maybe the message can be so darn complicated that it is difficult to distill down to concepts that are easy for normal, non-technical folks to understand.

Many in the digital asset space have said Bitcoin suffers from these difficulties. And some are also now saying that one of their own has grown into the ideal messenger to bring the message to the masses.

"You've been absolutely killing it, you've been relentless, you don't let up with the hosts," said Peter McCormack, the trailblazing host of the "What Bitcoin Did" podcast. "You don't let them interrupt you. You just came on, I've seen two specifically, you've come on like a fucking steam train, and some of the best clips I've seen of people talking about Bitcoin."

McCormack was referring to Natlie Brunell, the buoyant host of the *Coin Stories* podcast, who he welcomed onto his highly-respected program recently.

"I finally feel like I'm kind of in my zone and feel like I am, sort of, I found my calling," Brunell responded humbly. "I'm really passionate about Bitcoin and I want to spread the message and use my skills that I acquired over the last ten years to do that."

Brunell acquired those skills through her early career in journalism and it was only recently that she made the move full-time into Bitcoin education and programming. Just last week she helped anchor Bitcoin Magazine's live coverage of the Bitcoin 2022 Conference from Miami.

"We think you are the best we've got to be out there in the mainstream talking about Bitcoin. We think you are the best," McCormack said.

Going unsaid is one of the most obvious attributes she brings, that of being an eloquent woman in a space dominated by males. Most digital asset hosts openly admit that their audiences skew heavily male, an obstacle they feel the industry will need to surmount to reach the heights many of these insiders foresee.

Regardless of gender, breaking into the mainstream is a challenge for anyone.

"I want to get on more shows. It's funny, people ask me why haven't you been on CNBC yet? Why not CNN? You know, it's hard because for some reason Fox Business and some of the other outlets have been more prone to want to discuss Bitcoin, as opposed to some of the other outlets," Brunell replied. "I'm not a big CEO that purchased Bitcoin on my balance sheet, so I would love to get out there more if I can, and hopefully that'll happen."

"But you're an insider in that world," the intrepid McCormack responded, alluding to Brunell's stellar career in media and journalism. "You know how it works."

"Yeah, a little bit. A little bit," Brunell acquiesced. "But I still think that Bitcoin, there's still so much that people just don't understand, which has been an advantage to me, right? Because if mainstream media got it, I probably wouldn't be able to do what I'm doing right now and making a career of it. So I feel like I'm kind of running full speed because I got a head start sort of understanding and learning all this myself. But once mainstream media pours in, I don't know what will happen. They won't really need me anymore."

One of the traits that makes Brunell such a well-qualified Bitcoin educator is her deep appreciation for personal freedom. She was born in Poland and immigrated to the U.S. at the age of five, as her parents yearned for the opportunities America offers citizens, regardless of their place of birth.

"My parents have all these stories of what it was like when it was Communist. They really always dreamt of coming to the United States. My mom just had this vision of the American Dream, and coming to the U.S.," Brunell said. "She watched a lot of American films, which I think is why I was naturally predisposed to loving film and T.V. and just media in general. She always had things on and she loved the old classic Hollywood movies and how they depicted American life."

With her mother as the driving force, it took 20 years before her family was able to make the move to America, and the suburbs of Chicago. When Natalie arrived in an American elementary school, she didn't know a single person or speak the English language.

"It's like this feeling when you know you're different. Everyone kind of thinks you're weird and doesn't understand the food you're bringing to lunch, thinks your language and accent is weird," she recalled, remembering her early school years as a recently-immigrated student.

She eventually changed her name officially from Natalia to Natalie, in an effort to fit in. Financially, there were many challenges in her early days in Chicago. In their first apartment, she and her brother each had their own room, while her parents slept on a pullout sofa in the living room. Her family of four shared a single bathroom.

Brunell is bright, engaging and clearly a "people person," which helped her assimilate relatively quickly by talking and interacting constantly with friends. Even at her young age, she had the natural talent and desire to communicate and express herself, a skill set that today helps her make the sometimes-complicated topic of Bitcoin seem simple and understandable to the viewers. And not only understandable, but fun and exciting as well!

"I believe that the American Dream shouldn't be so hard to achieve. I feel like the country was founded on such amazing principles of self determination and freedom and we've lost that along the way. I've always been a believer that if you're a good person and you work hard, you should be able to achieve the things that you want," she told McCormack. "And it's not going to be all equal. We're not all equal and we don't all have the same motivations and desires, but I think you should have a shot, you know."

"I think certain types of journalists are predisposed to understanding or getting Bitcoin straightaway," McCormack complimented Brunell. "I think there's two types of journalists - they get it or they want to fight it. There's no middle ground, and the ones that want to fight it are usually shitty journalists who don't do the proper research. The ones who get it, they suddenly just want to work on it."

Brunell noted that, even in her younger years, she felt a strong pull toward media and journalism.

"I always wanted to work in T.V. or film and I grew up sort of having a ton of media on at home because it helped augment my parents' English skills," she said. "Whether it was T.V. shows that were more on the scripted, fictional side or just news. We were a family that watched a ton of news, like Diane Sawyer, Barbara Walters interviews, Oprah, all of it was on all the time." And as she matured, she felt even more compelled to the idealistic nature of true journalism.

"I remember being young and just thinking what an incredible job. What a noble profession, you get to interview leaders and big celebrities. I'm this little girl in the suburbs of Chicago who came from a foreign country. It just seemed like this amazing job," Brunell said.

Brunell eventually majored in journalism at Pepperdine University in Los Angeles. She then earned her Masters in Journalism at Northwestern. It was a continual rise of the ladder of success for the woman who once felt she would consider herself financially successful if she simply had a house with a garage. In fact, her family's financial struggle started after immigrating to America and worsened with the great financial crisis of 2008. During that time, the family lost everything, including their home, to bankruptcy.

And that led Brunell to Bitcoin.

"It took this ten year career being in news and exposing myself to some of the biggest crises facing this society - interviewing people on a day-to-day basis facing poverty, homelessness, civil unrest, public corruption - for me to finally start to connect the dots. Because when I discovered Bitcoin and finally went down the rabbit hole, I was like oh *this* is the problem. Oh *this* is the problem that's also impacted my hard-working, amazing, good family. And now I will do anything possible to help everyone I can, first understand the problem, and know that Bitcoin is the solution."

Today, Brunell delights viewers and listeners through her YouTube and audio podcast, discussing Bitcoin topics with the industry's leading voices. The best and brightest in the space appear with Brunell and watch with satisfaction as she so concisely and compellingly spreads the word on national media.

For McCormack and the other Bitcoin influencers, developers and O.G's, Natalie Brunell is officially one of them. And she is now also one of the most influential.

April 18, 2022

Some in Media See Impending Recession

As Americans experience economic pain to the levels not seen in 40 years, some in the media expect things to get worse.

Substantially worse. And needlessly so.

Chris Salcedo of Newsmax is one such broadcaster, who has had a laser-like focus on the recent American economic decline and what could be around the corner. On Friday he welcomed economist Stephen Moore onto his evening program to discuss the implications of current government policy and where the Democrat administration may be leading the nation.

Salcedo led off by highlighting the national budget proposal from the Biden Administration, which hits an eye-popping $5.8 Trillion and benefits "America's enemies, Joe Biden's pals over in communist China."

"When you talk about the rise and decline of great empires, you're exactly right in terms of tracking what happened," Moore, the author of *Trumponomics* said. "But another factor has been out-of-control government and out-of-control debt. It has also led to the demise of great empires as well. We'd better watch out."

Moore noted that when he first came to Washington in 1985, the budget was $1 Trillion. It's now nearly six times that.

The national debt was around $1 Trillion.
It's now 30 times that.

And these are bipartisan problems, Moore believes, created by both sides and exacerbated greatly in the past couple years.

"Nobody seems to bat an eye. Nobody in Congress, neither the Republicans nor the Democrats, seem to want to do anything about it," Moore pointed out. "If you're wondering why we have 8.5% inflation today, it's very simple. We've spent $3 Trillion that we didn't have, borrowed it and spent it. It's not Putin. It's not Trump. It's not temporary. It's not transitory. This is a result of out-of-control government."

Moore followed up by referring back to his 2020 prediction that if Biden were to win the election, the two biggest winners would be Russia and China.

"I didn't agree with everything Trump did. I worked for him. Some things I agreed with, some things I didn't," Moore, the co-founder of the *Committee to Unleash Prosperity* said. "I always believed that everything he did was oriented toward putting America first. This president, from the very start, from his first executive order of stopping the pipelines, then declaring war on American energy. Now, if you declare war on American energy and reduce our energy output, gee, what countries do you think benefit from that?"

"Mr. Moore, economists are telling me that Biden has so mismanaged the economy that the Fed is going to have no choice but to throw our country into recession to try to cool this massive inflationary spiral, this Democrat inflation. Is that your read?" Salcedo asked his guest.

"First of all we have to first recognize we have a problem," Moore continued, echoing thoughts from his latest 2021 book, *Govzilla: How the Relentless Growth of Government Is Devouring Our Economy—And Our Freedom.* "Joe Biden keeps blaming, have you noticed this, he keeps blaming it on Putin. 80% of the inflation we've had since Trump left office and Biden took over was before Putin went into Ukraine."

Moore then chronicled recent history - when Trump left office the inflation rate stood at 1.5%. Today, 14 months later, the inflation rate has exploded to 8.5%, with American families feeling the economic hardship that comes along with it. Pain at the grocery store checkout counter. Pain at the pump.

"How do you screw things up that quickly?" Moore asked Salcedo. "No, I don't think it's intentional, but it certainly has sabotaged our economy. I'm just aghast at how much our country has faltered. Now I lived through the 1970's, when we had the last episode of runaway inflation, and that did lead to a crash landing of our economy. I still think there is time to skate around a recession, but the longer we wait,the more this inflation metastasizes, the more painful it will be to get it out. We should be cutting government spending across the board by about 10 or 15 percent right now. We should be increasing our energy supply, and yes the Fed has to start sucking some of that money out of the economy by raising rates."

Both Moore and Salcedo view the current state of affairs as a government-created problem.

Only time will tell if government will enact their prescription for healing and a return to prosperity.

April 25 2022

Media Responds to the Speech Censors

The hallmarks of healthy discourse include passion, opinion, give-and-take, and sometimes, areas of agreement. This holds true in a friendship, classroom, marriage or country.

Unhealthy debate, however, might include an unfair playing ground, lies, innuendo, and perhaps most sinister of all, an effort to silence or cancel the opposing argument.

You can't make your case if your audience never hears your case.

On Friday's episode of ``The Five," the panelists took on the issue of free speech, labeling the opponents of such as hypocrites and highlighting those championing more freedom for everyday citizens.

Former Republican Congressman Sean Duffy opened the Fox News segment with his monologue.

"Battle lines are being drawn in the fight over free speech in America. On the side of freedom you have the world's richest man. Elon Musk getting one step closer to liberating Twitter from censorship-crazy Liberals. The Tesla CEO says he's secured more than $46 billion for his potential takeover," Duffy began. "And on the other side, you have former president Barack Obama, who is pushing for more censorship online."

A spliced montage then featured Obama saying, "The First Amendment is a check on the power of the state. It doesn't apply to private companies, like Facebook or Twitter. While content moderation can limit the distribution of clearly-dangerous content, it doesn't go far enough. As so much of the conversation around disinformation is focused on what people post, the bigger issue is what content these platforms promote."

The program then featured a new study from the Media Research Center, which said Big Tech censored criticism of Democratic Joe Biden 646 times over the last two years. The study investigated the censoring activities of Big Tech platforms, such as Facebook and Twitter, from March 2020 to March 2022.

"Big Tech's campaign to protect President Joe Biden and his agenda has continued unabated," an Media Research Center statement said. "The worst cases of censorship involved platforms targeting anyone who dared to speak about any subject related to the New York Post bombshell Hunter Biden story."

The main theme of the report is that censorship has increased as the Democratic Party and their Big Tech don't like what is being said.

"What I find most interesting is the timing of all of this," Judge Jeanine Pirro said. "Now we have Elon Musk getting closer to taking over Twitter. Barack Obama, former President of the United States, comes out and starts talking about the First Amendment and the moderation of that concept that is so fundamental to who we are. It makes us the freest country in the world. The First Amendment, the freedom to speak, the freedom to practice religion and the freedom to assemble. All of that is fundamental to who we are."

Pirro compared the methods of communication of centuries past to today's technological advances, such as email and electronic messaging. In her opinion, the vehicles of information exchange have changed, but the principles protecting that right have not. While we used to share ideas via pigeons and ink-penned letters, today we use social media and devices.

"This is the antithesis of the Constitution and what free speech is all about," Pirro followed up. "What Obama is doing, is he is cultivating now the concept that we can moderate things and content moderation, and now we can get rid of disinformation, which leads us to the place where if you don't agree with what I think you will be shut down."

Pirro said she is infuriated by the double standard - proven falsehoods being spread purposely by the media to bolster the Democratic political party, while material from other news publications disproving the information have been censored.

"Do they think that we're that stupid, that they need to tell us what we can and cannot read?" Pirro asked. "This infuriates me. He is wrong on this. This is un-American. Free speech is fundamental and when we lose it, we're gone."

Certainly, there are things published and shared via social media that are prosperous. Have you heard that President Trump colluded with Russia? Or that he said violent white supremecists were "very fine people?" Or that President Obama was a covert plant, born in Kenya? Or that he was groomed to infiltrate American and take it down from the inside?

There are those who have read and believed this "information," disseminated widely on social media and elsewhere. But many believe the solution is actually *more* information-sharing, not less. *More* media, not less. *More* true journalism, not less.

"Obama (in the montage) there started the speech off by saying I'm a First Amendment fundamentalist. You can't infringe on the First Amendment. Then he spent the rest of the speech undermining free speech in the whole speech," Duffy noted. "Free speech is not about protecting speech that we agree with. Free speech is about protecting speech we disagree with. Isn't it better that we all engage in the arena of debate and ideas and the best ideas will rise to the top?"

Former Democratic representative Harold Ford Jr. responded, pointing out some speech that courts have said is not protected, such as "yelling fire" in a crowded theater, but that he, at least, wants a free and open debate.

"I think it's important that we present ideas that may unsettle people, and for us to be able to have these conversations and have debates," Ford, long considered a remaining centrist in his party, said. "Even if the best ideas don't rise, at least we inform and educate people about what the issues are."

Ford concluded his thoughts by saying Musk is pursuing a purchase of Twitter for the most American of reasons - as a business venture with a large financial upside.

On that point, traditional Americans and centrist Democrats can mostly agree.

May 2, 2022

Michael Malice Takes on the Media, Again

"We've been trained since Kindergarten, in our government schools, to regard the media as authoritative, and as hardworking people fighting for the little guy and trying to present the truth."

Those, the words of Michael Malice, appearing on The Rubin Report back in 2020. He gave voice to the quintessential way American's "used to" view their media. Deserved or not, the media represented truth, authority and objectivity.

Malice then proceeded to list examples of that same media doing exactly the opposite - picking up propaganda spin and using it to metaphorically bludgeon that same little guy they purportedly represent.

The exchange was highlighted as part of an episode of Dave Rubin's program last week. The "best of" episode featured a compilation of excerpts from Rubin's conversations with Malice over the past five years, and ran with the provocative, YouTube thumbnail "It's Always Been Rigged."

An evergreen highlight reel that, to many, seems to be more true by the day.

While talking about the United States inserting itself into military conflicts over recent decades, Malice began by insinuating that the media has carried the water of war efforts, far and wide.

"The bloodlust of the establishment, which include the corporate press, cannot be overstated," he told Rubin in a 2017 clip. "2016, Trump's the nominee, we heard it every single day. He's crazy, he's going to get us into World War 3. He's going to get pissed off at a tweet from China and press the nuclear button. We heard this all the time. Carly Fiorina got asked this in the 2nd debate, first question, do you trust president Trump with his finger on the nuclear button. And now, China has hacked our systems, Russia has tried to interfere with our elections. And the press is constantly saying, do something about it, do something about it, do something about it, do something about Venezuela. So the fact that he's NOT getting us into World War 3 is now being used as a slight against him by the same people who regarded that as a problem when he was the nominee."

A remarkable clip from five years ago, while some of the biggest media deceptions had yet to be uncovered. Namely, the Trump Russia Collusion fabrication, the disingenuous January 6th "insurrection" narrative and the coordinated effort to hide the Joe and Hunter Biden scandal.

"It's horrific, and this has been a long time coming," Malice, never one to shy away from controversial statements, added. "We talked about yellow journalism in high school, remember, the Spanish-American War. And then they pretend it went away. It didn't go away. The same press, if it bleeds it leads. They can't wait to get us into another engagement. It's disgraceful."

And again, this was as trust in media was waning, but still before it had fallen to its increasingly low depths of 2022. As an example, a poll released Friday by Susquehanna Polling and Research showed that 73% of those surveyed said the mainstream media "misrepresents the facts to push a political agenda." An abysmally-low 17% trust the corporate media to tell the truth.

Rubin, a former liberal and lifelong Democrat turned Conservative, now hosts his program online and on BlazeTV. He pressed the issue in the 2017 clip, searching for a solution to lack of media trust.

"What has to happen with the press then? And I mean this in terms of cable news, mainstream news, network news, Vox, HuffPo, Buzzfeed, all of it," Rubin asked.

"The battle is won when the average corporate journalist is regarded with the exact same way as the average tobacco executive. They have a job. They're promoting their product. Their product is cancerous and deadly. They're often bright people, they're often good people, but be aware of what it is they're selling you."

For the 70-plus percent who don't trust the media, Malice's contentious remarks are a highlight reel well worth repeating again and again.

May 9, 2022

Katrina Szish: Charting the Uncharted Path

"You do too many things; we don't know what to do with you."

That advice from a senior cable news executive never hit home with Katrina Szish, and for that fact many Newsmax viewers are thankful.

Szish, the veteran television personality, announced last week that she has joined Newsmax TV as an afternoon anchor, pairing with Bob Sellers to host its daily 2pm-4pm program, *American Agenda*.

To say that Szish's path to this high-profile position has been unconventional would be an understatement. Her career has included red carpet conversations, discussions about pop culture and entertainment, interviews with political figures and four years hosting on QVC.

While most media personalities narrow down and find their niche - or rather, get shoved into one, with or without their approval - Szish has taken chances and grasped opportunities available to her. With or without the approval of traditional media managers or bosses.

After graduating with honors from Harvard, Szish interned for CNN's Political Investigation unit in Washington, DC and CNN Style with Elsa Klensch in New York. She was a correspondent for CBS News' *The Early Show*, an anchor, reporter and writer for ABC News Now, a freelance correspondent for E!, a correspondent and writer for CNN.com, a co-host on the Food Network, a host and correspondent for TBS and the host of Cindy Crawford's *Meaningful Beauty* television series. Just to name a few of her stops, as detailed on her website.

Szish even worked under Anna Wintour as a fashion writer at Vogue.

She has appeared with Barbara Walters and Larry King, Bill O'Reilly and Neil Cavuto. Szish spent time as a brand ambassador for clients including Yahoo, Mercedes-Benz, Calvin Klein, and others, and she worked in local news in major markets, such as New York, Los Angeles and Miami. She is a former fashion magazine Editor and hosted a weekly fashion and lifestyle show, *The Szish List*, on QVC.

So while many aspiring media professionals are content to fit in and let their career mold them, the 50-year-old Szish has chosen a different path, happy to take chances and build something unique. Her Twitter profile reads, "Truth-teller. Writer. Style Savant. Dog Mom."

Correspondent Caroline John, writing for *Earn the Necklace*, called Katrina Szish "the ultimate style goddess" in her April 22nd piece announcing Szish's departure from QVC, where she had been a premier fashion influencer since 2018. John wrote that Szish's "fans are dejected" by her exit, and that viewers have been "drawn to Szish's engaging and entertaining persona as much as her style and recommendations."

While many anchors would have trouble jumping from entertainment and fashion to news, current events and politics, Szish has fit in well in her first week with Newsmax. Her Friday broadcast concluded with a spirited segment regarding a contentious segment on *The View*, which discussed Liberal animosity toward Black Republicans.

"I think we often see on *The View* any of their Republican hosts tend to get completely lambasted, where there's not even an open discussion. It's immediately dismissive." Szish said during her program's final segment last week. "That to me is so much of what we're seeing. Whether it's between former friends, whether it's on-air, wherever it is. Is seeing something like this on-air, say with *The View* co-hosts, even make our society think, you know what, it's O.K. to be dismissive if someone's Republican, much less a Black Republican?"

Gone are the days of dishing on "party clothes." She now opines on political parties.

Szish's website says that another cable executive warned her, "You have to pick one thing -- TV producers need to be able to put you in a bucket."

Szish apparently took the advice to heart. She created an extra-large, multi-faceted, pliable bucket of her own making and jumped in to chart a distinctive path.

A path completely unique, personal and successful.

Dinesh D'Souza Fires Back Over 2000 Mules

2000 is a lot of mules. And yet that number pales in comparison to the number of reactions, critiques and commendations those 2000 mules have attracted over the past few weeks.

This month has seen the viral explosion of Dinesh D'Souza's latest documentary, *2000 Mules*, which chronicles the Democratic party's alleged, secret ballot-harvesting tactics during the 2020 election.

In episode 330 of his YouTube podcast over the weekend, the outspoken author and filmmaker directly answered some of the "fact-checking" that has been aimed at his latest blockbuster, where he claims to have uncovered the dark and allegedly illegal tactics that many think led to the election of America's current President.

D'Souza says his film has been very effective in "reshaping the way people think about our elections. Changing the debate about what happened in the 2020 election, all of that."

PolitiFact, the AP and Washington Post stand out as a few of the organizations that have officially "fact-checked" D'Souza's film, but he began his podcast responding to fellow conservative, Ben Shapiro. Shapiro, a staunch conservative influencer, if not card-carrying member of the populist wing, had some pointed questions about the film's validity.

D'Souza responded to the point made by Shapiro, stating that "we do not see in the film the same guy making multiple trips to a dropbox. In other words, making more than one dropbox visit. The same guy, not different people doing it. And we know you have video tracking showing it, but we don't see it."

D'Souza responded, "This is true. Let me tell you why it's true. It's true because most of these dropboxes, sadly, have no surveillance footage. They just don't. And so even though the geotracking, by the way, the geotracking is more reliable than video footage for the same reason that DNA is more reliable than an eyewitness. DNA show you left a hair or a drop of blood at a crime scene, and it's your DNA, you were there."

D'Souza continued, saying, "If geotracking showed a mule going from one dropbox to another, to another, to another, let's say between 2am and 3am in the morning, and it turns out that on the fifth dropbox there happens to be surveillance footage, and you know that this guy was there at a specific moment and day in time, and you look on the video at that day and that time and there he is - boom, you've proven your case. You've established it clearly. The geotracking supports the video, the video confirms the geotracking. So, it seems what Ben Shapiro is kind of asking for is unreasonable."

D'Souza went on to say that he also posted to his social media photos of who he says is the same individual in question, wearing different outfits, on two separate occasions "stuffing ballots, multiple ballots in his hand, in dropboxes." He says this is evidence of at least one case of the same person stuffing ballots into multiple ballot boxes.

"Frankly, if the states did what they said, if they followed the election rules, if they had video everywhere, we would have the mules at every drop box," he said. "We would have them at every drop box they went to." He added that some states didn't have video, others didn't have enough, and still other states had turned off their video.

He finished his point by quoting Chief Justice of the Supreme Court, John Roberts, in a 2018 case dealing with geotracking and privacy issues. In that ruling, Roberts said, "When the government tracks the location of a cell phone, it achieves near-perfect surveillance as if it had attached an ankle monitor to the cell phone's user."

2000 Mules, the most successful political documentary in a decade, goes deep into alleged voter fraud and ballot stuffing operations by Democrats, which many feel changed the outcome of the 2020 presidential election. The film has already crossed $10M in gross revenue, which is astounding for a political documentary.

D'Souza said there is a planned public exchange, perhaps this week, between himself and Washington Post national correspondent, Philip Bump, who has "in the last few months, written about seven articles focusing on the issue of vote harvesting, ballot trafficking."

D'Souza's other blockbuster documentaries include *Hillary's America: The Secret History of the Democratic Party*, *Death of a Nation: Can We Save America a Second Time?*, *The Plot Against the President*, among others.

Many of his earlier films have been launched with a more traditional theatrical release. Not so for *2000 Mules*, which included a limited theatrical release and distribution through SalemNow.com and at 2000Mules.locals.com

The mules will undoubtedly continue to rally the metaphorical troops and, simultaneously, ruffle plenty of feathers.

May 23, 2022

The Biggest Story in America

Bill O'Reilly says the biggest story in America this month is largely being under-reported by politicians and the media. And its impact may extend much further than we can currently comprehend.

It's not a Hollywood trial, exploding gas prices, economic pain or a potential Supreme Court ruling.

According to O'Reilly, the biggest development in the country in recent weeks is the disastrous situation at our nation's southern border. He joined the Glenn Beck Radio Program on Friday morning to discuss the country's ongoing disaster, and predicted that it will become the impetus for major developments in the next six to twelve months.

"Three million foreign nationals are estimated to cross just into Texas this year, this fiscal year," O'Reilly began, chronicling the emerging siege of Texas' border. "And a President doesn't call the Governor of the state that has to deal with that one time? So everybody listening just says, oh he's just incompetent. It's not that. And I keep telling everybody this and few believe me. I think you do, Beck, but I'm not sure. The President of the United States does not know what he is doing. He is incapable of assimilating - word of the day - information. You can tell him something, and he'll look at you, and maybe he'll understand what you're saying. But two minutes later, he will forget it."

O'Reilly told Beck there are actual, devastating consequences for citizens when the President cannot seem to effectively react to or deal with this ballooning crisis.

"So Biden, who has not been to the border, another unbelievable occurrence, because if you add up the human toll of this, plus the narcotics traffic that's killing hundreds of thousands of Americans every year, you add it up, this is a catastrophe," O'Reilly said.

"I don't believe the Constitution is a death pact. You know, it's not a suicide pact." Beck replied. "This is an invasion and the government is doing nothing, and the government has the constitutional responsibility for the border, not the states. So that's what's kept the states out of it. But again, are we in a constitutional suicide pact?"

Responding to Beck, O'Reilly predicted it is American citizens themselves who are poised to react decisively.

"You elect a President, he comes into office. Americans have this idealistic view of that. Many times you elect someone who is destructive to the country. Alright, I mean many times. Not a few. Many. So what happens now?" O'Reilly asked rhetorically. "Well, everybody can whine and complain and talk about it, but what happens is this. In November, there is a course correction possible, whereby the American people would say, I recognize what a disaster Joe Biden is, and I'm sorry he's the President. And if I voted for him I made a mistake. So now I'm going to correct that mistake, and I'm going to give Congress the authority to deal with Biden. That's our system. That's how the Founders set it up."

O'Reilly believes that this issue, among so many others going dreadfully wrong in America, such as punitive gas prices and unnecessary economic hardship, will galvanize voters to fight back in November.

"I fully expect that the Republicans will take both houses of Congress. I'll be shocked if that doesn't happen. Because of inflation, primarily, and the economy. That's the driver of the vote. But second is the border," O'Reilly predicted. "Now, once the Republicans take over, I can assure you articles of impeachment will be drawn up in January and February 2023 against Biden, on this issue. Dereliction of duty."

And while the country endured the Democrat-fueled impeachment of our 45th president, O'Reilly thinks this time will be different. This time, he says, will be based on substance.

"He's the commander in chief. This is dereliction of duty. Just like a corporal or a sergeant, if they were in the field with the military unit and they didn't follow orders, that's dereliction of duty. This is dereliction of duty," O'Reilly said. "Does everybody get this? Biden's President, but he's also the commander in chief of the armed forces. So you can impeach on those grounds. Now, will he be convicted in the Senate? Probably not. But it'll be such a hammer blow to the country. The Trump impeachments were jokes. Everybody knew what that was. A setup by Pelosi on any grounds at all to embarrass Trump. This is much more serious because the numbers are there. The deaths are there. Verifiable. Not a phone call to Zelensky in Ukraine. This is people dying every day because their government will not stop the importation of deadly narcotics from Mexico. That's what this is, and that is why this is the story of the week."

Time will tell if Bill O'Reilly's prognostication proves true, and that the lack of border security will continue to mushroom as a focal issue for voters.

If he is correct, what we are seeing in May will become an even bigger catalyst in January.

May 30, 2022

Freedom From Media Anxiety

Have you ever felt like you needed a break from something destructive or toxic in your life?

A relationship? A substance? A cable television channel?

If you did feel that way, and if you were successful in putting that nasty habit aside, did you notice how much more relaxed and less anxious you felt?

Once you got over the initial jitters, headaches and tormenting dreams of Tucker Carlson, did you feel a wave of relaxation pouring over your body and mind?

The truth is, we all get ingrained into our routines and comfortable in our way of life. We surround ourselves, as much as possible, and often unconsciously, with like-minded people.

In our homes. In our jobs. In our living rooms. And on our televisions and smartphones.

We surround ourselves with those that think the way we think and, therefore, inherently make us feel good. More often, however, they make us feel angry or anxious about something we *don't* like.

We are *attracted* to what we like. We are *addicted* to what makes us angry. And the news media puppet masters know exactly how to pull those strings, as long as we allow their programming to penetrate our minds.

On a recent episode of his *Pathway to Victory Podcast,* titled "Moving From Anxiety to Peace," Dr. Robert Jeffress discussed why turning away from negative, addicting influences can help lower our stress levels and calm our minds.

"It's not the size of what you're worrying about that determines your anxiety level, it's what you're focusing on," Jeffress said. "You determine your focus in life, and (Saint) Paul said one important antidote to worry is making sure you're focusing on the right thing."

Jeffress, who has made countless appearances on cable television programs over the years, pointed out that we have an obligation to ourselves to carefully guard what material we allow into our daily lives.

"This is going to offend some of you, I know. And my goal is not to offend you," Jeffress warned. "I'm talking to you as your friend and pastor. But I have to say this. There are many Christians who are feeling anxious right now because they have got the wrong focus."

In Jeffress' opinion, the media has become a much-too-important influence in many peoples' lives.

"Can I tell you a secret? The media doesn't care one thing about your level of anxiety. They don't care about your peace of mind, they really don't. And I'm talking about the left-wing media and the right-wing media," Jeffress said. "They don't care about your peace of mind. They care about one thing - getting you to click on their website or getting you to watch their television program. That's all they care about. And they're constantly thinking, how can we get more viewers?"

As the old adage goes - *if it bleeds, it leads.*

"And they've discovered the secret," Jeffress continued. "They've discovered the secret is to either make you angry or to make you anxious. If they can do either one, they can get you to tune in."

"Make you angry. *They canceled Dr. Seuss! Dr. Seuss is canceled, oh my, oh my, oh my! What are we gonna do?*" Jeffress mocked. "Now look, I like Dr. Seuss. I don't believe in the cancel culture. I'm sorry they canceled Dr. Seuss, but I've got some great news for you if you're all worked up about that. The Gospel of Jesus Christ does not depend on the Cat in the Hat. Did you know that? Isn't that great news?"

If one can't relate to Jeffress' specific focus on Jesus, it would also be true to extrapolate and say your job doesn't depend on the Cat in the Hat. Neither does your health or your family's wellbeing. In the scope of what is truly important and lasting in life, this example of a media-propelled controversy probably doesn't make most peoples' list.

Giving up that afternoon coffee might be difficult, but it may lead to numerous health benefits. The same with ditching the smokes.

And occasionally quitting the news cold turkey, at least for a spell, can provide a healthy dose of peace and tranquility.

June 6, 2022

The Media's Oversized Influence on Financial Markets

In the era of non-stop news and endless financial tickers, we have more investment-related information at our fingertips than ever before. When a stock sneezes, we know it instantly, as our phone alert jolts us into ready position. We have access to more company and industry analysis than ever before, and we have it faster than anyone fifty years ago could have anticipated.

And that's exactly the problem.

Television host Charles Payne concluded Friday's episode of his Fox Business program, *Making Money with Charles Payne*, by sharing his opinion of today's financial markets. In his opinion, abundant, minute-by-minute information doesn't always lead to higher levels of investing success.

"The stock market is confusing in so many ways, and in large part it's that way by design," Payne began. "Think about this, there are so many ways of measuring value. There's all these exogenous reasons for stocks being up or being down that often don't really have anything to do with the stock itself, or even the industry itself."

Perhaps Payne was referring to Tesla CEO Elon Musk, who's leaked emails laid out his company's plans to lay off 10% of salaried employees. In addition, Musk wants employees to report to work on location, rather than continue working from home. Tesla's stock dropped more than 9% on Friday, presumably as investors got the news-induced jitters. They received the news rapidly, and in turn reacted just as quickly.

Is it possible that type of news would never have hit investors' eyes or ears in bygone eras? And assuming shareholders did find out, it's possible that the trickling-out of information would not have the same quick impact on the stock's share price compared to everyone being deluged at the same time on their devices.

As a side note, regarding the substance of Musk's plan, wasn't the late business titan, Jack Welch, extremely successful in part due to his implementation of the same strategy? Wasn't it a net positive for his shareholders? And could that portend leaner and more profitable days for Tesla, as the company aims to fight through the difficult economic environment America has battled through during the Biden years?

In other words, do the hysteria, reactionary tweets and hot takes that have bombarded traditional media and the socials in the few days since Musk's emails became public match the reality of the announcement?

"A few decades ago, all of this stuff didn't matter as much because the average holding period was five or six years," Payne noted. "Now it's less than five or six months, and I gotta tell you something. Under the right conditions, like the whipsaws we're seeing these days, the holding period could be like five or six days. Wouldn't surprise me if it was actually five or six hours soon."

Payne brought up a recent report from Morningstar, titled *U.S. Stocks are Trading at a Rarely Seen Discount.*

He quoted from the article, saying *"Even with the market's bounce, the selloff provides a chance to invest in significantly undervalued stocks. Since 2011, on a monthly basis, there have been only a few other instances in which the market has traded at such a large discount to our intrinsic valuation. The current level of undervaluation is the greatest discount to fair value since the emergence of the pandemic in March 2020 and the growth scare that sent stocks lower in December 2018."*

"I think it's a breath of fresh air. It's not just because it's bullish, but because they're talking about intrinsic value. Not the notion your portfolio should be down because of the next headline, or even down because there's some kind of temporary thing that's going to impact the value, but intrinsically what this thing is worth longer-term," Payne commented.

Payne knows what Warren Buffett knows and what Jack Bogle and Benjamin Graham knew. Strong, well-run companies with real value are a strategy for investing success.

Not that this is the *only* strategy. But Payne's point is that staying focused and undeterred when bait-clicky media headlines appear in your feed nonstop is a foundation for long term investing success. Put the blinders on, block out the noise and stick to your strategy with valuable companies.

"I get the idea of trying to beat the market every day. It makes for good TV," the sagacious Payne summed up. "But pace yourself. You've heard that a lot today. Pace yourself, because investing can be a lot more simplistic. Think about the intrinsic value, and that's what you should be focused on. Don't let these markets whipsaw you."

June 13, 2022

DeSantis Basking in the Media's Ire

The mainstream liberal media clearly has their next big target. And their efforts are creating a mutually-beneficial relationship.

For decades before he announced his run for the Presidency, Donald J. Trump was a media darling, using his money, charm and influence to keep the mainstream press, and their closely-related pop culture, tied around his finger.

The moment he decided to run for President as a Republican, and therefore against the vast majority of the media, he became their Enemy Number One. And among many factors, this media opposition was key in propelling Trump to the White House. With distrust in the media at an all-time high, Trump became a leader willing to tap into these deep sentiments widely held across America. In essence, the outright media antipathy toward Trump directly fueled his success.

And the media now have their next clearly-defined enemy in popular Florida Governor Ron DeSantis.

Last week, DeSantis lambasted the media as he defended his Press Secretary against what he called a "smear campaign." Taking a page from the former President's book, the well-liked Governor took verbal aim at the press, speaking up on behalf of the outspoken member of his team.

The situation unfolded after DeSantis' Press Secretary, Christina Pushaw, was accused in a Washington Post story as potentially violating the Foreign Agents Registration act after working for the former president of Georgia.

Fox News obtained a statement from Pushaw's attorney, Michael Sherwin, which read, *"Ms. Pushaw did volunteer work helping to advocate for former Georgian President Miikheil Saakashvili, a close ally of Ukrainian President Volodymyr Zelenskyy, and the need for free elections and democratic institutions in Georgia where she was living at the time. She was then paid for some of that work, totaling $25,000 over two years, which covered some of her living expenses. Her efforts included writing op-eds, reaching out to supporters and officials, and advocating on his behalf in Georgis and in the United States. The work ended in 2020. Ms. Pushaw was notified recently by the DOJ that her work on behalf of Mr. Saakashvili likely required FARA registration. Ms. Pushaw filed for the registration retroactively as soon as she was made aware."*

Regardless of the merits of the media charges against Pushaw, the situation quickly became a golden opportunity for DeSantis. In the mold of Trump, he wasted no time firing back. During an appearance in West Palm Beach, he said, "I am not deterred by any smear piece by these legacy media outlets. The only reason they're attacking her is because she does a great job and she's very effective at calling out their lies and their phony narratives."

Perhaps the media antipathy toward DeSantis and his team stems from his success. While Democratic governors shut down their states during the pandemic, DeSantis took the side of freedom, becoming the most active - both in terms of words and action - in keeping Florida open. His reliance was on the personal responsibility and choices of his citizenry, and the results have proven him correct. He has publicly fought back against the woke, extreme agendas of certain Florida groups and corporations. Low taxes, economic growth and great weather have additionally fueled the migration from more controlling Democrat-led states down to Florida. This success for the Sunshine State, especially as it has become more Republican-leaning, has seemingly enraged Democrats and their media allies.

DeSantis, like Trump before him, continued last week, using the recent flap to position himself firmly on the side of the people, against what he considers the corrupt media.

"Whenever they're smearing somebody, you know that person is over the target and they're scared of them. I would be much more concerned with my press secretary if the Washington Post was writing puff pieces about her. Then I would think something was wrong." DeSantis said, "I think what we need to understand is that these legacy D.C. and New York outlets – we don't care what you think anymore. We know you peddle narratives. We know you lie. We know you don't care about the facts. And so you can try to smear me or anyone in my administration all you want to. All that's going to do is embolden us to continue moving forward for the people in Florida."

The jockeying has obviously begun. The Post rightly sees the Governor as the heir apparent to Mr. Trump, and a likely member of a future Republican presidential ticket. In other words, the liberal paper may be staking their claim early and reserving their prime seat in opposition to the popular, conservative leader.

On the other hand, were they not merely reporting the news surrounding the recent development? Ms. Pushaw's registration undoubtedly qualifies as news, being that she is so closely tied to one of the most high-profile and successful politicians in the country. Most objective observers would agree with the reporting and illumination of the facts surrounding her past work and how it may, or may not, have any influence regarding the work she currently does for the Governor of Florida.

Perhaps the likeliest scenario is that both parties - the liberal newspaper and the conservative Governor - are using the development to further endear themselves to their audience. DeSantis rightly knows his base of everyday citizens harbors growing distrust of the mainstream media. All recent polling confirms this trend across America.
So it becomes a wise political maneuver for the Republican leader to harness this distrust and use the opportunity to speak out against a media mob that Americans increasingly see as, at best, not representing their best interests.

And conversely, the Post understands that their readership skews heavily leftward, with their consumers largely preferring the Democratic policy positions. Their consumers delight when they attack Republicans.

Both sides get what they want and can claim the high ground. They each win and solidify their standing within their sphere of influence. A classic case of a Win-Win scenario.

Brats to Get a November Beating

The jackanapes are going to get what's coming to them. They don't listen. They always talk back. They think they are always right and when proven wrong they refuse to accept correction. Simply put, they just don't behave.

And in November, the Democrat brats are going to get an electoral beating, based on their mismanagement of America's economy.

This was the overarching message, albeit not as harshly-delivered, from Fox Business host David Asman last week.

During a Fox News appearance on *America's Newsroom*, where he spoke about the languishing economy, Asman opined that the Democrats have caused utter economic destruction to the country. And after a year of equivocation and word games with the public regarding inflation, Democrats are finally being forced to answer for their actions.

"The expectations have less to do with it than the reality of what's been happening," Asman began. "Inflation is too much money chasing what? Too few goods. We're not producing enough, it's that simple. That's why we have stagflation. It's not just inflation. It's a slowdown in the economy."

After the economy contracted in the first quarter of the year, many experts are expecting it to do the same in Q2, thus crossing the threshold to become an official recession.

"The answer to both, stagnation and inflation, is the same. Produce more goods," the measured Asman said. "Instead, Biden is beating up on the producers. He's beating up on the oil producers. He's beating up on meat producers. Anything. He's beating up on the producers. He should be incentivizing more production in the United States, by lowering tax rates even more and by getting deregulation. Instead, he's increasing regulation talk."

Asman said one clear way to jumpstart the economy would be to incentivize people to go back to work, rather than living off government subsidies that began during the pandemic.

"Joe Biden extended that long beyond the point in which it was necessary, if it was ever necessary to do that," he told hosts Dana Perino and Bill Hemmer. "You know, Elon Musk said about a recession, he said maybe it's a good thing. Americans are so used to not working, not working hard at full pace, that a recession might shake the tree, might shake them and wake them up, and wake the economy back up again. Instead we have this sleepy economy prodded on by exactly the wrong economic policies."

Indeed, Musk has made his opinions known recently. The lifetime Democrat says he's started voting Republican because of how radical and extreme the current Democratic party has become. Just this past weekend he commented that when the White House deliberately excluded Tesla from an EV summit, while at the same time inviting the United Auto Workers union, that "tells you everything you need to know." He also said that Joe Biden's praise of General Motors, and not Tesla, for leading the EV revolution was "next level insanity."

On a related note, many pundits have become more vocal in recent months, voicing their assumption that the push to increase gas prices over $5 per gallon has been a planned, deliberate effort, aimed at forcing drivers to transition to electric vehicles. And as gas prices skyrocket, food prices are creating financial fear across kitchen tables in many American households.

Asman finished the Fox News segment by pointing out that only West Virginia Democratic Senator, Joe Manchin, stood between his party and trillions more in wasteful spending.

"You go back to December and November of last year, and you look at what they were saying about Joe Manchin, how he was a traitor to the cause and feeding into the progressives' line that you could print money until the end of time without having any inflation. It was B.S.," Asman said. "It was kind of like these spoiled kids in the Upper West Side of Manhattan. I'm going to do a Greg Gutfeld analogy. You know, where you see these mothers that are indulging their children. Oh, it's all right. Oh, look at that. Oh, honey, don't kick that old woman in the knee. And they were indulging the young progressives who don't know a thing about the economy. And eventually they went a step too far, and they bought into the whole plan, whether it was in spending or in the Federal Reserve. And the house has burned down as a result of indulging these brats."

With the leader of their party, the President of the United States, historically unpopular with an approval rating in the 30's, the brats appear headed for a pretty brutal spanking come November.

June 27, 2022

Financial Media Finds an Example on the Hardcourt

On a recent episode of The Dave Ramsey Show, co-hosts George Kamel and Rachel Cruze discussed a story that intersected the pop culture world and financial news.

And they used one of the most polarizing athletes of our day to make their point.

According to a report from CBS News, basketball star Lebron James has officially become the first player to reach billionaire status while still in his playing days.

Kamel quoted the article, saying "After another monster year of earnings, totalling $121.2 million, before takes and agents fees over the last twelve months, Forbes estimates he's officially become a billionaire while still playing hoops."

James has both large numbers of admirers and detractors, often stemming from the argument over who is basketball's Greatest of All-Time, or G.O.A.T. Some say James, while others point to Michael Jordan.

In addition, James has waded purposefully into the political waters, as an outspoken supporter of Democratic politicians and their liberal policies. Many feel these policies hurt the very people James supports in so many other ways.

During the show, Kamel and Cruze continued discussing the article, which estimated the net worth of the hardcourt legend to be $1 billion. It quoted James as saying the milestone is an important one because he wants to maximize his business.

"He's commanded more than a $385 million salary from the Cavaliers, Miami Heat and Lakers, as the NBA's highest-paid active player," Kamel continued, quoting the article. "And off the court, to your point Rachel, he's raked in upwards of $900 million in income from endorsements and other business ventures. So he's a very smart businessman on top of being an incredible athlete."

"Kinda like Michael Jordan," Cruze added.

"So, here's the funny thing," Kamel said. "This isn't just why I wanted to talk about this. Yes he's a billionaire, that's an amazing milestone. And it's a thousand millions for those of you that need to get that picture in your head. But my favorite thing about this story is that he is known as the cheapest player in the NBA."

The show then cut to an audio clip of former NBA star Dwyane Wade, referring to James as "the cheapest guy in the NBA." James listed a few extras he's just not willing to pay for, such as data roaming, phone apps or commercial free streaming music.

"Let's be clear, LeBron James is not living in a shack. He's got a nice house, I'm sure he's got nice cars. He's done really well," Kamel joked. "But it's amazing to me the things he goes, I'm not paying three bucks for that."

"Hey, do you know who else who is not a billionaire, but listens to Pandora with commercials," Cruze asked.

"Rachel Cruz!" Kamel answered.

"I'm basically like LeBron," she quipped.

"I want to make it clear, LeBron James is not a cheapskate. In fact he's very, very generous," Kamel made sure to note. "And there's maybe a connection there, maybe you can speak to this. This is another article from CBS News. Lebron says he's opening a multi-million dollar medical facility in his Ohio hometown. He's built the I Promise School in his hometown in Ohio. He's pledged to send 2300 students to college debt-free through scholarships. So to me, I just go, this guy has a plan for his money. He's got a vision for where he wants it to go."

Cruze agreed, discussing the mental approach and discipline needed to make such a large financial impact.

"It's not the Pandora subscription that's going to make you a billionaire. That is not it. But it's a mindset too, of seeing what's wasteful, what's not. And it's the same ways of looking at life that really could lead you, I mean that kind of stuff can play into his business deals. Where he's like, hmmm, what am I doing. It's that same thought process that really can make you become successful."

Ramsey Solutions has preached for years the necessity of devising a plan for your money and then following it, rather than simply doing what feels good. They have always been strict adherents to a budget, regardless of how much one has flooding in on the income side of the equation. They also talk extensively about being a good steward and becoming incredibly generous along your journey.

Apparently, LeBron James shares many of the same deeply-held values.

"It's wisdom with money," Kamel added.

"LeBron, well done," Cruze summed up.

July 4, 2022

Media Fed Up With Biden and His Party

Frustration, toward the President and his fellow Democrats, is running hotter than ever.

Gas prices remain historically high. The stock market is tanking. American families are having a tougher time affording groceries and other necessities. This year's Independence Day cookout will cost considerably more than last years.

All at a time when the President and his party insist this is part of the plan to return the country to prosperity. Some even say these are necessary steps toward a new "liberal world order."

And now, added to this list are the Left's vitriolic reactions to the spate of recent Supreme Court decisions. Democrats are raging, angry that coaches can pray. Angry that babies can live. Angry with the notion that elected representatives of the people must create policy, rather than unelected bureaucrats.

But conservative, traditional media is where these waters have been boiling over for almost two years. And no talk radio host has been more outspoken than "The Great One," Mark Levin.

Levin began Friday's program, as he often has done over the last 18 months, by listing off a checklist of what he feels are the President's failures.

"Joe Biden has gone a long way in destroying our economy. Destroying our immigration system. Destroying women's sports. Destroying our currency. And destroying our national security," Levin began, pulling no punches. "And now he's trying to destroy the United States Supreme Court from the Office of the President."

One of Levin's most widely-acclaimed books is the 2005 title *Men in Black, How the Supreme Court is Destroying America*, which "dissects the judicial tyranny that is robbing us of our freedoms and stuffing the ballot box in favor of liberal policies."

A new court, thanks largely to the nominations of President Donald Trump, has led to a new outlook from Levin.

"The Democrat Party, in all of its manifestations, whether it's the Oval Office, Congress and the media, are now trying to destroy the Supreme Court of the United States. It had its way with the Supreme Court of the United States for 80 years. But it lost three decisions, and now it wants to burn it down."

Levin went on to point out how, in his opinion, the Left will do absolutely whatever is necessary to maintain power. He relied on recent news developments that, for whatever reason, the mainstream media has mostly avoided reporting.

"And let me be very blunt about this, they don't even care if a Justice is assassinated. Because even to this day, the seven Democrats on the January 6th committee, the Speaker of the House, and the Democrat Leader in the Senate, have said all but nothing about the plot to assassinate Kavanaugh," Levin noted. "And instead they continue to use rhetoric that incites violence. They didn't say peacefully and patriotically protest. They're calling the court illegitimate. Extremist. Rogue. Stealing rights from women. And the like."

The host then played a cut of President Joe Biden, divisively fanning the flames.

"I'm joined by a group of Democratic Governors. We work closely to protect women's rights, after this tragic reversal of Roe v Wade," Biden said. "The terrible, extreme decision, in my view, upending lives and impacting the health and safety of millions of women."

"No it doesn't," Levin interjected. "How does it do that? You're there with Democrat Governors. Democrat Governors. Do they not run their states?"

The clip of Biden continued, with the President saying, "Outrage that this extremist court has committed to moving America backward."

"Ok so his writers have said extremist court. Extreme decision. Go ahead," Levin mocked, as he proceeded to the next part of the President's comments.

"Fewer rights, less autonomy. And politicians invading the most personal decisions that, not only women, but you'll find if they expend, expand on…."

"Alright, you're rambling on like the moron that you are," Levin said, ending the clip of Biden. "But you were a moron before you couldn't put three words together. Notice how they keep talking about women now. Women. Women. What's a woman? Women. Women. They hate women. And they hate their children. They hate the children of women. Trying to brainwash them in our schools, if they ever get there. They're not for women, and they're not for babies and they're not for children. Let's be blunt. And let's be even more blunt - what this party supports is infanticide! Hello! Infanticide! That's what the Democrat Party supports."

The host then said 49 Democrats in the Senate voted for infanticide in February, and that all but one of two Democrats voted for infanticide in the House.

"The media supports infanticide," Levin, the author of the 2021 bestselling book, *American Marxism*, said. "Chuck Todd. Fake Tapper. Jeffrey "Keep Your Pants On" Toobin. I guess we should call him Rocket Man now Mr. Producer. But you understand my point ladies and gentlemen."

If the past two years are any indication, Levin and other talk radio hosts will continue to find ample material to exemplify what they perceive as failures of the current president and his political party.

July 11, 2022

Van Susteren Captures Both Horrors and Kindness Amid Ukrainian War

Believe it or not, there are amazing signs of goodness emanating from amid the violence and strife in Ukraine. The situation remains dire. Many people are suffering beyond comprehension.

But hidden among the dreadful conditions, there are some glimmering sights of hope. Signs that the American spirit - more precisely the *human* spirit - is alive and well.

Greta Van Susteren spent an hour on Friday to document both the horror of war and efforts by one of the greatest humanitarian groups in the world today.

Van Susteren opened Friday's special episode of her Newsmax TV program, *The Record,* from the cabin of a cargo airplane, headed to the region along the border of Ukraine and Poland. The plane, owned by Franklin Graham's Samaritan's Purse, has made the journey more than 20 times since the conflict began in February.

Samaritan's Purse, Graham's international humanitarian aid organization, has gone to the aid of the world's sick, poor and suffering for over 50 years.

"Tonight, I'm going to do something special," Van Susteren began. "I'm not going to tell you about an international relief organization. I'm not going to tell you about Ukrainian refugees. I'm actually going to bring you along on a journey. I'm going to show you what an international relief organization like Samaritan's Purse does to help people. And I'm going to bring you along to meet Ukrainian refugees, people who have lost everything. They've lost their homes, they've been reduced to rubble. And they are fleeing a war to their new home, which is going to be in Toronto, Canada."

Van Susteren began the show with the plane's cargo area stocked full with medical supplies and clothing, which would be distributed to field hospitals upon arrival. The return trip from the border of Poland would carry many refugees looking to escape the horrors of war.

The host continued her program, featuring an interview with the Christian humanitarian group's Vice President of Operations, Edward Graham.

"God brings us the best people that want to serve Him. And it's just not the doctors and nurses that go. Like you say, we have to supply that. So we have companies, organizations that help us and that sometimes it's gifted to us. But we also have to purchase a lot of it," Edward Graham explained, detailing where his group acquires the resources and supplies so desperately needed by the refugees. "We have the best logistics people out scouring the globe, getting this material. And it's hard right now, during a pandemic, with the war going on, gathering this stuff, but they're doing an incredible job."

The planes have been loaded and prepared for each trip by volunteers and load masters in Greensboro, North Carolina. The supplies are then offloaded by members of the Samaritan's Purse Disaster Assistance Response Team when the plane lands about an hour outside of Krakow, Poland. The supplies are then shipped across the border, to those waiting in Ukraine.

As they have done in other conflicts around the world, the group has also helped supply and start temporary field hospitals, to serve those in need of medical attention in and around the war.

Van Susteren also detailed the emotional, human aspect of the current conflict, with discussions about bombings, attacks and families doing their best just to survive.

"We didn't have any light. We didn't have bread to eat. We didn't have water to drink," a female refugee told Van Susteren. "We know how the bombings look like. We know how helicopters attack. We know how it sounds. We were lying on the floor, myself with my children and their kids, my grandkids. The windows would just be broken, everything would be destroyed. It was super hard and scary. We were terrified."

The refugee said that after retiring following 42 years of work, she had to escape, carrying only one small bag and her passport.

"What I have is on me right now," she told Van Susteren. "We don't have any plans because we don't have a place to go to. We are very confused."

"You talk to these people who have lost everything, knowing that this is something that you could never experience yourself. And you meet them, and they tell you these stories about their families are destroyed, their homes are destroyed," Van Susteren noted, capturing the gravity of the situation. "And you end these interviews, or you end these conversations, and what do you say to them? I'm sorry? Or, good luck? Anything you say seems so inappropriate, because they have lost everything."

The episode provided viewers the chance to peek behind the curtain at the devastatingly bad, and unseen good, that is currently taking place amid the violence of war.

Rising Star Offers Perspective on the State of Journalism

When two of the country's brightest minds collaborated recently, the conversation morphed into an engaging, informative discussion about a seemingly unrelated topic.

It was less about Bitcoin, as initially intended, and more about the underbelly of the television news business. So informative and enlightening was the hour-long episode, that any aspiring television news journalist should take note.

Natalie Brunell recently hosted Aubrey Strobel on her *Coin Stories* podcast, and the two discussed Bitcoin, the crypto industry, public relations and their college years. But perhaps most interesting was their in-depth discussion about the challenging, and often pernicious, side of the television news business.

Before transitioning to the main topic of the program, the promise and future of Bitcoin, Strobel explained how a girl from New Mexico ended up living in New York City.

"I actually came out here, because my Mom, it was for journalism. Back in the day I was in the Roger Ailes reporter program, before Roger Ailes was taken down," Strobel, host of the new show, *The Aubservation*, said. "I basically lived the movie Bombshell, if anyone's seen the movie Bombshell. I was living that when I came to New York."

After graduating from New Mexico State University, Strobel faced the dilemma confronted by many aspiring journalists - whether to begin in a large or small market.
The question is not a small one for graduating professionals looking to make their mark.

A large market may provide connections, however the prospects for rapid advancement may be limited with one's lack of experience. At the same time, a small market may offer opportunity, albeit with meager pay and relative obscurity.

"I had offers to go and work in these smaller markets" Strobel told Brunell. "Because you know you never go to a number one market. New York City for a journalism degree, after college, is unheard of. You never do that. But this program for Fox, my Mom wanted me to apply."

While providing a springboard for Strobel, the Fox program was about to undergo a major change. On August 5th, 2016, TheWrap.com wrote that Fox News would drop Ailes' name from the apprentice program.

"The Ailes Apprentice Program will now be called the Fox News Apprentice Program. Ailes, who stepped down amid a sexual harassment investigation, started the program and named it after himself back in 2003," Brian Flood wrote for The Wrap. *"The program recruits and develops diverse talent who are given a salary and training for their careers. Several past graduates have gone on to work at Fox News. The minority journalist program is in its 12th class and the current group is scheduled to finish in November."*

In her opinion, the time during which Strobel began this phase of her news media career was considerably different than it is today.

"This was also before Fox was like, not that it's different now, it's just a different climate in terms of political reporting," Strobel said. "This was before the election. It was a little bit more, I think they've moved a little bit more opinion based, but all of these networks have. Every single one. It was just more covering the election cycle, which I was really excited about the opportunity to do."

When her time in the apprentice program ended, Strobel decided to remain in New York, rather than to begin in a smaller market.

"I know that lifestyle, because I worked my way up from a little, tiny market to a big one," said Brunell, who's early career was also in television news journalism. "My first market was Palm Springs, but I visited so many more. It was great because it was like the backyard of Los Angeles and I was with a great station and all of it. But it was market 150, and that's where you start. You're making no money, you're covering a little bit of everything. I looked at stations in different states such as Texas and Missouri, and this and that, but I was really excited to start in Palm Springs. But a lot of people, especially if they interned in, let's say, a big city like New York City, they have to make that decision like, should I stay and work kind of in the network or behind the scenes, or do I go to one of these tiny markets that may or may not even have an airport?"

The daughter of two teachers who taught on the Navajo reservation in northern Arizona, Strobel always felt that journalism was a natural fit for her talents, background and interests.

"I really, really just always loved politics. And because my Dad is an American History teacher, it was just something that felt important," Strobel said. "And I really also loved Clarissa Ward from CNN. She covers wartorn situations, Syria, Libya. I was following all of her coverage and I thought it was so amazing, and sort of heroic that she was putting herself on the line in a way, and serving."

Strobel has seen the evolution in the news media business over the last decade, since she began her career.

"I just think content has changed and storytelling has changed. The way we're even having this conversation right now," she told Brunell over the remote connection. "And I saw that trend happening too, back then. I saw news networks like Cheddar pop up, which you probably saw too. Things were going more digital, and you could have a voice and talk about these things that were important to you and that mattered, without being on *Good Morning America* and being an anchor."

Not that the traditional media was altogether bad, but today's news consumer simply has different needs and preferences.

"Yeah, it has all the, like, credentials and, you know, validation and people love watching that show, but actually the generation shift of Millennials and Gen Z, they're not consuming news from *Good Morning America*. They're just not," Strobel said. "Everyone's talked about news has been dying for years, but it wasn't even how I consumed my news any more. So I felt like you can have a voice and an impact and tell stories, but it doesn't have to be for, you know, Fox, *Good Morning America, Today Show*, whatever. But I did love *The Today Show* growing up, so that would have been great."

"It's so interesting, because the change in the industry happened so quickly, between when I was young and when I went to college and graduated, the technology shift and social media coming out and all of the sudden everything's digital, and you're a one-man-band instead of having a crew. Everything changed," Brunell, who has embraced those changes to become one of the most eloquent voices on the emergence of Bitcoin, agreed.

A twin from Gallup, New Mexico, Strobel found that her time in the apprentice program taught her what television news was really all about. She said every other woman there "looked stunning" and "everyone was gorgeous," and much of her time was devoted to changing outfits, fake eyelashes and gobs of makeup.

"We both know that broadcast does care about what you look like. Fox cares about what you look like," Strobel said, detailing stories about having her wardrobe changed because she didn't have the correct look. "And they also put so much makeup. I mean, I did not even look like the Fox-i-fied look. There's a whole thing that they do. And at the end of the day, Fox is selling an image. They're selling a person and a brand and the people that work there. And so it was a moment where I did question, was I here because I'm talented, I'm smart and I'm good at reporting?"

Based on their enlightening conversation, Brunell and Strobel agree on much. They both hold tight to the ideals of principled journalism, and used those standards to fuel the early stages of their careers.

Both believe journalism has evolved, but that it should always hold true to the noble precepts that initially attracted them, and continue to attract others, to the industry.

And while much of their conversation was devoted to the changing news media business, they both agree that Bitcoin has bright days ahead. A future that, quite similarly in their opinion, offers so much good to so many people around the world.

Mike Lindell Still Pursuing 2020 Election Truth

If you thought the ink was dry and the door was shut on the alleged cheating scandal related to the 2020 Presidential Election, think again.

In many respects, it may only just be beginning.

Late last week, a federal judge in Arizona heard arguments related to the dependability and corruptibility of electronic voting machines. The hearing was part of a lawsuit brought forth by Kari Lake, the Republican who is surging in her candidacy for governor in the state, and Republican Secretary of State candidate, Mark Finchem. The two are suing the Arizona Secretary of State's office, saying that voting machines simply cannot be trusted.

As the hearings were taking place Thursday, entrepreneur and entertainer, Mike Lindell, joined RSBN's Brian Glenn to discuss the issue.

"It's a big breakthrough, it really is," he told Glenn. "This is a preliminary injunction to get rid of the machines. Remember, January 9th is when I got the full blown evidence out that it was all machines with the bigger numbers. Obviously now we have *2000 Mules*, all the other kinds of cheating. But if we don't get rid of the machines, we lose our country. It's as simple as that."

Lindell, the iconoclastic CEO of My Pillow, has been on a very public mission to uncover the truth since multiple irregularities have surfaced related to the election results.

RSBN has been one of the few media outlets allowing their hosts to voice independent, non-mainstream thought regarding the 2020 Election results, and also to unabashedly voice their support and advocacy for President Trump.

Lindell has indeed been a vocal Trump supporter, who says it should be a non-partisan issue to foster clean, accurate, unassailable elections.

"This was a different kind of evidence. It was showing that all machines, no matter what brand, it doesn't matter what brand they are. They are all either A, they can make mistakes, such as in Georgia. This primary a couple months ago. Three Democrats, she got zero votes in her own precinct. Now call it a cheat or whatever, they shoulda gave her at least two votes, her and her husband. But they didn't," Lindell said. "Let's say it was what Brad Raffensberger called it, because they found three thousand, seven hundred some votes. They found the votes, they say, and it put her from third to first."

As of this weekend, the full, detailed conversation between Lindell and Glenn could be viewed at RSBNetwork.com.

Lindell said the main theory behind his activism on behalf of President Trump was actually brought up during last week's arguments.

"When one person can hit a button and take millions of votes. The other way, with paper and hand count, millions upon millions of people would all have to be a big cabal and cheat together and go 'come on, they're not going to notice us all cheating.' And that's where it becomes basically an impossibility of this kind of....we're in another era," Lindell said. "It's kind of like this. If you're a teller at a bank and you're stealing any cash or any kind of money, how much can you take as one person? Under camera, how much can you take, physical money? Or how much can you take if you hack into the system and go, blip blip? That's it. That's where we're at."

Glenn referred to the testimony of a witness from Alabama, who said he hacked voting machines in five minutes "despite what the experts say."

Lindell recalled an incident from the Cyber Symposium he hosted last August, which delved deeper into electronic voting integrity.

"We had all the cyber guys there, from all parts of the country, all parts of the world. We were doing a mock election with the machines in the other room," Lindell recalled. "We had it all set up Brian. We went to do the mock election and somebody hacked in from the table out in the main floor in less than five minutes. We had to do a complete reset!"

On Friday evening's RSBN broadcast, preceding President Trump's rally speech in Prescott, Arizona, Lindell said Biden's questionable win in 2020 will be seen as a long-term blessing-in-disguise. He told Glenn and co-host Christina Bobb that only because of that outcome, and the myriad of inconsistencies it brought forth, are Americans now able to see the true, untrustworthy underbelly of mechanized voting across the country.

Indeed, a Rasmussen poll from late last year showed that a whopping 56% of voters feel that cheating had an effect on Joe Biden's victory over Donald Trump in 2020.

As Lindell dined Thursday evening with Lake, one can imagine the two discussing the possible steps they could take to protect election integrity should she become the nominee and win the state's governorship in November.

"No matter what happens, this is a start," Lindell said, noting that last week was just the 2nd judge to date who has looked at evidence related to alleged voting machine irregularities. "I've said it before everybody. The judges are gonna help bring back our country."

Millions of Americans sympathetic to Lindell's views may feel that this modern subset of leaders, activists, politicians and media voices will also play a crucial role.

August 1, 2022

Political Polling: Cream Rising to the Top?

It's that time of the political cycle again.

They face off against each other, trying to prove who really has the pulse of the American electorate.

And on Election Day, voters will finally determine who is right, and who is wrong.

And by *they*, we don't mean the politicians.

We mean the pollsters.

With primary season in full swing, major national pollsters have stepped into their cyclical period of prominence, trying to predict - or for some, shape - the trend of electoral opinion.

Among the most accurate in recent years have been Rasmussen Reports and the Trafalgar Group, to name just a couple. But the most ubiquitous, via his online weekly programming and various news media appearances, has been Richard Baris and his Big Data Poll.

Baris, "The People's Pundit," hosts weekly YouTube programs, occasionally with renowned attorney and political analyst, Robert Barnes. He has appeared on national news programs, with hosts such as Tucker Carlson, as well as with more regular spots with Steve Bannon's *War Room*, and others.

With all eyes looking toward November's Election Day, the Big Data Poll has already resumed its position as a frontrunner, giving an electoral snapshot heading into August 2nd's primaries.

For example, two weeks ago Baris released his Arizona statewide polls, showing considerable, and growing, leads, for GOP Senate primary candidate, Blake Masters, and GOP Gubernatorial primary canidate, Kari Lake. His data showed Lake leading by 17 and Masters by 13.

And for being first with these developing snapshots, Baris was roundly derided and dismissed in many mainstream political circles.

But just a week later, many outlets are now coming to the same conclusion as the Big Data Poll.

On Friday, the headline for Laurie Roberts' opinion piece for the Arizona Republic read, "Kari Lake, Blake Masters and Mark Finchem are all surging toward victory. Democrats cheer." The piece detailed the recent surge by both candidates. The same surge that was picked up early by Baris, and simultaneously disbelieved by most analysts.

Roberts wrote Friday, "What was a 39-31 split in early July is now 51-33, according to the OH Predictive Insights poll, a combination of live callers and text. That resembles several other independent polls released in recent days. I didn't believe them. Until now." To her credit, she based her outlook on the emerging trend, first picked up by Baris.

On Friday, Rasmussen also released polls also showing similar leads for the duo - Masters by 12 in his GOP Senate primary race, and Lake by nine in her primary for Arizona Governor.

And just a day earlier, Trafalgar Group showed Masters up by eight and Lake by nine. Each of these reputable polls verifying what Big Data Poll had shown a week earlier.

Baris began last week's program by taking a victory-lap of sorts.

"I just want to say before I start this, that you might have noticed Doug Ducey's own pollster. Just all the abuse last week I took with that poll, and Doug Ducey's own pollster just came out. And so far I've just seen the Governors. I'm sure it says the same thing with the Senate if they're polling that as well. But the fact of the matter is, the CD Media Poll definitely had Kari Lake leading, and our next guest (Blake Masters) leading."

Regarding Arizona Governor, Doug Ducey, Baris was apparently referring to a newly-released Data Orbital poll out of Arizona, which also showed Lake leading by 11 over Karrin Taylor Robson.

When political writer, David Catanese, tweeted the final @OHPredictive polls before this week's primaries, which also showed Lake leading by 18 and Masters by 15, Baris tweeted, "Damn that looks familiar. Looks like our final interviews. That's rather remarkable."

The Big Data Poll has been correct with most of its polling over recent years. In 2020, he was correct in calling Florida and Ohio as big blowout states in favor of President Trump. He was also cautious, stopping short of saying the President would carry Nevada, Minnesota or New Hampshire. His data also showed Trump would do well in Georgia and Arizona. Regarding those two electoral outcomes, both Baris and Barnes shared hours of analysis in the months that followed the 2020 election.

"I'm not being arrogant here. I don't want it to come across as arrogance. It's just that this happens every time," Baris said with a laugh. "I release a poll, this is the way it is, this is what we're finding. And there's always these critics that say, 'oh no Lake does not lead by that much. Blake Masters is not winning by that much.' Ok, whatever."

Baris has spent countless hours over the past few years, detailing the shortcomings of the current polling industry - from their methods to their agendas. He has often detailed the difference between reputable pollsters, whose goal is to take an accurate snapshot of public opinion, versus those groups that incorrectly skew their samples or simply build a model based on flawed surveys. He also notes that as much as *who* you poll and how you weigh the samples, it is crucial to examine *how* you ask the question.

On last week's program, he specifically cited certain data-collecting methods as being better than others. Specifically, he said that, faced with a months-long pandemic shutdown, many people signed up for internet polls and panels out of pure boredom. These people, Baris says, now make up a much higher percentage of online polls and surveys, dramatically skewing the results.

"A lot of these people are just really high interest voters, and they don't represent the entire electorate," Baris said. "So these consumer panels are really blowing the metro vote way too, it's way too much in the sampling."

On Saturday, Baris tweeted, "It's just crystal clear at this point that certain pollsters have no interest in correcting their repeated failures."

Over the years, Baris' *People's Pundit Daily* and *What Are The Odds, with Baris and Barnes* programs have become YouTube staples for political junkies and data nerds alike. Master classes in statistical analysis, demographic trends and trending political issues.

Last week, Baris also made a few additional predictions based on his mid-year polling and gauge of the current electoral mood.

Number one - Kari Lake is the early favorite to win the race for Governor of Arizona, regardless of the mainstream media narrative that she is "unelectable."

Number two - in a break from the popular media narrative, his surveys found that those supporting the overturning of Roe vs. Wade are 10% more "certain to vote" than those opposing it.

And number three - Donald Trump and Ron DeSantis would be an "unbeatable ticket" en route to Republicans re-capturing the White House in 2024.

This week, we will see how Big Data's polling holds up during the primaries. And over the next few months, and couple years, viewers will watch Baris' programming to see if his results remain predictive of our nation's most crucial races and issues.

Calling Out the Inflation Shell Game

If anyone doubted Will Cain's ability to jump from sports media back into news, the past two years have laid those questions aside.

The Fox News host has fully hit his stride and shown the versatility network executives knew they were getting when they brought him to the network roughly two years ago.

Cain filled in for Tucker Carlson on Friday evening's *Tucker Carlson Tonight* and, as is his style, he wasted exactly zero minutes making his opinions known.

"If you want to know what is in a bill in Congress, and what it's actually going to do, take a good look at the name of the bill. Whatever it is, you can be sure the legislation will do the exact opposite," Cain began. "The American Recovery and Reinvestment Act of 2009, for example. It led to the worst economic recovery this country had seen since World War 2."

Cain referred next to the "Marketplace Fairness Act," which he said is nothing more than an internet sales tax, which helps bigger players "price out smaller competitors."

"So we should all be very nervous. Very, very concerned, that Congress just passed something called the 'Inflation Reduction Act.' It mandates hundreds of millions of new dollars in spending that will increase the money supply in this country," Cain told his viewers. "That will, in turn, devalue the currency. And that, in turn, will cause more inflation. That's basic supply and demand."

Relying on the basics, Cain believes the real-world results matter far more than any fancy title, talking point or political spin. More money printing equals more inflation. Two quarters of negative GDP equals a recession. Higher gas prices equals less money left over in Americans' pockets.

"Life is already so expensive in this country that we literally have bread lines in major cities," he said, cutting to a segment where Camden, New Jersey residents said they couldn't even afford rice and beans. "That's America. And that's happening all across America, and you have to wonder, why then is the Biden Administration devaluing money when we have bread lines?"

True enough, political leaders of both parties have fired up the money printer to go Brrrrrrr for decades, and there is plenty of blame to be shared by any politician unwilling to make the necessary, but tough, choices. In this instance, however, many feel it is ridiculous to cite global warming as the impetus for heaping more economic pain on middle and lower-income Americans.

"Well, their justification for the bill is that it will stop the climate from changing. That's why the bill includes 50 billion dollars in subsidies for electric vehicle purchases, which by the way will lead manufacturers to jack up the price of electric vehicles. We've learned that lesson from healthcare subsidies and subsidies for college tuition," Cain pointed out. "There's also billions of dollars for the postal service to buy new mail trucks that don't pollute as much. And of course there's 100 billions dollars for the so-called renewable industry."

Cain then explained how China, while at the forefront of the "renewables" industry, continues to see annual carbon dioxide emissions increase, while the United States has experienced a steady decline in such emissions over the past couple decades. In his opinion, "China wants the rest of the world to run on so-called renewables but China doesn't want renewables for themselves." He pointed out the financial and strategic benefits to China when Western countries "sabotage their own energy supply in the name of protecting the climate."

"Like any good dealer, they don't get high on their own supply, and most Americans recognize that," Cain said, referring then to a recent poll by Rasmussen. "People in this country care about, of course, things like inflation, the economy, crime, immigration. By contrast, most Americans recognize the media is far more interested in pushing false narratives about climate change."

Cain asks, where is the media drumbeat against China or India for their world-leading levels of emissions?

"Instead, the media blames Americans," Cain said, leading into footage of cable media hosts and analysts downplaying the pain caused by higher prices and monetary inflation.

Cain briefly highlighted the 80 billion dollars in the bill designated to grow the IRS, and wondered aloud "why do we need to make the IRS even more powerful, exactly?" He noted that the bill keeps the carried interest loophole, benefiting "wealthy individuals and institutions, in particular," along with "hedge fund managers, who are some of the Democratic party's biggest donors."

Will Cain believes inflation is real, and it is painful for most everyday Americans.
He also seems to believe the media, and their Democrat partners in Washington, don't seem to care or have any interest in leveling with citizens.

"What do Americans get out of the deal?" Cain asked. "Probably a lot more inflation, and a lot more audits."

August 15, 2022

Democrats Raise Taxes on Americans Again

With less than three months to go until a midterm election that most feel will strip Democrats of much of their congressional power, the Party decided now was the best time to push through a tax increase on Americans. Assumably, they figured voters will push back on their policies in November, so it was now or never to hit the gas on their tax and spend agenda.

On Saturday morning's episode of *Fox and Friends*, Fox News host David Asman began the program with a summation of why the recently-passed "Inflation Reduction Act" will soon have middle-class Americans in the financial crosshairs.

"Democrats passing new taxes in their huge spending bill on Friday. Now they say it will only hit people making more than $400,000 a year, but the Congressional Budget Office, CBO, says it will raise $20 billion from Americans earning below that amount, sometimes far below that amount," Asman opened.

Historians and economists alike have often noted that the income tax was originally designed to impact only high-earning taxpayers, before it gradually spread to lower-earning levels.

Karen Kerrigan, President of the Small Business and Entrepreneurship Council, joined the program to discuss her concerns about the ramifications of the tax hikes, which many feel will indeed hurt lower and middle-class income earners.

"When you're beefing up the IRS to the tune of $80 billion, and focusing those resources on compliance, and looking historically at who is audited the most, it is taxpayers of moderate means," she began. "As much as the President says, oh no no no no, we're not going to do that, and Secretary Yellen sending a memo to the IRS, saying you can't do this when you get this money. The fact of the matter is, there's going to be a lot of small businesses, a lot of taxpayers of moderate means who are going to be audited. And I will have to say, this is only one tax impact of this bill, David. If you look at the taxes on big corporations, this is going to have a downstream impact on many small businesses. Many small business suppliers. So this is a tax increase on all America."

Some have offered praise for the Inflation Reduction Act's tax credits and subsidies for energy efficient purchases and upgrades. Surely, tax credits for those purchasing costly electric vehicles are sure to be popular among wealthy drivers looking to land a new Tesla. The bill has been considered by many mainstream media voices to be the most aggressive "climate-related" legislation ever passed.

Others believe taxing Americans in the name of global warming amounts to nothing more than virtue signaling, having little or no effect on the Earth's temperature. Many economists have mused at the bill's inflation-reducing title, predicting it will actually increase inflationary pressure due to the additional increase in spending.

Asman juxtaposed the idea of Americans tightening their belts during the Biden-era stagflation - featuring skyrocketing prices for food, gas and other essentials - with the newly-passed bill, which increases the number of IRS agents six-fold.

"The Joint Taxation Committee, also a non-partisan group, found that 78 to 90 percent of the hits of the money that would be received as a result of supersizing the IRS would hit people making below $200,000," Asman said. "So that's way below the President's pledge."

Kerrigan went further, citing the JCT, saying those making $75,000 or less will contribute $20 billion of the increase in the bill.

"No one is saying that the IRS shouldn't have the resources that it needs to do its job, but there are a lot of problems that are plaguing the agency right now," Kerrigan said. "Small businesses are fair about this, but giving the IRS $80 billion, there are so many things broken over there, and specifically focus on compliance, again, specifically means that many small business taxpayers are going to be targeted. There is no doubt about that. Small businesses, self-employed and people of moderate means."

Asman noted that Republicans requested to add an amendment to the bill, "to keep the President to his word that this won't affect people below $400,000" per year.

Rather than give Americans that assurance, Democrats instead pushed the bill through without the amendment.

August 22, 2022

Secrets to Finding News Media Mentors

There is one particular ingredient in building a lasting career in news media that seems to be incredibly predictive of lasting success. If you do this one thing, you'll be off to a great start and you'll have a stronger foundation to jumpstart your career journey.

The secret ingredient? The ability to find and cultivate mentors.

In an industry such as media, with its unique challenges and pitfalls, the people you know are often more important than your talent, experience and media chops.

As the cliche goes, it can be WHO you know, rather than WHAT you know.

And at the beginning of your career, the WHOs you need are experienced professionals in the industry where you hope to eventually become an experienced professional. In other words, you need mentors.

The benefits of mentorship are plenty. A mentor can impart priceless information and advice that leads you in the best direction for career growth. They can answer your real-world questions to give you perspective and insight. Often, they can provide tips and tricks to help you avoid difficulties and sniff out opportunities not available to the masses.

In short, mentors can help you avoid mistakes, supercharge your news media career and advance much faster than you would have otherwise. And the best part - many successful news media professionals are willing and able, as time permits, to help the next generation of up-and-comers. In fact, sometimes the most successful are the most willing to share and help.

So if having mentors is such a crucial part of building a successful news media career, how does one go about finding such people?

Online radio host Dan Miller devoted a good portion of this weekend's program to discussing some key steps to finding a mentor. During his *48 Days to the Work You Love* podcast, Miller said a colleague named Tanner recently sent him the following five steps to finding a mentor and a better future.

Don't Seek a Relationship.

"Don't assume that somebody who you really want to have as a mentor is just going to be your best buddy and just hang out with you all the time," Miller said. "Don't come in with that expectation. Just see them as a teacher, where you want to share their wisdom. You want to learn from them and grow from them."

Ask for Work
Miller says "that may mean going to a workshop, going to a seminar, going to a conference, buying a book, buying a course. Those are the ways that you can ask for work and actually get the wisdom of the person."

Disappear
"Leave. Don't show up the next day," Miller, who has mentored countless career-seekers in his day, advises. "Go do something and then be able to come back."

Do The Work
"This tends to be the nail in the coffin for many," Tanner told Miller. "Unfortunately, we can't overnight our growth. We have to do the work. We have to lose ourselves in what the teacher asks us to do and then we have to do it. This is hard and this is where a lot of people get stuck."

Return and Report
Miller agrees with Tanner's assessment that "this is what the teachers love the most. That thing you told me to do, well, I did it, here are my results. The teacher then knows that there is a willing student."

Dan Miller has become a leader in this space, writing repeatedly about the benefits of mentorship over recent decades. He says he has benefited greatly from the value of mentors in his own life, and he teaches that mentors can be anyone, from personal friends we know, to authors, podcasters and professionals we learn from via books and other media.

Also over the last week, author and pastor Andy Stanley discussed mentorship on his *Your Move* podcast, putting it this way.

"Choose a destination, and then borrow a map. Every season of life requires a different set of skills in order to be successful," Stanley advised. "And the thing is, it's true of all of us, every time we move into a new season we've never been there before. Which means we really don't know what we're doing. And by the time we figure that out, we've moved into another season of life."

Stanley says mentorship is the key to getting through the "seasons of life" with the most success and least amount of pain.

"Determine what you want your life to look like in this season - and here's the trick - find someone who is a little bit further ahead, that has successfully navigated this season, and ask them for their map," Stanley implored. "Find somebody who is where you want to be and ask them how they got there." He adds that the way you ask is just as important as the fact that you are asking in the first place.

"Never, ever, ask anyone to mentor you. Never do that, because mentoring sounds like a homework assignment," Stanley said. He suggests requesting a quick meeting to ask just a few questions, as well as following up to continue nurturing the relationship.

The juicy little secret captured in what Dan Miller, Andy Stanley, and others have taught about mentorship - it works in virtually every industry.

Business. Higher Education. Construction. Real Estate. Retail sales. You name it.
Mentors always play a crucial role in rapid and sustained success.
And especially in the people-centric world of news media.

The Days That Create Fortunes

These may be the days when fortunes are made.

As the saying goes, "Be greedy when others are fearful, and fearful when others are greedy."

And with the country engulfed in increasing economic pain and hardship, some experts say this may be exactly the right time to jump into the stock market, as many others are scurrying frightfully toward the exits.

CNN Business held a discussion on this very topic over the weekend, and a financial strategist shared her opinion that now could be precisely the time to jump in the market with a long-term outlook.

"We've seen the summer rally run into a little trouble recently," CNN Business host Alison Kosik began. "But you say investors should buy stocks when it feels terrible. So can you talk us through the risk-reward scenario right now?"

"This has been a good strategy for long term investors," Anastasia Amoroso, Chief Investment Strategist at iCapital said. "And what I mean by that, buy stocks when it feels terrible to do so, when you're buying stocks when they're valued at 20, 22 times multiple, as they were in the beginning of the year, that's probably not going to yield the best long-term returns. Historically we see that over a one year, or a five year timeframe, if you invested at that high multiple, your returns were pretty subpar, pretty muted."

The S & P began this year sitting at 4793. As of August 29th, the S & P stands at 4057, down roughly 15% since we turned the page to 2022. Most investment and retirement accounts are likely down a similar percentage, adding to the financial difficulty caused by higher prices for food, gas and other essentials. Not to mention rising interest rates for mortgages and other loans.

But where there is pain, there also may be opportunity for those willing and able to seize the moment. And that outsized opportunity may take a relatively-short time frame to materialize.

"If you bought stocks when the S& P was trading in the 16 times forward multiple range, the forward returns tended to be a lot better on a one-year basis and on a five-year average basis," Amoroso said, alluding to the market's yearly low back in June. "And so as we trade today at somewhere around 18-times forward multiple, I would say it doesn't feel terrible to actually buy stocks. But we are going into September where things tend to be seasonally a little bit weaker. So to the extent that we get a pullback, maybe not all the way back to 3700, but somewhere in that vicinity, I think that's when investors should step in with some conviction and buy those stocks with a long-term investment horizon."

In other words, for those with a long-term strategy, she believes now is a good time to buy. Recession or not, layoffs or not, high gas prices or not - many companies are on sale compared to what their value will be when the nation eventually gets its financial motor humming again, as it was just a few short years ago.

CNBC.com ran a similar story by Ryan Ermey on August 1st with the headline, *65% of Americans are doing 'the exact opposite of what they're supposed to,' says investing expert—here's what to do instead.* In the piece, the conclusion brought forth by Kelly LaVigne, Vice President of consumer insights at Allianz Life, was that most investors have it backwards.

LaVigne said, "When the market is doing well, people are throwing their money at it. When it's doing poorly, they're keeping their money out," he says. "It's doing the exact opposite of what you're supposed to be doing." He suggests buying more when prices are low and avoiding trying to time exact market bottoms. In his opinion, buying consistently near market lows will provide much better long-term results and help investors take advantage when markets see cyclical upticks.

But if today is a good time to buy, coming weeks may provide even better prices at which to gobble up high-value equities that may appreciate considerably in years to come.

"The risk-reward, the closer we get to 3700, the more compelling the buying opportunity is," Amoroso summed up. "The closer we get to 4300 on the S & P, where we were recently, that's probably where you run into a little bit of a ceiling and I probably would shy away from buying stocks right there."

Will this outsized opportunity materialize in the coming weeks? And how quickly will investors be willing to jump in?

Only time will tell if these painful economic days will lead to future fortunes.

September 5, 2022

Gen Z Needs a Break From the News

Perhaps we can all learn a lesson from self-aware Zoomers.

Not a lesson on proper emoji use, dating apps or the current hip language of the day.

Rather, some of Generation Z sense they need a break from the news. In fact, they *know* they need a break. In an age of constant stimuli, negativity, advertisements and sensationalism, some of the youngest and most savvy media consumers are planning to temporarily check out.

With news networks barraging our senses daily with click-bait material, it's no surprise that many of us eventually feel we need to step away. Negative news sells, and we are all extremely willing buyers.

This politician was caught in a scandal, while another made a decision that will ruin the country, if not the planet.

How could citizens possibly vote for him? How could our neighbors possibly trust her?

Gas prices have skyrocketed! Groceries are through the roof! The earth is freezing, or melting!

All this and more, with the dawning reality that the political season is just heating up for the fall.

With all this "good" news enveloping our culture and refusing to let us breathe, who's to blame *anyone* for needing a break?

On her Thursday Gettr livestream, Gen Z thought leader Isabel Brown began by urging her generation to take a mental health break and turn off the noise, at least temporarily.

"I just want to say, I've kind of hit a wall the last couple of weeks, and I don't know if everybody else is feeling this way," Brown began. "I saw Allie Beth Stuckey post something about this earlier in the week and I think I brought it up in my stream on Tuesday. I think there's just this overwhelming feeling of, for lack of a better term, impending doom."

It's possible, even probable, that many Americans share similar sentiments with Brown, with record-high inflation and a plethora of news items to buoy one's political persuasion.

"Overwhelming negativity, everything is awful," Brown continued, sharing a mood that she has seen infiltrating her circle of influence over recent weeks. "There's a trending Tik Tok sound from the news that's like, *And in tonight's breaking news everything is awful.* And I think it literally does feel like that because it just kind of feels like we are in this limbo situation of things not moving forward, of not going our way, of constantly being drug back into this crazy culture war that we're consistently fighting. And it just feels really overwhelming."

A contributor to Turning Point USA, the energetic Brown has garnered a loyal and growing following for being a refreshing, counter-culture voice for freedom, morality and traditional American values. And during the episode, she was taking the pulse of her audience.

"I don't know if you guys are feeling that way. I'm certainly feeling that way. The post I mentioned from Allie Beth earlier this week, was on her story" Brown said, referring to Stuckey, a fellow rising media star. "She said, tap yes or no if you're just feeling really overwhelmed and over politics and the news and all of it. And 99 percent of the people in this poll said yes. And I've really been feeling that way lately too."

And in Brown's opinion, the timing for a temporary hiatus couldn't be better.

"I don't know if you guys just need a break or you need some time away from all of the constant noise and information and negativity being thrown at you from every single direction. I certainly feel like that, working in this world of politics all the time. But I just really want to encourage you this weekend, when you're gathering with your friends and your family, and you have some down time on Monday. Maybe you have tomorrow remote or tomorrow off, because a lot of companies are doing that this year for Labor Day," she said. "Take the time - this is a big challenge but it's a good one. Take the time to literally turn your phone off. Turn it off. Not silent. Not vibrate. Turn it off, leave it at home, and go do something outside. Go for a hike. Go for a walk. Spend some time with your family. Go fishing. I'm hoping to go fly fishing this weekend. But I'm realizing when I get really overwhelmed and I am struggling with the overwhelming amount of negativity and just horrifying information going on in the world, I always feel so much better when I take the time to step away from screens. You guys need it too."

Isabel Brown seemingly has more energy than most, with which she engages viewers and continues building a network of like-minded young Americans. And even she plans to take a short break, putting the news aside and connecting with other essential areas of her life.

She urges her friends, family and followers to do the same.

"Read a book. Go for a hike. Go outside this weekend. Please, that is my challenge for you because I think we will all be a lot better for it."

September 12, 2022

From the Gas Pump to the Grocery Store and Back Home Again

That pithy phrase, coined by Richard Baris of the Big Data Poll, sums up the cost-of-living catastrophe that most Americans are struggling through. And while he and other political experts expect that the President and his party will undoubtedly face the electoral consequences of that inflation this November, it could be a longer wait still until remedial policies are enacted to counter the destructive trends of recent years.

On Friday's edition of *Your World*, Fox News' Neil Cavuto welcomed an economist and a political consultant to discuss a new Gallup poll, which shows that 56 percent of Americans are indeed feeling financial hardship due to the nation's current inflationary crisis.

"This is the big deal here, that this has now crossed party lines," Cavuto began. "You don't have to be a Republican or Democrat to know what it's like to pay through the nose when you go to the grocery store or department store. It's real now."

He asked if these pocketbook problems are resonating with voters.

"I think it is, and I would predict that notwithstanding the tightening of the polling recently with Biden's slight uptick, that ultimately in the November election, it will redound to the benefit of the Republicans, the out party, as it typically does midterm of a new administration," thoughtful Democratic strategist, Doug Schoen, answered. "This is still tough conditions. Something of an upturn after the passage of the so-called Inflation Reduction Act, but bottom line, even with prices moderating, as the sound byte you played suggests Neil, people are hurting and hurting badly."

Cavuto then lamented the current trends that began with fuel and other energy prices. He asked economist Steven Moore about the fact that there doesn't seem to be any specific "plan in place" currently, other than hope that the Fed can simply "rate-hike it away."

"Well, first of all it's not just travel, but obviously that's something that's really been affected. And the major reason , Neil, that the gas price is down this two or three months is because people are traveling less, they're taking less vacations, they're not packing the kids into the station wagons and the mini vans and going on trips because they can't afford the five dollar gasoline," Moore said. "I'll give you one statistic that kind of amplifies what Doug was saying. The average family, median household family, has lost about four thousand dollars of purchasing power since Biden came in, when we went from one and a half percent to seven percent inflation."

Even with other issues and stories in the headlines - and with Democrats and some Republicans trying to divert attention toward those shiny objects - Cavuto wondered aloud if anything could possibly steal the spotlight from the cost-of-living agony being inflicted on American families.

"I don't think the Democrats have much of an answer, Neil," Schoen said. "I'm a Democrat and I wish we did, but I don't believe that the Inflation Reduction Act which, best case, will reduce inflation over the next ten years modestly, is going to do anything in the short term. And longer-term I think what the Democrats are seeing is that the Republicans are in disarray, they're divided, and that Trump becomes a convenient target. It's a lot easier to campaign against someone and something than it is to tout your own accomplishments. Particularly when you have a political achilles heel, as is inflation and the cost of living for the Democrats."

While things are bad in the U.S., many experts look around the world and see even more financial hardship possible in the near future. The solution, however, is in our control if only we'd enact policies that, according to Moore, would start alleviating the kitchen table pain across the country.

"Britain and Europe are the canaries in the coal mine," Moore said. "Look at what's happening in Europe, they are in a severe recession right now. A friend of mine who lives in London tells me that they are paying nine to ten dollars a gallon for gas right now because of this kind of war on energy. And you see it by the way in California as well. So we've got to start producing American energy. This has been the driving force of higher prices, no question about it. The fact that we're producing less oil, less gas, and let's keep nuclear power in the equation as well. That would help bring down energy prices."

From the gas pump to the grocery store and back home again.

Citizens are feeling the cost-of-living pain, and they are becoming increasingly impatient waiting on solutions.

September 28, 2022

Massive Market Crash Still Looming

Current economic conditions, and the reaction of the American government and Federal Reserve to deal with them, may lead to a market crash worse than 2008.

Those are the sentiments of two recent guests who appeared on Kitco News in the past week. They expressed an outlook that, although temporary in nature, will be extremely painful and jarring for investors and American families.

In an episode published Saturday on Kitco News, Bloomberg Senior Commodity Strategist, Mike McGlone, joined Lead Anchor, Michelle Makori, to discuss the possibility of an impending financial market catastrophe. He believes the "Fed has taken away the punch bowl and we just need a reset."

"I've never seen this," McGlone said. "The Fed will not be easing any time soon, and it's classic human nature because now we have the benefit of knowing how far and the mistakes they made by easing too much. So that's the key thing I like to see. Looking in the rear view mirror, it's very clear the pendulum for risk assets swung way too far to one side. And looking forward, into the front where this car is going, it's very clear that the pendulum's going to be swinging back significantly the other way."

McGlone, a big fan of Bitcoin, believes that the digital gold, and other digital assets, have been a leading indicator of what has transpired in 2022. He eventually feels that these assets will lead the charge back when maximum capitulation has occurred.

Others, such as Ray Dalio, Chief Investment Officer at Bridgewater Associates, have said they expect the markets could be staring at an additional decline of 20% or more in the near future. And even with this possible short-term pain, McGlone does not think the Fed will blink and make a knee-jerk decision to lighten up.

"The Fed is a leading part of that but it's just not gonna happen that they're gonna ease like they did during the '87 crash and during this when we plunged in 2018. And most significantly when we plunged in Q1 2020 because they know now they are somewhat responsible for this massive inflation."

The market largely expects a 1% rate hike from the Fed at the next meeting, and many think it is much too little, much too late. Financial thought leader, and author of the groundbreaking book, *Rich Dad, Poor Dad*, Robert Kiyosaki appeared with Makori last week and said his predictions are now coming true. He referred to a previous interview with Makori and some predictions he made nearly ten years ago.

"It says why the biggest crash in stock market history is still coming, this is 2013," Kiyosaki said, holding up a copy of another book he authored, *Rich Dad's Prophecy*. "I gotta change the book now. It's here. And the reason I could predict it is because, as you know, in 2008 they didn't fix the problem. They made it worse. And so today I'm more bullish than ever on gold, silver and oil. Hard assets."

Makori noted to Kiyosaki that the value lost during this year's stock market decline, as a percentage of national GDP, is more that the value lost in the last 40 years of market crashes. And for his part, Kiyosaki has often spoken about the national dependance on shaky pension programs and other's he refers to as nothing more than socialism, Marxism and communism.

"I am a hardcore, hard assets person. I am hardcore," Kiyosaki explained. "I stopped trusting my government in Vietnam. They would report the news, I'd listen to Walter Cronkite. You're too young to listen to him. But I'd be watching Walter Cronkite in the evening news from Vietnam. And I'd be involved in many of those battles they wrote about. What they reported wasn't the truth. I don't trust the news at all."

The S&P 500 sits roughly 17% down so far this year, and investment management giant, Morgan Stanley, said last week they expect the market to drop another 17% to 27%.

"That's why I think the macro is overwhelming, and when I see a storm coming I think it's somewhat my duty to warn people," McGlone told Makori. "And I'm just telling, this is my true feelings of what's happening. I ask people, and I'll ask you this, and even our listeners. What stops this? Is it going to be the Fed? Is it going to be a stronger dollar? Does the dollar have to reverse? No. Is it going to be a global economy coming out of it? No. Is it going to be China coming out of this? That's very unlikely. I don't see what stops it at the moment other than risk assets going lower, and reaching a lower plateau and us resetting."

McGlone said this is finally the cleanout event we have needed for decades, while acknowledging that there seems to be nowhere to hide.

"This is the worst I've ever seen. I mean, I've never seen bonds, and stocks, go down this much. And I hear on a global basis it's one of the worst ever," he said. "And it's early on. Why do I say it's early on? I keep asking myself, what's gonna stop it? Not the Fed. We need to see that pivot. I don't say they're going to ease, but at least for them to signal we're done tightening. Inflation's not going to be a problem, we expect it to decline. If the stock market, we wake up one day and it's down 10%, and it's down 10% another day and 10% another day, that's what happens. That's what we typically, I think, need to shut off this sledgehammer."

McGlone and Kiyosaki both believe that for financial markets, the worst is yet to come before the good times eventually return.

September 26, 2022

A Promise to Save America From "Living Hell"

So much has gone wrong, and there doesn't seem to be an end in sight to the economic, kitchen-table pain being forced on Americans in recent years. But there has finally been a commitment to change course and fix the problems.

Republicans last week unveiled their "Commitment to America," a series of legislative promises they say they will put forth if voters give them control of the United States House of Representatives in November.

On Friday night's edition of *Rob Schmitt Tonight*, just before former President Donald Trump took to the stage for his Save America Rally in Wilmington, North Carolina, Representative Ralph Norman of South Carolina joined the Newsmax program to discuss the GOP's plans to rescue the country from the current state of affairs.

Schmitt began with a sound byte of House Minority Leader, Kevin McCarthy, highlighting the promise to repeal the Democrat Party's recent move to hire an additional 87,000 IRS agents during Friday's announcement of the Republican initiative.

"How do you do that," Schmitt asked Norman. "They obviously just got this big bill passed, they're so proud of it. Their Inflation Reduction Act, which doubles the size of the IRS. How do you just take that away?"

"Well, it's going to take some bold action, Rob. And I was happy that the pillars for Commitment to America is out there. We know what we have to do. Strengthen the economy, national security, protect our freedoms and government accountability. But it's gonna take more than just slogans," Norman said. "We've got to put the details to it. As they say, the devil's in the details. But I'm optimistic that we will. This is the first step of laying out a blueprint of what Republicans will do. And the thing about it, on the Commitment to America, the Democrats are doing everything to destroy the pillars that made this country great."

The Republican outline is much in the mold of a similar legislative agenda put forth by the party during the 1994 congressional election season, under the leadership of former House Speaker, Newt Gingrich.

Schmitt honed in on one of the more painful parts of President Biden's economic crackdown, asking Norman what his party would do differently.

"When he talks about gas prices, his administration intentionally spiked the price of fuel in this country. We all know it. The actions were very clear. They wanted to push green energy in order to push that agenda. You gotta get people out of regular fuel cars and you gotta get them buying electric cars and buying solar panels and all that. Then they panicked and lowered gas prices when their poll numbers tanked by emptying out our reserves, and then here is the President today talking about gas prices," Schmitt said, cutting to a clip of the President boasting about bringing down gas prices. "You raise em up to a ridiculous level and then you're putting us at risk by emptying our reserves to bring them back down, intentionally just for political reasons, and then you brag about it. I mean, it's astonishing to me."

"Everybody knows when gas prices were going up, who did you blame it on? Vladamir Putin. Now when they're coming down, why aren't you giving him credit? No, it's laughable if it wasn't so serious. The only way you're going to get gas prices down in this country is to use our natural resources here in America," Norman said. "We've got a 300-year supply of natural gas and oil. And he's buying, the sad part about it, he's buying from OPEC countries that hate America. So everything is self-inflicted by this administration. The last twenty months have been a living hell and we've got to stop this. And it comes with bold action. It comes with putting people in Congress who will do something, and I think the American people are going to do that."

Reputable polling indicates the American people, indeed, will make that choice and give Republicans more power in roughly 40 days. They'll then wait to see if GOP politicians will keep their commitment and fight back on their behalf.

October 3, 2022

30 Years of Ramsey

You can touch a lot of lives in the course of the day if your goal, when waking, is to help and serve as many people as possible.

And you can help, counsel, motivate and love untold numbers of people when you build a team to share that aim, and you do so for nearly 11,000 days.

That is the legacy, to date, of *The Ramsey Show* and Ramsey Solutions, which has helped people get out of debt and become financially independent for 30 years.

Last week, the show released a bonus episode on YouTube and podcast, with the current team of Ramsey personalities reminiscing with their leader, Dave Ramsey, on the evolution of the program, and its mission, over the last three decades.

The show began 30 years ago when Dave Ramsey made a guest appearance on a friend's real estate program on a local Nashville radio station. The host of the show quit shortly thereafter, and Ramsey was asked if he wanted to take over the time slot.

"I'm not doing radio," Ramsey said at the time. "Radio people don't get paid nothing. They're like bankers - big egos and titles and no money. I need money. I am broke, my kids are hungry. I am not doing this." Ramsey had just gone through bankruptcy, after watching his personal real estate empire crumble, leaving his family in financially dire straits. He had emerged with the goal of helping others avoid the pitfalls and pain he had brought on himself.

Eventually, Ramsey agreed to host the radio show a couple days a week as a way to promote his self-published book, *Financial Peace*, which he was promoting and selling out of the trunk of his car. Ramsey said the awful *Money Game* program was "hillbilly, red-neck radio." In time, Ramsey took over the program on his own and re-branded it *The Dave Ramsey Show,* based largely on the example laid out by other top radio stars, such as Rush Limbaugh and Dr. Laura Schlessinger.

"We shifted everything to Dave Ramsey, branding off the single person brand. And then everything drove through that brand," Ramsey recalls. "That focus is what helped us move everything. Events, books, website started working. It was in the early days of the web."

About fifteen years ago, the brand began to look toward the future, branching out to include multiple personalities and build an eventual succession plan.

"In my mid-40's I said this thing's not going to outlive me if we don't decide how we're going to carry the message in the next generation," Ramsey said. "As we started thinking about that we said well, we don't really say anything that's unique. Lots of people have said, live on less than you make, get on a budget. You know, lots of articles that were boring, written by boring financial people. The only thing that's unique is that we actually love the people. We actually care about people, and we actually help them. We've got compassion for them and we're sassy and smart-aleck and funny and tell stories and entertain and convince them in the midst of that to go through their transformation. So we realized at that point that the business, the whole thing we built, would just die with me if we didn't have other people that could do the same thing."

Enter new personalities, such as those who appeared with Ramsey on the special 30th Anniversary episode - his daughter, Rachel Cruze, Ken Coleman, Dr. John Delony, George Kamal and Kristina Ellis.

When listeners visit the Ramsey Solutions headquarters in Franklin, Tennessee, they are greeted like friends, with Janelle graciously checking them in and offering them a cookie and cup of coffee. Over three decades, the radio program - like the brand itself - has become much more than a radio show about money.

"I would say it's a place that people call in with their questions about their life, and it's more heavily geared towards money. But yeah, it's just a couple people sitting in a radio studio, friends, and taking people's calls." Cruze said.

"We're kind of diving into whatever mess is going on in life and going, here's how we can help," Kamel interjected.

The program has evolved into areas such as relationships, boundaries, career growth, mental health, college planning and small business building.

"The pressure for someone to call in live on the air and talk to somebody, that's a terrifying proposition for a lot of people, so there's that," said Coleman, who focuses heavily on his role as a career coach. "And then they're dealing with something where they go, I feel like I need a breakthrough. And so, regardless of the topic, like Rachel said, it's just a real person with a real struggle who needs real help."

In addition to the flagship *Ramsey Show*, many of the personalities now also host individual podcasts, which focus on their specific areas of expertise. And during this special anniversary episode, the hosts recalled some of the more memorable calls they've taken on the air. From the hilarious to the emotional, Ramsey and his co-hosts have tackled it all on the air over the years.

The man planning to get out of debt.
The war vet dealing with PTSD.
The college student searching for Biblical principles for handling money.
The millionaire developing a plan to become incredibly generous.
The main considering installing a pay phone in his home.
The brother forming a business partnership with his sibling.
The frightened mother cowering in a back room, hiding from her angry and violent spouse.

"I remember the first couple of calls I took on my podcast, and it came out organically. My first response to their question was, why are you calling me? That's a huge thing. Why haven't you called your friends or your pastor or your family members?" Dr. Delony recalled. "And to a person every response was, dude I got nobody. Like, you're the only person to call. And so if you'd have asked me right when I was starting, what is the role of the show, how do I explain it? I would have said it's a show people call about life. Now I think my answer would be different. It's - We'll Be There. When you've got nobody, we'll be honest with you. And we'll tell you what we think. We think we're pretty smart. We think we know what we're talking about, but we'll be honest with you."

In many respects, the *Ramsey Show* has become a place where callers can talk about subjects they may not even feel comfortable discussing with their own friends and family. After all, money conversations can be sensitive.

"I also think it's just like a safe space. These topics we talk about, sometimes there's a stigma around them. People feel shame and they feel intimidated to talk to their friends and family. It's like this is a spot where we're comfortable with this," Ellis said. "You can bring us your ugly stuff. You can bring us the things that you don't want to mention to anyone else and we'll work through it."

It's a long way from the "awful, hillbilly program" on local Nashville radio. But through constant growth and evolution of the program and the organization, the company has helped countless people around the country and around the world. And judging by the trajectory, this group plans to help a whole lot more over the coming decades.

"The thing is, when you tell people the truth about how to get a job, or the truth about, here's how you do this relationship, or the truth about what you got to do with your money, they hear it even if they don't like it," Ramsey summed up. "Truth has a way of getting to you. And they know you love them. And we love them. We care about them."

Thanks for Reading!

If you enjoyed this book.....

Connect with Barrett News Media today!

Visit SportscastersClub.com to Become a Better Sportscaster and a Better Sports Fan

Follow Rick Schultz on Twitter - @RickSchultzNY

Other Books By Rick Schultz (Available on Amazon, Kindle & Audible)

Secrets of Sports Broadcasting: Practical Advice for Sportscasting Success

Minor League Baseball Revealed: A Secret Tour Inside Our National Pastime

Untold Tales From the Bush Leagues; A Behind The Scenes Look Into Minor League Baseball, From the Broadcasters Who Called the Action

A Renegade Championship Summer: A Broadcaster's View of a Magical Minor League Baseball Season

101 Things I Wish I Knew Before I Bought My First Home

101 Things I Wish I Knew Before I Sold My First Home

How to Buy or Sell Your Home: 202 Real Estate Tips for Success

Sales Surge: 50 Secrets to Propel Your Sales Career With Less Stress

Sales Surge Sequel: Another 50 Secrets to Boost Your Sales

If you enjoyed the book, check out BarrettNewsMedia.com

Made in United States
Cleveland, OH
09 December 2024

11570319R00144